Adolphe Valette

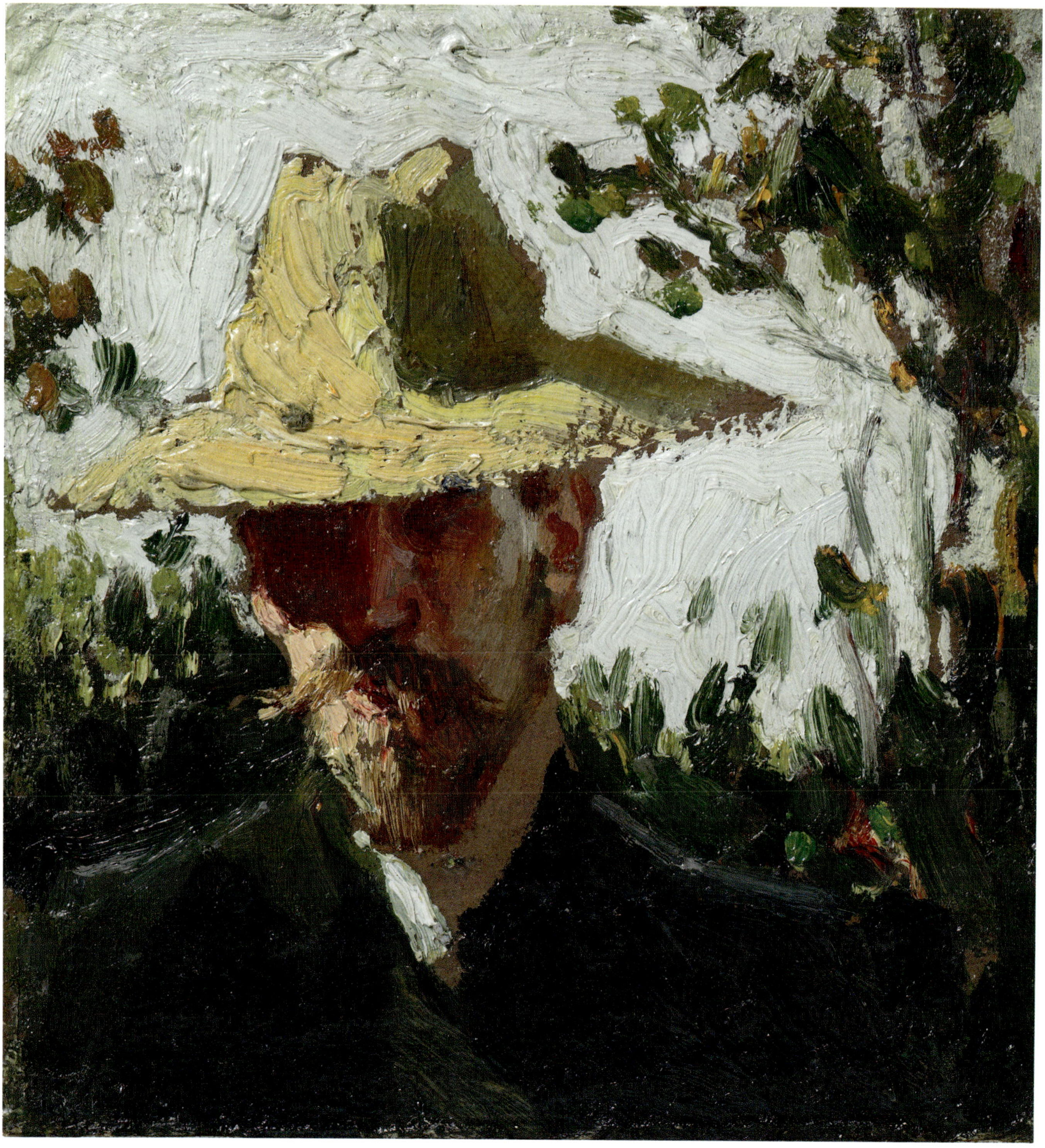

Self-Portrait wearing Straw Hat

Oil on board or card, 15.1 x 14.1

Private collection

Adolphe Valette

Cécilia Lyon

Phillimore

2006

Published by
PHILLIMORE & CO. LTD
Shopwyke Manor Barn, Chichester, West Sussex, England
www.phillimore.co.uk

ISBN 1-86077-426-1
ISBN 13 978-1-86077-426-3

Printed and bound in Great Britain by
CAMBRIDGE UNIVERSITY PRESS

Contents

Photographic Acknowledgements
Clive Digital; G-Ten Photography of the University of Manchester; The Lowry Collection, Salford; Manchester Art Gallery; Yves Bresson/Musée d'Art Moderne de Saint-Etienne Métropole; Bill Clark; Sefton Samuels; Wolseley Fine Art; Geoffrey Lyon.

Illustrations
All sizes of illustrations are given in centimetres, height preceding width, many are sight sizes only.

Acknowledgements

This book on the life and work of Valette has been the source of great joy for me.

The first joy was that which I had knowingly contrived, and which I anticipated: having fallen in love with Valette's paintings in April 2002, in the Manchester Art Gallery, and having felt a second similar impact at the house of my friends, the collectors Alan and Caroline Harrison, I felt a pressing need to live in a world surrounded by Valette. I wanted to know more about his life and works. So it was that in the four years that ensued I immersed myself in the life of Valette – travelling to research it, where he had lived, both in France and in England. I had a wonderful time doing so; this was a hedonistic pleasure that I allowed myself, which I had planned, because it corresponds to my aesthetic temperament and my reflex for academic research, and around which I gladly constructed my life during these four years.

The second joy, and this is where I would like to come to in these pages of acknowledgements, is the joy that I really had not anticipated or arranged for, and which took hold of me like the gift of life: namely that of friendship and the pleasures of meeting people. The infectious enthusiasm I found in contact with all those who contributed their assistance in piecing together the fragments of Valette's life was something I had really not imagined to this extent, and was a revelation of optimism.

It was the pleasure of meeting so many exceptional people: I will never forget the confidence and generosity of Madame Desdier, the niece by marriage of Maria Lafond, one of Valette's muses. Madame Desdier was interested in my project from the first moment and gave me access to her family archives. I am also very mindful of the determination of Madame Louisgrand, who, at the age of over 90 and braving an earthquake and a snowstorm, took me to the Beaujolais region to retrace Valette's steps. I remember those animated conversations, most often over a glass of Beaujolais, with those of Valette's entourage in the region to which he retired, who were kind enough to share their memories.

Another abiding memory is that of an afternoon in the company of Jan Green, Tim Chapman and his daughter Liz and my husband Geoffrey, when the conversation was focused on nothing other than Valette for many hours, which still seem to me like nanoseconds, as we were all so enthusiastic about the subject. The warm-hearted evenings spent with Alan and Caroline Harrison will henceforth be an integral feature of my life's almanac. This book has enabled me to create bonds of friendship and collegiality with a very large number of enthusiasts for Valette whom I would have never otherwise met and with whom I have spent fine moments, and found new friendships, which I hope can continue through our shared admiration for the works of this painter.

I would also not have imagined the support for, and interest in, my project proffered by those who, through their professions, were able to provide me with information on Valette, that has been so vital, and without which this book could never have been written. I think it is fair to say that I have detected a genuine élan for my project, and a curiosity for the subject that has been substantiated in the generosity of the assistance I have received.

In France, I would like to begin my thanks with Jacques Beauffet, Head Curator of the Musée d'Art Moderne de Saint-Etienne Métropole, who has supported me from the very outset, has obligingly provided me with all the information he could find on the painter and has also done me the honour of contributing the Foreword to this book. The Musée d'Art Moderne de Saint-Etienne Métropole is the only institution in France that owns works by Valette. I would also like to thank Christian Gay, librarian of the Musée d'Art Moderne de Saint-Etienne Métropole, for his willingness to make his time available to me and for all the information he has provided.

My thanks also go to Christophe Tillière, the territorial attaché at the Archives Municipales de Saint-Etienne who also embraced my project from the outset and provided me with a mine of very important information, as well as archive images.

I would like to thank Henri Chauve and the Amis du Vieux St-Etienne, Nicole Daydrein, librarian at the Ecole des Beaux-Arts de Bordeaux, Cyril Lopez and Agnès Vatican, Curator of the Bordeaux Municipal Archives, Serge Fernandez and Olivier Le Bihan, director of the Musée des Beaux-Arts de Bordeaux, the Mairie of St-Jean-Soleymieux, the Mairie of St-Bonnet-le-Château, Madame Jouvinroux, librarian of the Ecole Régionale des Beaux-Arts in Saint-Etienne, Alain de Bompuis, President of the Société des Arts du Forez, André Maire of the Archives Municipales in Lyon, Dominique Dumas of the library of the Musée des Beaux-Arts in Lyon, Corinne Raviol, librarian of the Ecole Nationale des Beaux-Arts in Lyon, Julie Solly and Anne-Marie Ellezière of the Musée Paul Dini in Villefranche-sur-Saône, Philippe Branche of the Maison du Patrimoine in Villefranche-sur-Saône, Joëlle de Couëssin, in charge of documentary studies at the Ecole Nationale Supérieure des Beaux-Arts in Paris, Nathalie Muller, Isabelle Rollet and Cyril Duclos of the Institut National d'Histoire de l'Art.

Still in France, I would like to extend my warmest thanks to the Mairie of Blacé in the persons of Jean-Jacques Sandrin, Guy-Noël Texier and particularly Madame Martine Morion, in charge of cultural affairs for the Mairie, who has been very supportive.

My sincere thanks to the various people of the Beaujolais, too numerous to be mentioned here and whose privacy I want to respect by not naming them personally, who had known the entourage of Valette and have provided invaluable assistance.

In England, as in France, I have been extremely touched by the great interest shown in my project and the assistance I have been given.

Most naturally my very sincere thanks go to the Manchester Art Gallery and individually to Sandra Martin, Principal Curator of Fine Arts, Marcus Chase, Trading

Manager and Tracey Walker, Picture Library Manager. The catalogue of the 1994 exhibition 'Adolphe Valette, a French Influence in Manchester' written by Sandra Martin, has been a well documented and most useful companion for the writing of this present work. The Manchester Art Gallery is the museum that gave Valette institutional recognition for his talent. For some years, following the renovation and extension of the Manchester Art Gallery, Valette's works have been on permanent display in one of the finest rooms. I would unreservedly recommend anyone who appreciates the work of Valette to visit the gallery.

At the Manchester Metropolitan University, the institution that now incorporates within its structure the Municipal School of Art, where Valette spent nearly fifteen years of his life, the enthusiastic and very friendly contribution of Jeremy Parrett, archivist at the Manchester Metropolitan University, was invaluable. The same applies to Caroline Furey, who catalogued all the School's archives. They both found rare and interesting documents on Valette and I am extremely grateful to them.

I would also like to extend my warm thanks to Lindsay Brooks and Ruth Salisbury, respectively Head of the Galleries and Collection Administrator of 'The Lowry' gallery in Salford. My very particular thanks also go to Andy Firth, exhibition officer of the Stockport Art Gallery. I often visited the Manchester Central Library and my thanks go to all the staff of the Arts section as well as to George Turnbull in Local Studies who gave me indications of the various addresses of Valette in Manchester and to Kath Lapsley who provided me with archive images. I also wish to thank Mary Griffiths, Curator of Modern Arts of the Whitworth Art Gallery, Robin Griffin of The Garrick Society, Stockport, Dr James Peters, University Archivist of The John Rylands University Library, The University of Manchester, Moira Lindsay, Curator at the Walker Art Gallery, Liverpool, Peter Ogilvie, Collections Manager of the Salford Museum and Art Gallery, Ron Thorn, Honorary Librarian of The Silk Museums in Macclesfield.

I also wish to thank Tim Chapman for having provided me with the registry office documents relating to Valette in England. My warmest thanks go to Christina Bolton, Denis and Barbara Btesch, John Evans, Patricia Ferguson, Leslie Gibbs, David Goeritz, Jeanine and Colin Gordon, Muriel and Gordon Hay, Barbara and John Lee, Brigid O'Hagan, Mary, Bob and Imogen Peers, Anne and Sefton Samuels, Canon Aiden Turner, Jeannie and Paul Willan and Bill Wrather. My thanks also to a list of people far too long to name individually, who provided such friendly and personal assistance in support of bringing this book to fruition.

At this point I would like to give particular recognition to Jan Green of the Tib Lane Gallery and to highlight the important role that her late husband Geoffrey played, as she did, in the recognition of Valette in England in the 1970s; the coincidence of their numerous exhibitions in their private gallery with the bringing to the fore of the historic masterworks of Valette by the Manchester Art Gallery, was responsible for raising Valette to the status of being the first artist to have portrayed the radiance of the city of Manchester. I wish to thank Jan for the very significant help that she gave me throughout this project.

I also benefited from the support of other art dealers in the context of this project. My sincere thanks go to Bill Clark of Clark Art, who has shown an unfailing interest in the book, and for providing significant technical assistance through his photographer Clive Good, to whom I would also like to convey my sincere thanks. My thanks also go to Martin Heaps of Collect Art. I am also grateful to Ruppert Otten of Wolseley Fine Arts for the image provided, and to John Falle of John Falle Fine Arts who provided archive documents originating from Jersey. I would also like to thank Mark, Oliver and Simenon Wardle, sons of the late Elaine Grace. My thanks also go to William Gregory of Capes Dunn.

My thanks go to the photographer Michael Pollard of the G Ten Photography studio of the University of Manchester. I also thank Patrick Maguire for IT support throughout the project.

I would like to pay tribute to Elisabeth Lee, whose undergraduate thesis prepared in 1976 for her degree at the University of Manchester was the first work ever to be written on the painter Valette. Its scope and relevancy, after more than thirty years, is still remarkable.

The original text of this book is written in my mother language, French, and I would particularly like to highlight the excellent work of the translator Paul Ratcliffe, who, having found himself engaged by the subject of the book and also bearing in mind the deadlines imposed upon him, has provided me with a remarkable translation.

I also particularly wish to convey my very sincere thanks to Philip Woods, whose spontaneous, supportive and wise counsel was particularly apposite at a critical moment of the project.

I would also like to thank my publisher, Noel Osborne, whose enthusiasm for the project gives the lie to the reputation of the profession of publishers, notorious for taking months to respond to an author's submission. Noel replied by return of post, to say that he would like to set out on this great adventure retracing the steps of Valette. From that point I can only consider myself fortunate to have had the level of support he has given me throughout this project.

And finally, I give my special thanks to my husband Geoffrey, with whom I share this overwhelming passion for the painter Valette, who has been tireless in his encouragement and assistance throughout the project and without whom this book would not have been completed.

This book is a work of admiration for a long neglected painter; I have invested in it all my knowledge to the best of my awareness, and if it contains errors or omissions, I take upon myself full responsibility for them, and I would ask all who may be in a position to assist me in finding further information that may yet remain to be discovered about this fascinating painter, to feel very free to contact me.

Foreword

Art history as it has been written for the past century could be viewed as a history of the *centres* as opposed to the *periphery*. As such it forms part of a manifestation of a totalising, even totalitarian conception, of an incorrectly truncated history of art, omitting entire fields that remain open to the work of researchers.

It would be futile to deny the significance of artistic centres. They are identified as places of distillation of thought, characterised by their capacity to focus discussion and to provoke theoretical emulation and confrontation and are often mistaken for locations where political, economic and of course cultural power is expressed; similarly art history from the Renaissance to the 20th century, tends above all to be that of the large metropolis and of the cities whose attractive force tends to group together creative individuals, collectors and infrastructures involved with the distribution and commercialisation of art.

While one cannot neglect the impact of the cities as 'centres' upon the artistic production of a given period, an art history that neglects the periphery would remain at best incomplete, at worst a vector for actual falsification. Against the centre as a unifying principle imposing its models and codes, it has been possible in the case of more than one artist for the choice of the periphery to stem from a deliberate affirmation of their distinctiveness. When actively embraced and claimed, being at the periphery is no longer, as it has often been represented, a sign of a withdrawal, failure or resignation. For those who make of it a life principle governing their work, it is, on the contrary, a mark of autonomy and freedom. Positioning oneself at the fringes, placing oneself outside the dominant system, does not represent an option for any lack of dynamism or presumed comfort zone. While it is a risk in terms of recognition and standing, such a choice is often productive, distancing the artist from the dangers of becoming derivative.

It has always seemed that this had been Adolphe Valette's standpoint, whose itinerary from Saint-Etienne, to Manchester, to Blacé was a conscious removal on his part from the powerful draw of the artistic capitals, most probably in order to evade their inhibiting and profoundly ossifying thrall. Therefore, while he was indeed thoroughly acquainted with the art of his period he did not on the other hand allow himself to be aligned with any given school, or become the epigone of any master. He was thus able to develop an oeuvre that stood outside the avant-gardist obsession for novelty and a 'breaking away', an oeuvre whose depth and irreducible originality still engage us to this day. Cécilia Lyon's work shows us a body of work in its full extent and complexity, which has remained to transcend the reserve and modesty of its creator and, notwithstanding the initiatives of the Manchester Art Gallery, awaits further illumination and exposure to a yet wider public. Such has also been the rationale of this book.

Jacques Beauffet
Conservateur en chef du Musée d'Art Moderne
de Saint-Etienne Métropole

Introduction

The phenomenon of the critical fortunes of artists can be a disconcerting one. Some achieve immediate recognition during their lifetime, while others must await the verdict of posterity. Sometimes their success is also bounded by frontiers.

Adolphe Valette was no exception to this. In France, through the geographical vagaries of his life, including his time abroad, he failed to enjoy the conventional artistic recognition that he earned during his stay in England, where he lived and worked at the beginning of the 20th century.

When Valette died in 1942, a short tribute was published in his memory in the local press in Saint-Etienne, his birthplace.[1] In it, the author praises Valette's excellent artistic qualities, his pictorial sense, his effortless and subtle technique, his talent as a colourist, all of which were qualities that had enabled 'the creation of works of depth and seriousness'; however, he regrets implicitly that Valette had not received public recognition, particularly in France. The writer concludes his obituary with the conviction that 'the future will do him justice'. However, more than sixty years after Valette's death and the publication of that article, little has changed in France in terms of the reputation of this great artist.

In Great Britain, on the other hand, Valette is still appreciated, even increasingly so, by the English, who recognise in him a multiple talent, and apart from anything else for having assimilated French impressionism to the Northern English industrial and urban landscapes from the beginning of the 20th century. The English are grateful to Valette for having taught L.S. Lowry, one of the most interesting and totally atypical artists of 20th-century English painting. It is on these two counts that numerous works by Valette now hang in English public galleries, especially in Manchester, where they are proudly exhibited in the City Art Gallery.

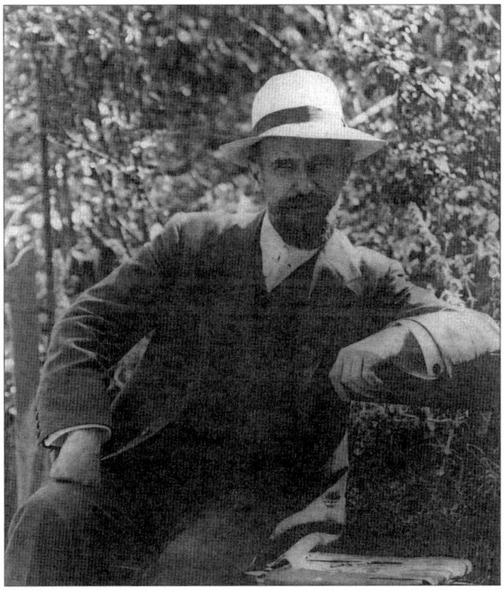

Valette
Collection of John Falle

Unfortunately, in France Valette still remains unjustly unrecognised: unrecognised by the general public, due to him remaining in the shadow of the great impressionist painters who he himself so much admired; unrecognised, too, by himself having perhaps had insufficient faith in his own talent. While very attentive to what was going on

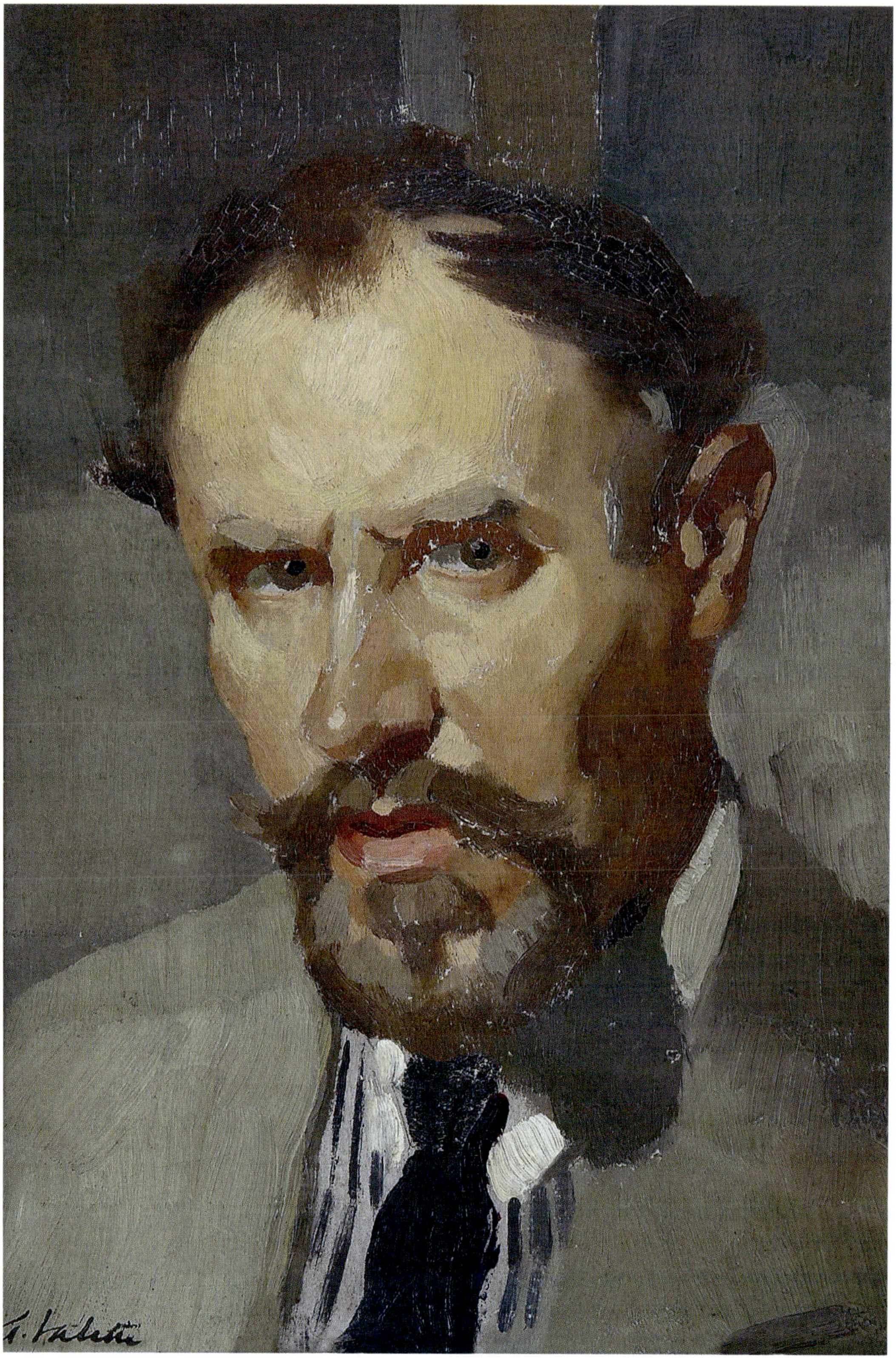

Self-Portrait

Oil on board, 23 x 15

Sefton Samuels collection

around him in the art world, Valette found himself outside the traditional circuits of the artist's trajectory; he was far from the Parisian *mêlée*, which sometimes expected not just talent but also personality, that could contribute to an artist's rapid success. There was nothing in Valette, in his behaviour, in his lifestyle, in his decision to live and work abroad, that pertained to the careerist artist, who focused on social climbing and recognition for his work. He did not seek glory, fortune or the consideration of others.

The research we have carried out on Adolphe Valette was, in this regard, extremely difficult. Valette did not write, nor did he keep a diary. He was not a man who confided in people, or who cared about his own posterity. He was equally not given to manifestos or exalted relations with other artists; he did not communicate in the press, and he hated fuss and publicity. He was quite simply a man with a great mastery of his art, who sought neither medals nor honours.

In his paintings he conveys an expression of his fondness for his family, friends and disciples, as well as his admiration for the places where he spent the two longest periods of his life: Manchester in England and the Beaujolais region in France. He portrayed the two places differently, in the light of the different stages in his life: Manchester in the fog and pollution of a city in an economic and industrial ferment that mirrored all the artistic revival to which he bore witness, and the Beaujolais region with the calm perspective and appeasement of the end of his life.

The life story of Valette, with a foot in two countries, is one of exemplary modernity, anticipating the removal of frontiers in the artistic community. His frame of reference was not bound by the confines of a regional or even national artistic school. His talent, which was very personal, transcends such frontiers. Adolphe Valette's career is the proof that, without belonging to an aristocratic or grand bourgeois élite, an early 20th-century artist could be involved in a rich European culture that had strong traditions and yet was going through a period of profound changes.

The aim of this book is to present the talent of this artist for the appreciation of the art lover, as someone who already features in the artistic and cultural heritage of Great Britain but who also deserves a place on the roll of honour of French painting of the first decades of the 20th century.

1 The Formative Years in France

Saint-Etienne, Early Education

In many ways, the life of Adolphe Valette continues to present something of an enigma for the art world. We shall attempt to unravel these enigmas in the light of discoveries we have made about the artist in the course of our travels in Valette's footsteps, both in France and in England.

The starting point of this journey should be with the simple, straightforward facts which are documented in the official records. The painter Pierre Adolphe Valette – Valette being a common surname in that part of France – was born in France on 13 October 1876 in Saint-Etienne, an industrial town, about 60 km south-west of Lyon. His father was 30 and his mother 29 years old.

At that time Saint-Etienne was one of the most dynamic industrial centres in France, whilst, in England, Manchester also was going through a similar rapid industrial expansion. We shall see later how these two cities played a major role in Adolphe Valette's artistic development.

The manufacturing activities of Saint-Etienne dealt primarily with metal and with silk. Its metallurgical industry had begun many years earlier, with the Manufacture Nationale d'Armes de guerre [French national armaments factory]. The 19th century also saw developments in coalmining and steelmaking industries; factories sprang up everywhere in the area, with manufacturing associated with the railways, armour plating and artillery pieces, bicycles, and motor cars. Silk was woven with cotton to make velour cloth, curtain and furnishing trimmings, as well as ribbons and thread.

In contrast, during these same years coinciding with Adolphe Valette's education, the intellectual and artistic life of Saint-Etienne was rather featureless; businessmen were too occupied with commerce and industry to support the visual arts. Art was essentially contingent on its potential industrial application, such as where engraving could have applications in the arms industry and where flower painting had similar industrial applications for textiles.

In the context of the economic expansion of the period, Adolphe Valette's father not unsurprisingly worked in a profession that was representative of this industrial growth: he was an armourer. Adolphe's father, and, as we will see, his mother, were far from poor. His father's occupation and social position were clearly associated with middle-class attributes; they were certainly hard working but also reaping the fruit of their labours. His father, Ferdinand (Jean Baptiste) Valette was born in 1846 in Saint-Bonnet-le-Château, a village close to Saint-Etienne. When he married Madeleine aged

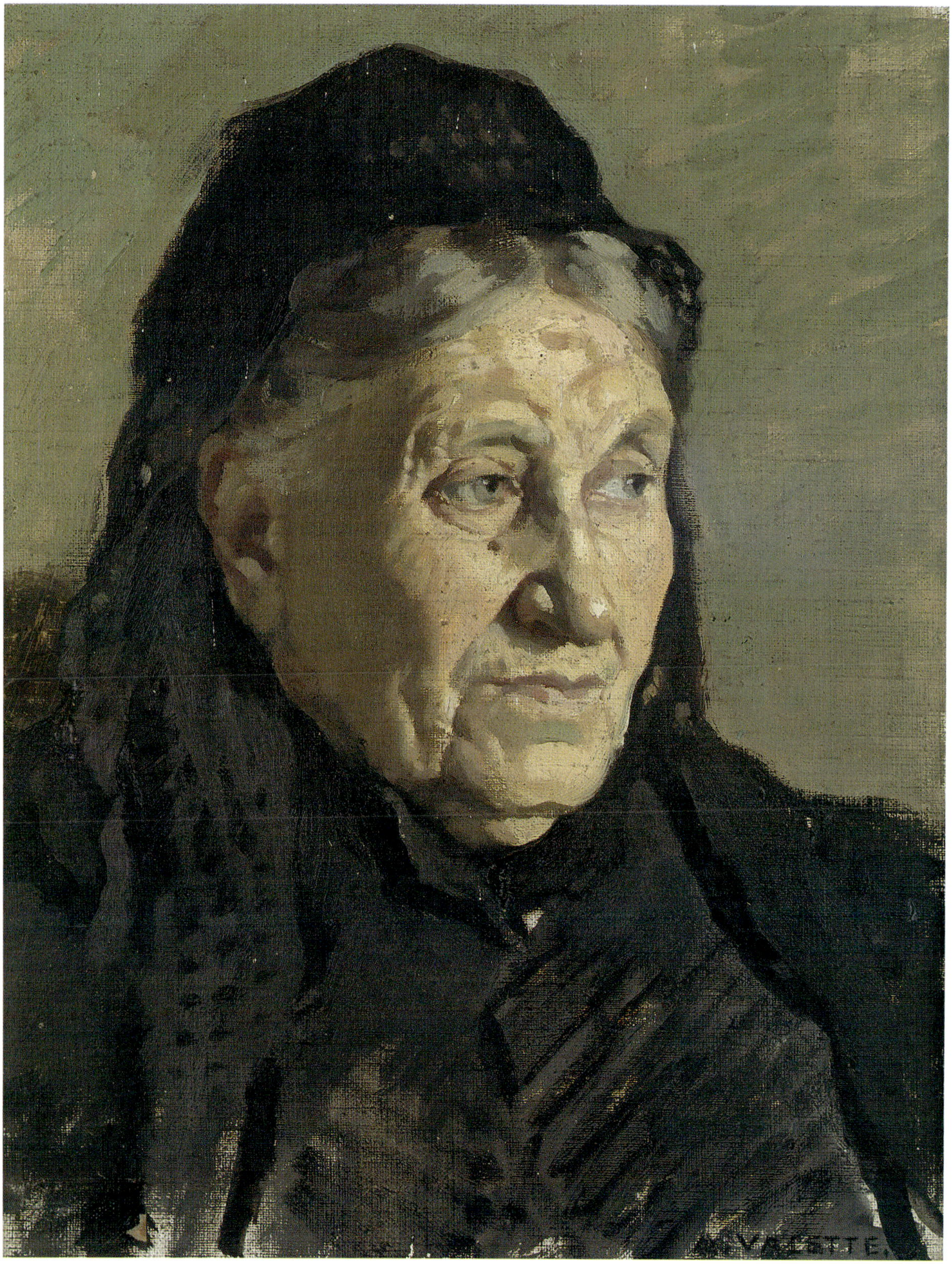

1 *Portrait de la Mère de l'Artiste*

Oil on canvas, 43 x 32

Musée d'Art Moderne de Saint-Etienne Métropole

26, he was already working in the armaments firm of Claude Brondel, his future father-in-law, whose prosperous workshops occupied a prime site in the centre of Saint-Etienne, next to the town hall.

The rearmament of France after the defeat of 1870 and also the equipping of Piedmont and South American countries and colonies entailed a strong resurgence in the production of arms and this industry was in full swing. Sporting guns for hunting were a speciality of Saint-Etienne, and the engravings on these guns would give rise to generations of talented artists. However, it is known that Adolphe Valette's father did not work all his life in the armaments industry, perhaps because of a downturn in the business, and at a later stage joined the Army and completed his career as a Captain of Artillery.[1]

Adolphe Valette's mother Madeleine was born in 1846 in Saint-Jean-Soleymieux, close to the village where her husband came from. Ferdinand and Madeleine were born in the same year.

We have also researched Adolphe Valette's grandparents and we know that his paternal grandfather, Pierre Valette (from whom Adolphe Valette obtained his first christian name), was born in 1806 and had been a locksmith in Saint-Bonnet-le-Château. Pierre had married Marie Daval, who bore him a son, Ferdinand, Adolphe's father, when Pierre was forty. Adolphe Valette never knew his paternal grandfather, who had died in 1864. Pierre's other son, Louis, Adolphe's uncle, continued the family locksmith tradition, whilst Adolphe's father, Ferdinand, at the beginning of his career, entered the armaments profession of his future father-in-law.

Adolphe Valette's maternal grandfather, Claude Brondel (born in 1807), had started his professional life as an innkeeper in the village of Saint-Jean-Soleymieux, where he married Antoinette Tissier. Life as an innkeeper was undoubtedly a hard one, but certainly provided a good living. The inn was a popular meeting point of the village. Claude Brondel's first child, Madeleine, Adolphe Valette's mother, was born when Claude was 39 years old. He later moved to Saint-Etienne and set up in business as an arms manufacturer, taking into the firm his future son-in-law, the father of Adolphe Valette.

Adolphe Valette's parents were thus both living in Saint-Etienne when they were married on 12 March 1872. Ferdinand Valette was 26 and Madeleine was twenty-five. Already by this time they must have had some property, because otherwise they would not have drawn up a marriage contract prior to their wedding.

At the time of her marriage in 1872, Adolphe's mother Madeleine is described as a dressmaker. In the 19th century, occupations related to dress and fashion, such as making ribbons or other trimmings, were important to the prosperity of the capital of the Forez region, as the making of the extravagant dresses worn by fashionable ladies was very labour-intensive. Many women in Saint-Etienne were involved in this burgeoning industry and very often worked in family workshops. However, just two years after her marriage, in 1874 the official records describe Madeleine as a housewife, without profession, which would indicate a degree of financial security; she would therefore have been able to stay at home and look after her children.

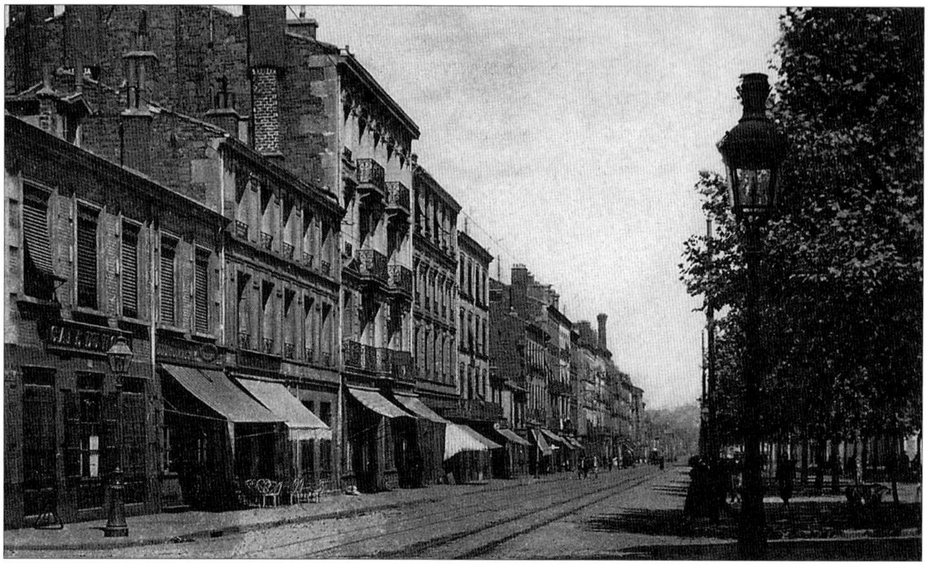

2 *Rue de Roanne in Saint-Etienne, where Valette was born*
Archives Municipales de Saint-Etienne

Shortly after their marriage Adolphe Valette's parents moved house within Saint-Etienne to 28 rue de Roanne, one of the main thoroughfares of the city. Many years later this street would be renamed Avenue Charles de Gaulle.

They had a family very quickly, of whom (Pierre) Adolphe was the third of four. His oldest brother, Ferdinand (Claude Marie), was born in Saint Etienne on 15 January 1873. He lived for a long time in Lyon where we know that he was twice married, before retiring to Cagnes-sur-Mer on the French Riviera, and he died in Nice in 1959.

Of the second child, Antoine (Emile, Edouard), born on 20 September 1874, we also know very little. He was married in Soissons and is reported to have died in a car accident.[2]

The third son was Pierre Adolphe, born on 13 October 1876 in the family home on the rue de Roanne (fig 2 page 4). Later in life, Valette opted to be known by his second name, Adolphe.

Finally came a girl, Louise (Marguerite Aglaée Nathalie), born 25 June 1881, who had a slight mental handicap. She spent part of her life in the Beaujolais region, at Blacé and Coichat, at first with her mother and then close to her brother Adolphe. She was known to be stooped (the village children called her 'hunchback'), and she spent her time pushing a pram full of dolls, with lots of little medals pinned to her blouse. Louise survived her brother Adolphe for another further twenty years, and lived at that time in Coichat with a foster family. She died in 1961 at Véron in the Rhône valley.

The paintings of Valette's mother (fig 1 page 2) and of Louise (fig 3 page 5) show already the two greatest qualities of Valette's work, namely his innate skill as a draughtsman, together with the delicacy of his brushwork and of his use of colours, which give his work an impressionist feel.

But to return to Adolphe. Adolphe Valette was therefore a town child, furthermore from a cold, damp and polluted industrial town, just like Manchester, the town he would later choose to live in.

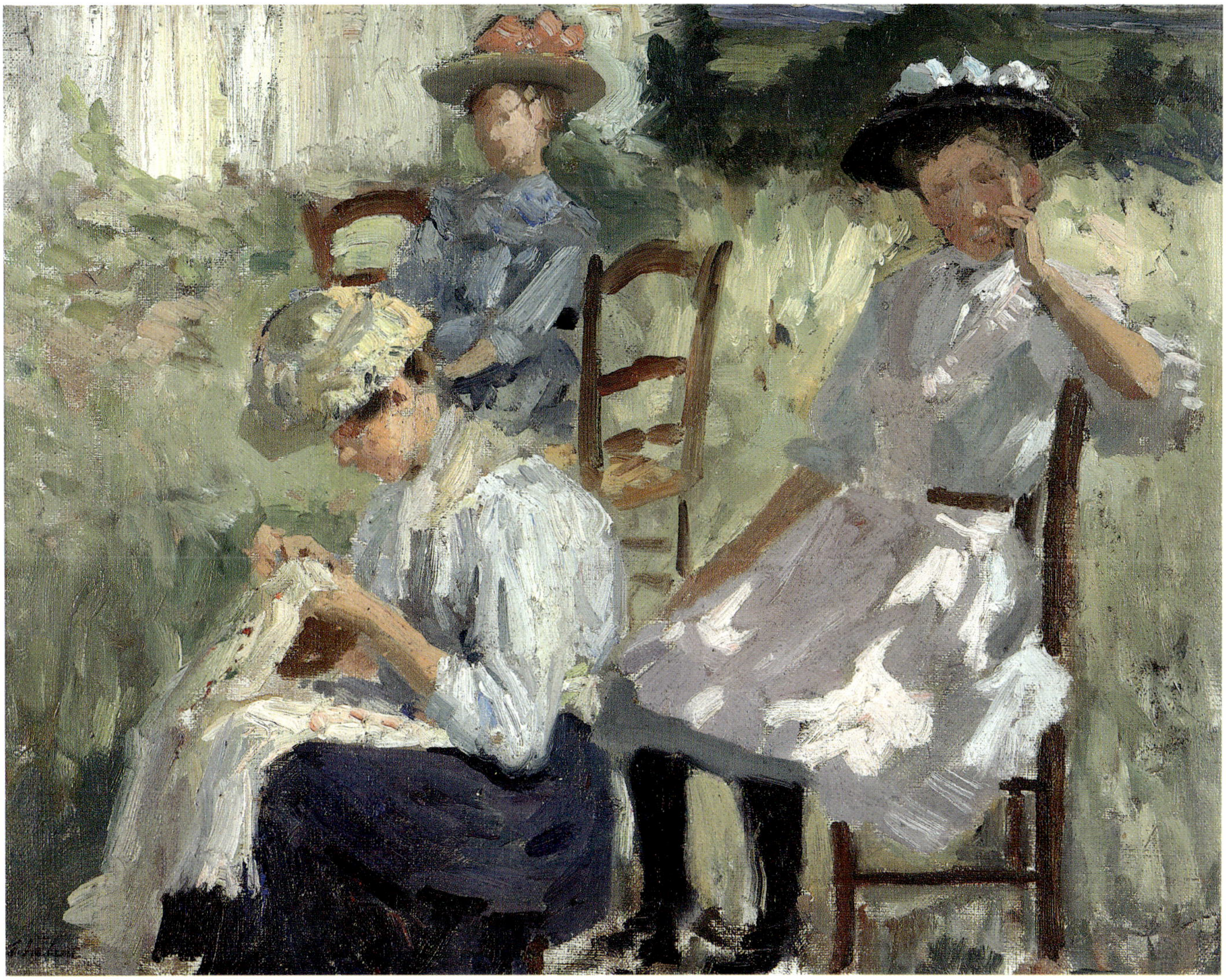

3 *Louise sewing with Two Friends*
Oil on canvas on board, 32 x 40
Tib Lane Gallery

The Saint-Etienne of Adolphe Valette's youth was an industrial town, as was Manchester, his future artistic home. The first French railway had been built in Saint-Etienne in 1832, with horse-drawn wagons, and from 1844 with steam locomotives. It is a valley town, stretched along the valley floor where most of the monuments and public buildings are to be found. Then it expands into the side valleys, filling in all the available space. Just like Manchester, it looked blackened, unpleasant, the public buildings grimy with soot and fissured due to underground mine subsidence. Nevertheless, in a praiseworthy effort, the town council had built some pleasant parks such as the Botanical Gardens and, as if to prove its interest in the arts and in cultural matters generally, the Palais des Arts contained some well-endowed museums (artillery, botanical specimens, and paintings) as well as a fine library. The town also set up an Ecole Spéciale des Mines, an Ecole des Arts Industriels and an Ecole de Dessin.

One can imagine the young Valette, a native of the city, living right in the centre, going to the armaments workshop of his father and grandfather, walking in the streets, smelling the air, soaking up the almost unreal atmosphere of economic prosperity, and finding a certain empathy with the smog of industrial pollution. The little boy, during his early years at school, would certainly have been fascinated by what he could learn from the probably frequent visits to the Palais des Arts, which had on display a wide range of the artefacts and industrial technologies of the period.

His father enrolled young Adolphe, while still very young, at Ecole Régionale des Arts Industriels in 1891.[3] As indicated in its name, the school placed an emphasis on convergence between the arts and industry, a matter vital to the development of this prosperous industrial city. Metallurgy as well as textiles both had a huge need for young people capable of applying their creative talents to the requirements of industry. It is likely that Ferdinand Valette, by registering his son in the special class for engraving, was hoping to perpetuate the family firm of gun manufacturers. Ferdinand Valette would also have most certainly observed in his son a natural talent for drawing, and perhaps he hoped as a result to open up the way to the artistic side of the profession of gunsmith: an important aspect of the study of engraving dealt precisely with engraving on arms.

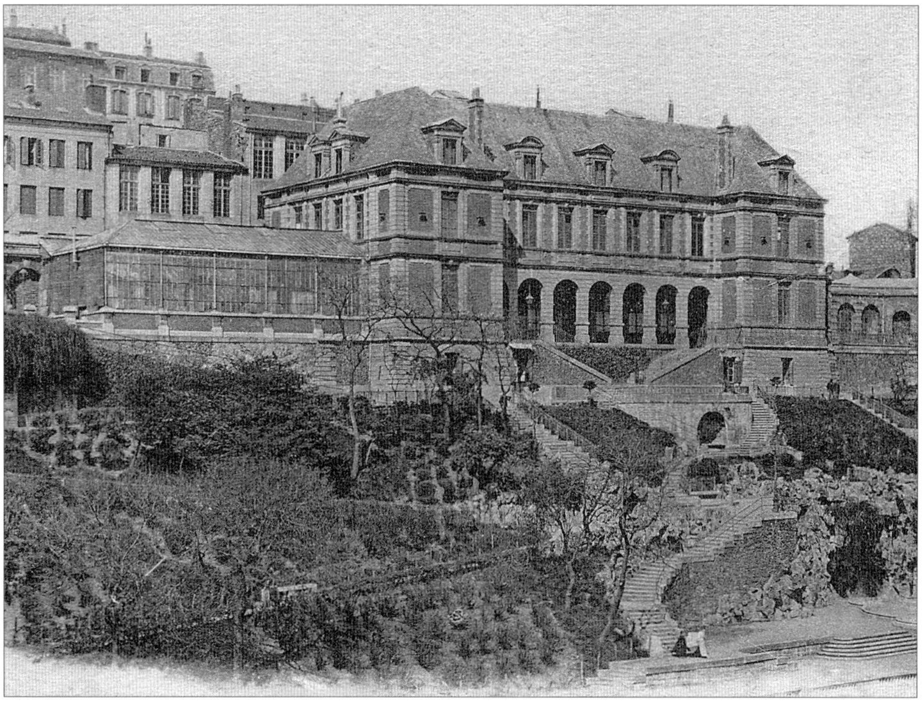

4 *Saint-Etienne School of Art, where Valette studied*
Bibliothèque de l'Ecole Régionale des Beaux-Arts de Saint-Etienne

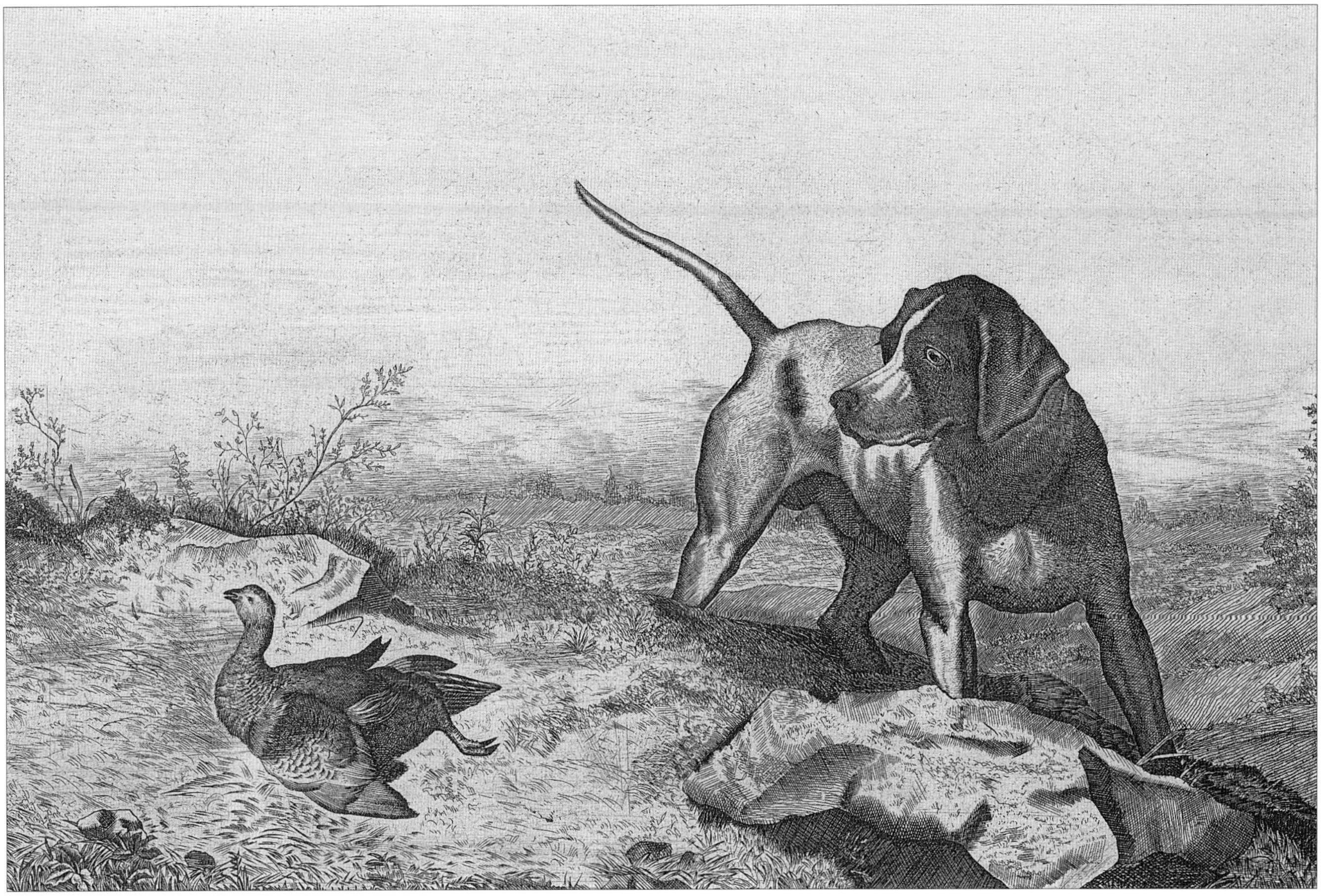

5 *Dog surprising a Partridge, 25 Septembre 1890 (?)*
Engraving, 9,5 x 14.3
Tib Lane Gallery

The school (fig 4 page 6) occupies a prominent site in the centre of the town. The building had been completed in 1860, and it reflected architecturally the ambitions and the value that the town of Saint Etienne placed on the arts and their professional application. Valette attended the school, much as it can be seen today: the building dominates the town from its bold location on the hill of Sainte-Barbe. The construction is of brick, stone and slate, which echoes a style from the time of Louis XIII. In the front, the garden is laid out in a mixture of flowerbeds and lawns, artfully arranged to conceal the slope of the hill. One can imagine the effect on the boy of this building of indisputably venerable appearance. The advanced studies undertaken by the students would, moreover, have reflected the serious impression made by the building.

The specialist engraving class had been created by the Ecole Régionale des Beaux-Arts in 1884, and until 1887 had been directed by Jean Guichard, the 'Courbet' of engraving, who became a teacher at the school having been curator of the Musée d'Armes.[4]

We found in the school records the examination marks for the 1st section of the Advanced class for the academic year 1893/94; Valette was third in Anatomy, and got a special commendation in History; not surprisingly, in view of his tremendous talent, he came first in the class for Engraving, with a mark of 36 out of 40. We have also found a record of the enrolment of Valette for 1894/95, from which we learn that the family had moved from the rue de Roanne to 11 impasse d'Isly, and that Valette, now 18, declared as his profession that of engraver: thus Valette was plunged at a very young age into the world of work, while at the same time continuing his studies. This also seems to be the case for the other students in the class, who all declared a profession (photographer, lithographer, teacher), but who were all older than Adolphe Valette.

Working by day, studying at night: very early on we can see one of the dominant traits of Valette's character, his determination and physical toughness in the face of long working days. All through his career in Manchester he taught during the day as well as in the evening, starting at eight in the morning and finishing at nine in the evening, while in parallel with this activity producing paintings of his own. He was tireless and tenacious, a characteristic that was only weakened through illness towards the end of his life.

One of Valette's teachers at the Ecole Régionale des Arts Industriels in Saint-Etienne was Jean Dablin, who subsequently went on to set up the local Société des Arts du Forez. The two men were to meet again years later in 1929, after Valette's return from Manchester when he rejoined this group of artists with whom he had always kept in touch. The School had recruited Jean Dablin in 1892, following a competitive examination, to teach Flower Drawing, as well as the Life class, the discipline Valette himself was subsequently to teach. Jean Dablin involved himself in the life of the town of Saint-Etienne, and exhibited portraits and also rural landscapes of the Forez region. Dablin was also struck by the industrial landscapes and aspects of the coal mines, which he painted, for example in 'Les Crassiers à Terrenoire' ['The Slag Heaps at Terrenoire']. His painting also seems to have been influenced by symbolism, with Baudelairian references.[5] Given this similarlity of choice of subjects, Jean Dablin may have been Valette's first mentor, albeit that there is no formal confirmation of this.

We do not know what prompted Valette to leave Saint-Etienne. Nevertheless, it reveals another constant in Valette's character, which is that from the time he was very young he had an urge to keep moving, to change his surroundings, and to travel. Perhaps Saint-Etienne no longer brought him satisfaction in his work, or perhaps he wished to expand his artistic horizons; whatever the reasons, he went to live in Lyon.

Lyon was in competition with Saint-Etienne, as much concerning the arts applied to the textile industry, as in the fine arts themselves. Moreover, Lyon saw itself as slightly superior. For a young artist from Saint-Etienne with a degree of ambition, establishing a reputation in Lyon would certainly have been regarded as an essential step on the road to professional success constituted by the cachet of recognition in Paris.

Lyon, Academic Honours

In Lyon, as in Saint-Etienne, Valette, full of pugnacity, led a very full life, a double life in fact, working by day as a professional engraver, while in the evening putting the finishing touches to his artistic education, attending courses in the Lyon art schools.[6] From September 1895 he was enrolled at the Ecole Municipale de Dessin de la Guillotière, 279 rue Vendôme.

Recognition of his brilliant artistic talent was not slow in coming. In fact academic accolades came thick and fast. In the list of successes at the examinations for the year 1895/96, he obtained a silver medal, for Figure Drawing. He also came top of his class in the male class, for which he received a vermeil medal, which was effectively a first prize.

The next year the school organised a competition, which included making a drawing in eight hours without any guidance from a teacher. Valette received the first prize, a 'rappel de médaille de vermeil', and a further vermeil medal in the Figure Drawing category.

In the awards of 21 July 1898 for the academic year 1897/98, in the Figure Drawing category (première division), Valette was awarded a special commendation and an art book 'having twice in succession repeated the winning of the same prize, and to whom the Jury expressed its wholehearted congratulations on his drawing.' ['qui a deux fois obtenu un rappel de prix et à qui le Jury adresse toutes ses félicitations pour son dessin.']

At the 1899 awards, Valette once more received a special commendation and an art book, this time for his work in the Sketching from Nature class.[7]

These accolades won in only a very few years show the talent and promise of the artist. To appreciate the extent of Valette's talent, one should not forget that these awards were granted on the basis of an evaluation of the work of all students from all the municipal schools of drawing in Lyon, as well as the Ecole Nationale des Beaux-Arts de Lyon.

As was the case in major industrial cities such as Saint-Etienne and Manchester, these schools had initially been established to meet the needs of industry; specifically in Lyon, factories working with silk needed talented artists to decorate their fabrics. Nevertheless, over time, these schools increasingly developed by placing the emphasis on artistic creativity in its purest form.

Among Valette's teachers at the Ecole de la Guillotière were Pagny, Eugène Flachat, Tony Tollet, and Perrier.

Tollet taught Valette figure drawing, and Tollet had become by this time one of the key personalities on the artistic scene in Lyon. As a holder of the Prix de Rome, and partisan of traditional styles of painting, Tollet was in particular distinguished for his paintings of historical scenes and in portraiture. Tollet was certainly very accomplished technically, but it is not certain that Valette shared his artistic ideas. In spite of this, many years later during the 1930s at the Salons in Lyon, Valette was described, or allowed himself to be described, as a student of Tollet; was this affiliation claimed by Valette, or was it imposed for commercial reasons? It is difficult to say. As father and breadwinner for a family of six children, in order to make ends meet, Tollet had to accept commissions for innumerable portraits, as well as religious decorations for churches, stained glass windows, and

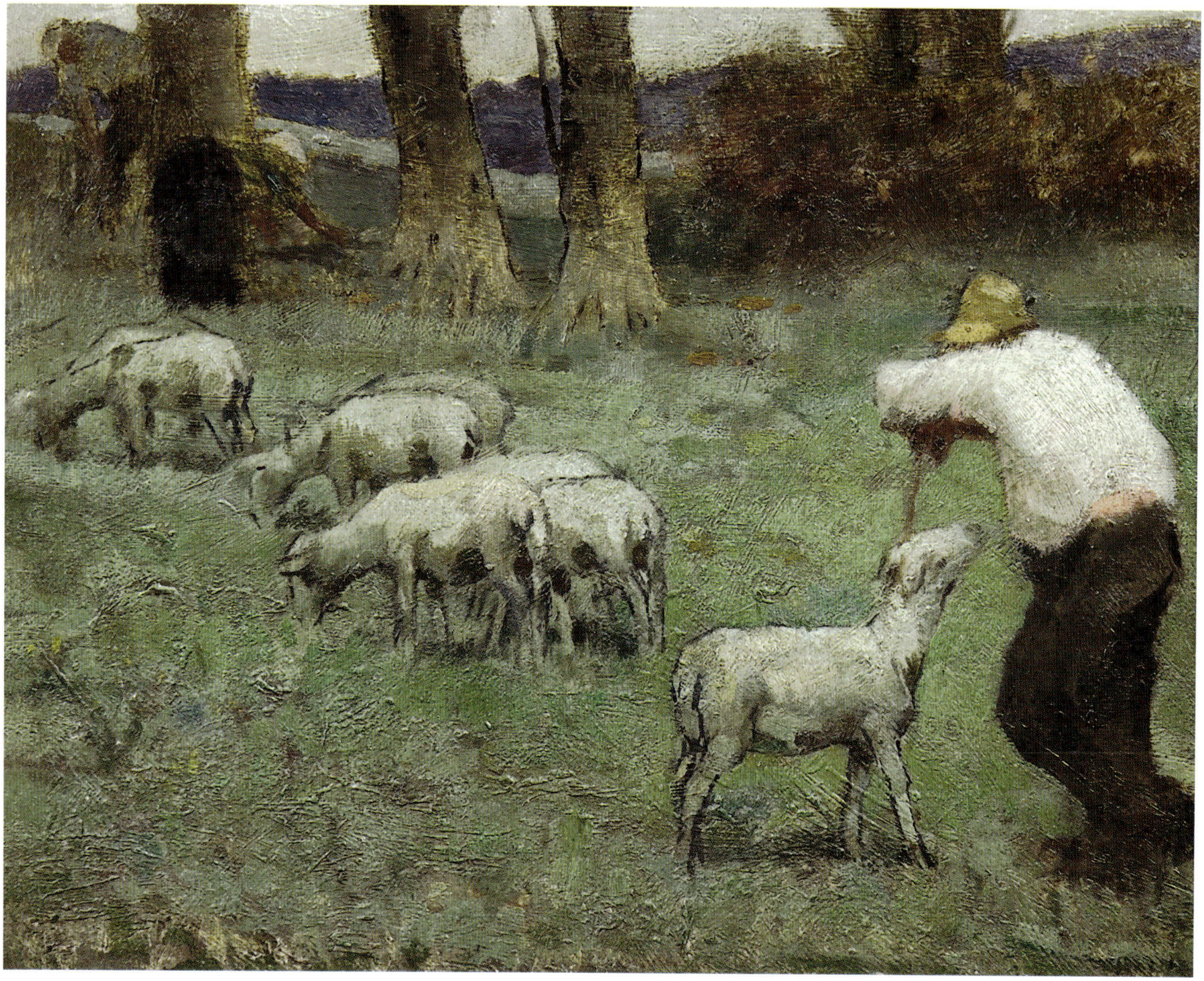

6 *Le Berger et ses Moutons*
Oil on board, 32.5 x 40
Private collection

civic commissions. We will see later that, faced also with the need to earn a living, Valette performed similar work in England for private clients, after he had left the Manchester Municipal School of Art.

It is interesting to note that at this time all the schools of art, in Lyon and also throughout France, suffered from a significant backlash towards austerity and a rise of puritanism including some retrograde reforms such as the suppression by presidential decree in 1899 of the use of nude models in the life class, and their replacement with rubber models. Perhaps this, among other issues, drove Valette several years later to move to England where such restrictions did not apply.

Nevertheless, it would be reasonable to suggest that it was in Lyon that Valette, then aged 20, finally mastered his craft and began to develop into a mature artist.

Lyon offered the young artist many opportunities to enrich his art. It is certainly the case that, in the collections of the Palais Saint-Pierre art gallery, Valette had the opportunity to see many different schools of painting, from Italian painting of the 15th to the 18th centuries, Dutch and Flemish paintings from the 17th century, as well as the Spanish school. French paintings of a very high quality and many diverse styles were on display. The art gallery also took a very healthy interest in local Lyon painters and in modern art, with purchases of contemporary living artists.

A few years before Valette arrived in Lyon, an important event had taken place, namely the decoration of the main staircase of the Palais des Arts, a commission granted in August 1883 to Pierre Puvis de Chavannes (Lyon 1824-Paris 1898). His paintings were done on canvas which was then affixed to the walls and their pale colours created the effect of fresco. Puvis de Chavannes painted monumental compositions to decorate the walls of the various aisles of the art gallery. At first he painted 'Le Bois Sacré Cher aux Arts et aux Muses' [The Sacred Wood cherished by the Arts and the Muses] which was affixed to the south wall of the stairwell in 1886. 'Vision Antique' [A Vision of Antiquity] was painted in 1885, and affixed to the east wall in 1886. That

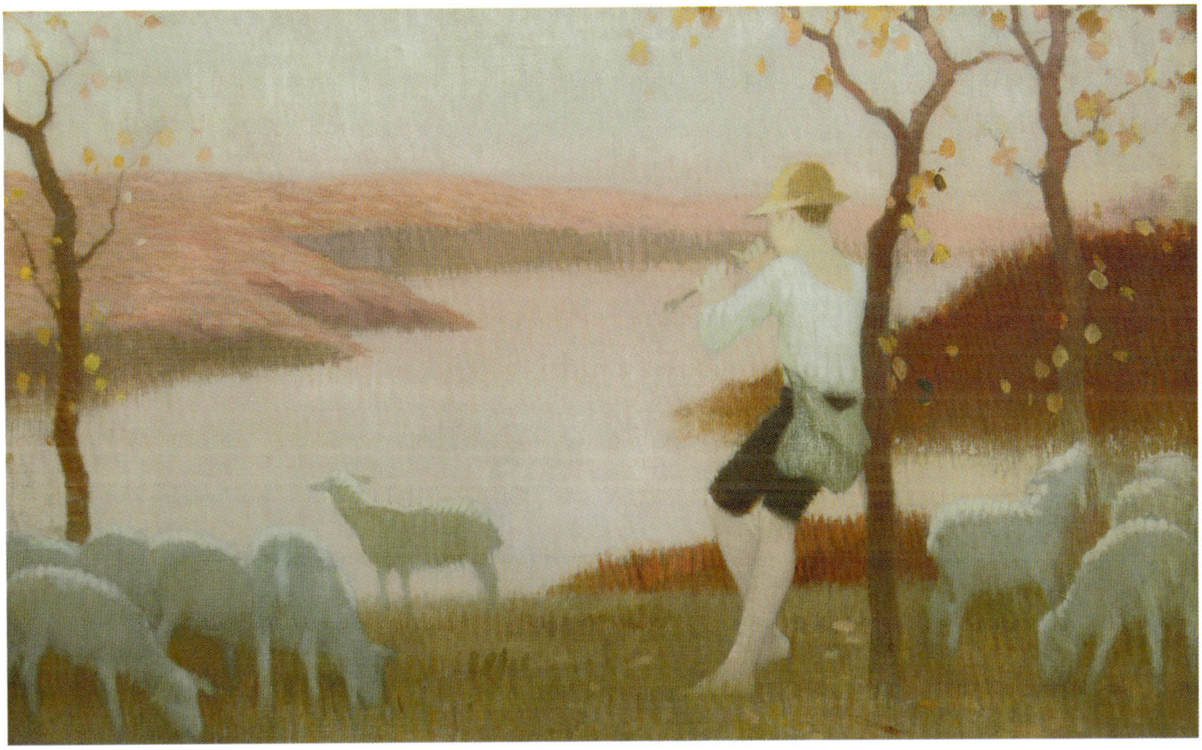

7 *Shepherd and Sheep under Trees*
Oil on canvas, 76 x 120
Private collection

same year 'L'Inspiration Chrétienne' [The Christian Inspiration] was affixed to the west wall of the stairwell, and 'Le Rhône et La Saône' went on the north wall. These decorative frescoes, where Puvis de Chavannes deliberately avoided any attempt at conveying contours, and only made a play on the balance of masses and harmony in different shades of soft monochrome colours, drew their inspiration from the antique and allegorical repertoire. At the time these entirely innovative murals aroused great controversy, but they had a major influence on their contemporaries and consolidated the reputation of Puvis de Chavannes as a master of symbolism. In some of Valette's canvases one can detect this influence of symbolism (without the mythological subject matter), particularly the use of diluted colours and monochromes in pastoral themes where Valette gracefully depicts gentle landscapes, valleys and fields, in which he places, with careful observation, the peasant working in the field, or the shepherd and his flock.

Paris at the end of the 19th century had finally accepted the impressionist movement, and painters there began to acquire increasing prestige and universal recognition. Monet triumphed, the pictures of Pissarro and Degas were purchased or accepted by the State, retrospective exhibitions (Berthe Morisot in 1896), solo exhibitions (Sisley in 1897), exhibitions of paintings from legacy (Caillebotte in 1894), auctions (Duret in 1894, Choquet in 1899) – everything contributed to arouse the public's appreciation for this style of painting, which then swept through the French provinces and across Europe. Valette found his masters and his inspiration very largely from amongst their number.

Bordeaux, Honours, Disappointments, and a Springboard of Fate

Our investigations in Bordeaux have led us to refute some widely accepted beliefs about Valette, which had been presented as indisputable by his admirers. We have made some most edifying discoveries.

But to start at the beginning: after Lyon the Valette trail leads to Bordeaux. We do not know the reasons that led Valette to move once again. After Lyon, why did he not go 'up' to Paris, which would seem to have been the obvious move for such a gifted young painter? We do not know. The archives of the two most famous Paris arts schools of that time, the Ecole Nationale des Beaux-Arts and the Academie Julian, bear no record that Valette ever enrolled there.

In Bordeaux Valette immediately found work as an engraver and professional draughtsman, at the same time enrolling at the Ecole Municipale des Beaux-Arts et des Arts Décoratifs.

We have found the results of the examinations for 1901 and 1902. In 1901 Valette received a commendation in Decorative Painting (working on a compulsory subject), and a commendation for his work during the year in the Croquis de Groupe [Group Sketch Drawing] class. In 1902 out of 414 students he received a commendation for Tête d'Expression [Drawing of the Head], and again for Sketch Drawing of figures in a group.[8] The prize-giving ceremonies were held in the presence of local politicians and municipal dignitaries in the concert hall of the Grand Théâtre of Bordeaux. It is

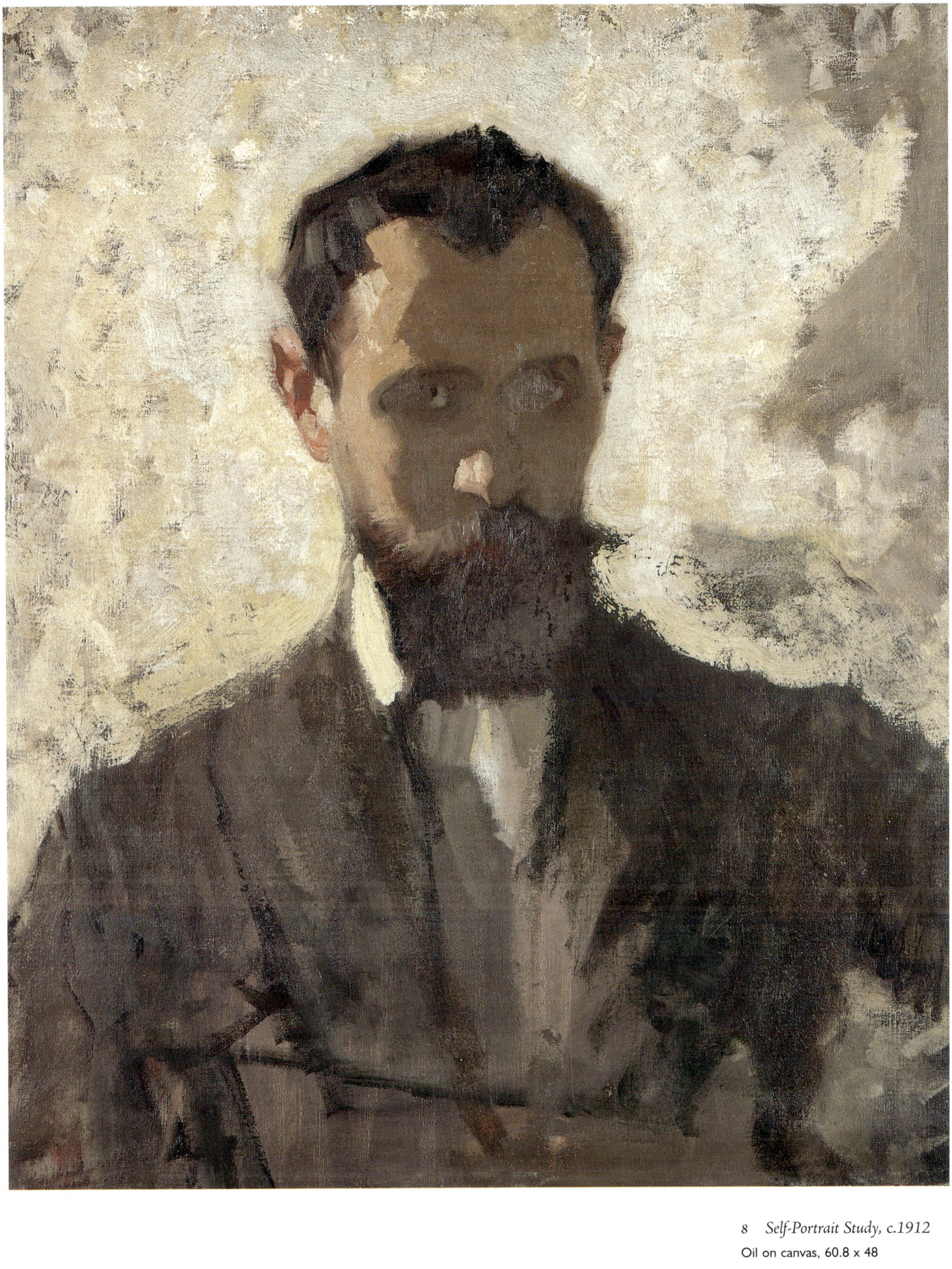

8 *Self-Portrait Study*, c.1912
Oil on canvas, 60.8 x 48
Manchester Art Gallery

clear from the list of award winners from among the students at the school, as well as the curriculum and range of courses on offer (Painted Sketch Composition, Head Life Drawing, Figure Life Composition, Figure Composition from the Antique Individual and Group Sketching, etc.), that these studies were wide ranging, well documented, and thorough.

At the Ecole Municipale des Beaux-Arts et des Arts Décoratifs, Valette was tutored by Quinsac, a fashionable portrait painter of the Bordeaux upper class. Quinsac also painted scenes from ancient mythology, and was subsequently appointed director of the Ecole des Beaux-Arts. However, it does not seem that Quinsac had any determining influence on Valette's artistic development.

Valette took up residence at 30 rue de la Course, a street of small houses half-way between the residential district of the Jardin Public and the bustling Chartrons area, where the activities of the Bordeaux wine merchants were concentrated.

Here we can see a third feature of Valette's life, namely his capacity to integrate into the local artists' community. He showed his work at the Salons d'Automne of the local Société des Arts Girondins; in 1903 he exhibited two charcoal drawings, one of which was an autumn landscape, and in 1904 two dry-point etchings. It seems, however, that this local society was fairly conventional and reflected the ambient provincialism that prevailed at the time.

Valette is recorded also as having been granted a scholarship by the Bordeaux Chamber of Commerce.

The Ecole Municipale des Beaux-Arts et des Arts Décoratifs in Bordeaux, founded as early as 1690, was a prestigious academy, and wherever possible it sought to encourage the most talented students. Several scholarships were available to support able students while learning their craft. There was a scholarship funded by the municipality, and one from the Chamber of Commerce which was at pains to demonstrate that, in the context of the interests it represented, art was not divisible from industry and commerce, and there were prizes funded each year by the Société des Arts Girondins.

There was the important Poirson scholarship, awarded every second year to a young painter to enable further study abroad. In the 1903 report by the Jury, we read that Valette had been recommended for this prize by Pierre Paris, director of the school and also Valette's art history tutor. This involved financing a trip to Japan to study the influence of Japanese art and prints on French impressionism. Japanese art had reached France in the wake of the Great Universal Exhibitions and thanks to reports by learned collectors who were fascinated by the Japanese prints. In some of Valette's work one can detect a faint influence from the Far East in the way he underlined certain features, a purity of line, as well as his choice of certain still life objects or the way he emphasised certain views in a landscape.

The Poirson scholarship, worth 400 francs, came from a legacy of 50,000 francs left by the eponymous art lover to the town of Bordeaux, to whom he had also bequeathed his collection of paintings.

Unfortunately, Valette's application was turned down 'on the grounds that he already had an income from his skills as an industrial draughtsman' ['dans la mesure où il tirait déjà des revenus de son talent car travaillant déjà comme dessinateur industriel']. A vote was taken, but the application was finally rejected in favour of another student, Bournac.[9] This is specifically mentioned in the report of the Jury of the Ecole des Beaux-Arts of 1903.[10] Nevertheless, it is still common to see documents written about Valette describing him as having actually received this scholarship, and suggesting that it was the outbreak of the Russo-Japanese war that prevented him from going to Japan.

We now know that the usurped reputation of having won this scholarship followed Valette and enhanced his reputation even after his death. This begs some serious questions regarding certain aspects of his character or his close circle of family and friends, questions hitherto obscured. Did Valette personally wish to allow it to be believed that he had won this scholarship? Did he think he had 'morally' won it, given that he had been recommended for it, and that it was only his status as a professional designer, which had resulted in his being turned down? This is an enigma, as Valette does not seem the sort of person to claim a distinction that he had not won. What is possible is that, somewhat as legends are created, the truth was distorted by popular enthusiasm and the excessive bias of his admirers (perhaps by his second wife, Andrée), and subsequently believed and amplified by public opinion. Did Valette go along with this concept by not firmly denying it, or was this a fiction created after his death? We do not know. Perhaps there are other documents, not preserved in the Archives and library of the Ecole des Beaux-Arts, that may have played a part in giving credence to the scholarship thesis. Conversely, only documents clearly stating that he was not the beneficiary have been found.

Valette would certainly have been very disappointed not to have been awarded the scholarship and, having travel in his blood, and with the ambition to improve his skills and to face new challenges, he decided to emigrate to England.

Other famous French artists had shown the way. Already by the second half of the 19th century the artistic community had become increasingly international, and a number of French artists had gone to learn from the great painters of the English countryside, such as Constable, and to discover the very original way in which Turner portrayed the effects of light. Later it had been the turn of Monet and Pissarro, who had originally gone to England to escape the consequences of the Franco-Prussian war. Here they discovered unexpectedly the potential for powerful artistic inspiration of mist over the Thames, smoke above the factories, and the variety of the English countryside. So it was that, years later, Valette decided to follow in their footsteps.

Nevertheless, one may ask, what were the underlying reasons for the specific choice of England? To emigrate seemed a normal enough reaction for a young man who must have been hugely disappointed at having been rejected for the Poirson scholarship. But why England? One can only conjecture. England at the time was a country where it was not difficult to find employment, and Manchester presented many similarities to Saint-Etienne, the town of Valette's birth.

2 The Manchester Years: The Flourishing of an Artistic Personality

Manchester, as seen by Valette: An Economic Effervescence in the Haze and Fogs of Northern England

According to certain witnesses, it seems that Valette, prior to Manchester, first went to London and in 1904 enrolled at the School of Art at Birkbeck College.[1] His stay in the capital was brief, as from 1905 we know for certain that he was in Manchester, where his name appears as a student on the registers of the evening classes of the Municipal School of Art, in the Life Drawing and Engraving classes, a technique already familiar to him from his time in France.[2]

Manchester was at the time a city with many similarities to Saint-Etienne, the town of his childhood and youth. It is even interesting to note that there were also tenuous industrial links between Saint-Etienne and England from the 19th century; the first steelworks in Saint-Etienne was founded by an Englishman by the name of Jackson and production of bicycles was introduced in Saint-Etienne by another Englishman, Duncan, of the Rudge company.[3]

The Municipal School of Art in Manchester had been founded, like those in Saint-Etienne and Lyon, to meet the needs of textile manufacturers and the first classes were focused on Landscape, Figure, Flower and Ornamental Design. From the first half of the 19th century, we know that there were contacts with the Ecole des Beaux-Arts in Lyon, whose facilities were the envy of the Mancunian lecturers. In Lyon, 'Their school occupies a palace with botanic gardens attached to it', railed the tutors in Manchester. 'Here we occupy a ruin … and a few cut flowers are our botanic garden.'[4]

Combining the words 'industrial revolution' and 'cotton' immediately triggers an evocation of phantom-dark, grimy towns, factory towns whose pulse is that of the steam engines driving machinery or a forest of chimneys pouring out smoke. In fact, the cotton mills were present throughout the Lancashire region, but popular imagination very often associates them with Manchester.

The only really notable French visitor to provide us with an account of Manchester was Alexis de Tocqueville, in 1835, of course well before Valette's arrival there. At that time, Tocqueville pilloried Manchester as being guilty of all the errors of the industrial revolution: 'Raise your eyes and all about this place you will see immense palaces of industry rising up. You will hear the roar of furnaces, and the whistling of steam. These vast edifices overshadowed the dwellings of the people living there, and prevented the penetration of air and light; they envelop them in a perpetual fog (…). A thick, black smoke covers the city. The sun is visible through it only as a disk without rays of light. It is in the midst of this incomplete daylight that 300,000 human beings toil ceaselessly.' ['Levez la tête, et tout autour de cette place, vous verrez s'élever les immenses palais de l'industrie. Vous entendez le bruit des fourneaux, les sifflements de la vapeur. Ces vastes demeures empêchent l'air et la lumière de pénétrer dans les demeures humaines qu'elles dominent; elles les enveloppent d'un perpétuel brouillard ... Une épaisse et noire fumée couvre la cité. Le soleil paraît au travers comme un disque sans rayons. C'est au milieu de ce jour incomplet que s'agitent sans cesse 300.000 créatures humaines'] (...).[5]

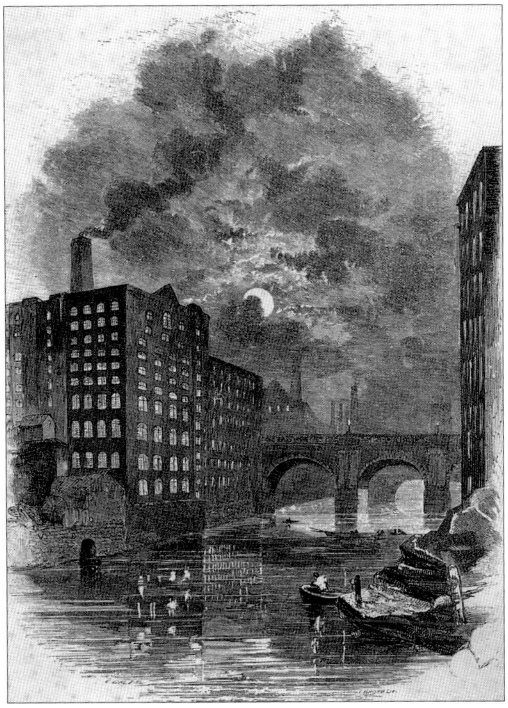

9 *River Irwell, factories at night, 1890*
Manchester Archives and Local Studies

Valette arrived in Manchester seventy years after this description of it by de Tocqueville. Manchester had certainly changed since 1835; Valette's canvases, on the contrary, were to reflect the beauty that the artist saw in the town; he wished to reveal this to the local population, albeit perhaps solely occupied, as Tocqueville imagined, 'in the pursuit of accumulating riches' ['à vouloir amasser de l'or'].

This pursuit on the part of Valette of a beauty in modernity was certainly appreciated by art critics of the time. In 1910, the first of the monumental canvases by Valette was exhibited in the Walker Art Gallery in Liverpool in the 'Continental Room'; On 17 September the *Liverpool Courier* reported: 'The imaginations of these men, whetted and quick, are constantly whipping about in fresh directions, pouncing on new motives and fresh finds. It takes Mister Valette for instance, to discover that "Oxford Street[*sic*], Manchester" with its taxi-cabs and high poised cranes is just as genuinely romantic as Oxford itself.'[6] *The Daily News* also shared this opinion in the following appreciative terms: 'Pierre Valette's "Oxford Road, Manchester" is a fine impression conveying all the greyness and sombre dignity of the city, with a motor car in the foreground to symbolise its wealth.'[7]

Equally, on the occasion of the exhibition of the 'Society of Modern Artists' that took place in 1912, the critics were enthusiastic: 'If any citizen desires to realise how really beautiful parts of Manchester may appear under certain lights he should inspect the canvases of Adolphe Valette.'[8]

Valette's Mancunian canvases reflect the atmosphere of smoke, fog and pollution, but also the industrial and economic dynamism of the city and its inhabitants. The Manchester smog was an inspiration for Valette, just as it inspired Monet in London, when he found in this industrial mist a chromatic and pictorial challenge worthy of him. Monet ultimately grew to hate Sundays in London in that the reduction or cessation of industrial activity diminished the effects of pollution: in his own words he complained: 'As always on Sunday, there wasn't a wisp of fog, it was appallingly clear' ['Comme toujours, le dimanche, pas l'ombre d'une brume, même c'était d'une netteté épouvantable'] and 'What a sad day is the English Sunday, nature feels its effects,

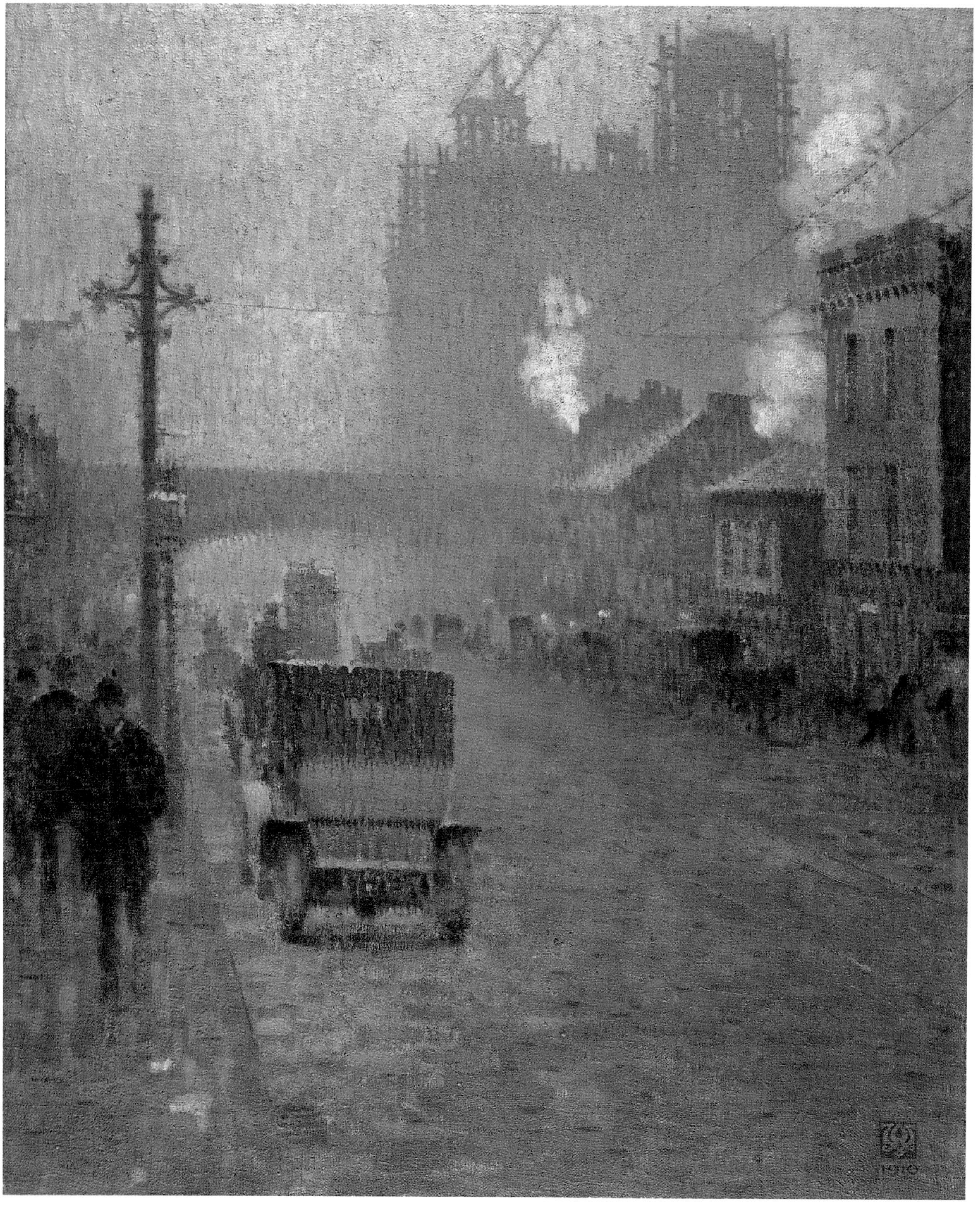

10 Oxford Road, Manchester, 1910

Oil on jute, 127.4 x 101.5

Manchester Art Gallery

everything seems dead, not a train, no smoke, no boats, nothing that stimulates the imagination.' ['Quelle journée triste que ce Dimanche anglais, la nature s'en ressent, tout est mort, pas de train, pas de fumée ni de bateaux, rien qui excite un peu la verve'!][9]

Manchester, in Valette's day, was involved with the development of many different types of industry: engineering and the manufacture of all types of industrial machinery, but above all 'cotton was king'. The scale of the cotton industry was reflected not only in the cotton spinning and weaving mills, but also in all the derivative activities, in other words the dyeing of cotton yarn, the printing of the woven cotton cloth, the marketing and distribution of products, and the creation of clothing. Employment in Manchester encompassed a vast number of cotton mill workers but also clothes pattern designers and draughtsmen, seamstresses, milliners, and hatters.

So it was that Valette, from 1904, gave his services to the printing company Norbury Natzio and Co Ltd. Valette's main task was to paint portraits of young women which would be then used on printed piece tickets for textiles to be exported. He also designed calendars.

The Manchester textile industry traders had won a supremacy in the new ready-to-wear clothing industry and the influence of fashion cycles had transformed the dress habits of young female workers and women of the petite bourgeoisie and middle classes.

The Mancunian traders, thanks to the development of the railways, had unquestionably captured the market by sending their commercial travellers to visit drapers and sellers of fabrics in all countries, but had also monopolised the markets in the colonies (Australia, New Zealand, Canada, and South Africa) and in Latin America and China. Consequently, a certain segment of the population in Manchester was rather cosmopolitan, and Valette enjoyed their company such as that of the Venezuelan Gabriela de Bolivar who was later to become his first wife and the Egyptian poet Ahmed Loutfi (fig 56 page 57).

Between 1870 and 1913, each year Manchester sent to India over a thousand million yards of fabric.[10] It was also in Manchester that the rainwear industry was born, which was created in 1824 by the eponymous Charles Macintosh, and by the early 20th century it had attained an undisputed supremacy.

The advances in telegraph technology and improvements in communication rendered the growth and development of markets even more rapid. At the end of the 19th century, the train linking Manchester to London took only three and three-quarter hours.[11] In 1910, the French aviation pioneer Louis Paulhan, just a few months after Louis Blériot's crossing of the channel, achieved an even more remarkable exploit: he flew from London to Manchester, a distance of 183 miles. Louis Paulhan was honoured at the Manchester town hall and this feat by a compatriot would certainly not have escaped Adolphe Valette, who had already been living in Manchester for over five years.[12]

By 1901, the population of Greater Manchester including the suburbs had increased from the 300,000 inhabitants to which Tocqueville refers in 1835 to 2.1 million inhabitants. In fact, the centre of Manchester reduced in population size,

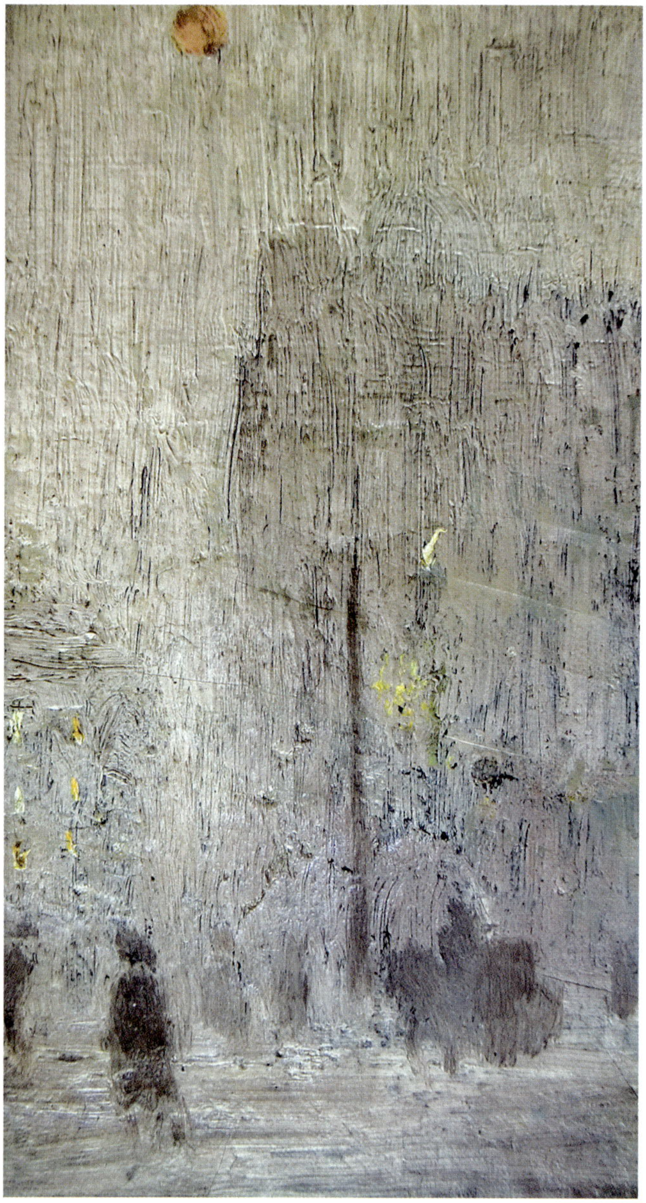

11 St Peter's Square
Oil on board, 15.2 x 7.6
Private collection

while retaining its administration, commerce and businesses, as well as restaurants and cafés. Large hotels were already a feature of the major locations where business was done. It was at the *Midland Hotel*, also frequented by Valette and located on St Peter's Square (fig 11 page 20), that Charles Rolls met Henry Royce in 1904 and thereby determined the destiny of the most famous motor car to be produced in the region.[13]

Vast fortunes were made due to the advent of the industrial age in Manchester and some of the warehouses located along the commercial avenues in the centre assumed the bearing of Florentine and Gothic palaces. The warehouse was a pivotal component in the business trading centre of Victorian and Edwardian Manchester: it served as a place for the presentation of merchandise, as an office, as a packing and dispatching hall and as a loading and unloading hub.[14] In present times, these warehouses, which have an undeniably venerable appearance and are as such testaments to the quality of industrial architecture, have now been converted into offices and luxury hotels, and, most recently, into apartments.

These warehouses, offices and industrial buildings, through which so much economic activity passed, are magnificently represented in one of Valette's most famous canvases, 'India House' (fig 12 page 21), painted in 1912. Through their rear façade the buildings communicated with the rivers and canals for the water-borne loading and unloading of goods delivered by barges on the water which 'industrial activity has tinged with a thousand colours' [que les travaux de l'industrie ont teinté de mille couleurs].[15] The smoke of a train and the twinkling of the lights in India House, the office building that occupies the entire background of the composition and is located on Whitworth Street, show us the

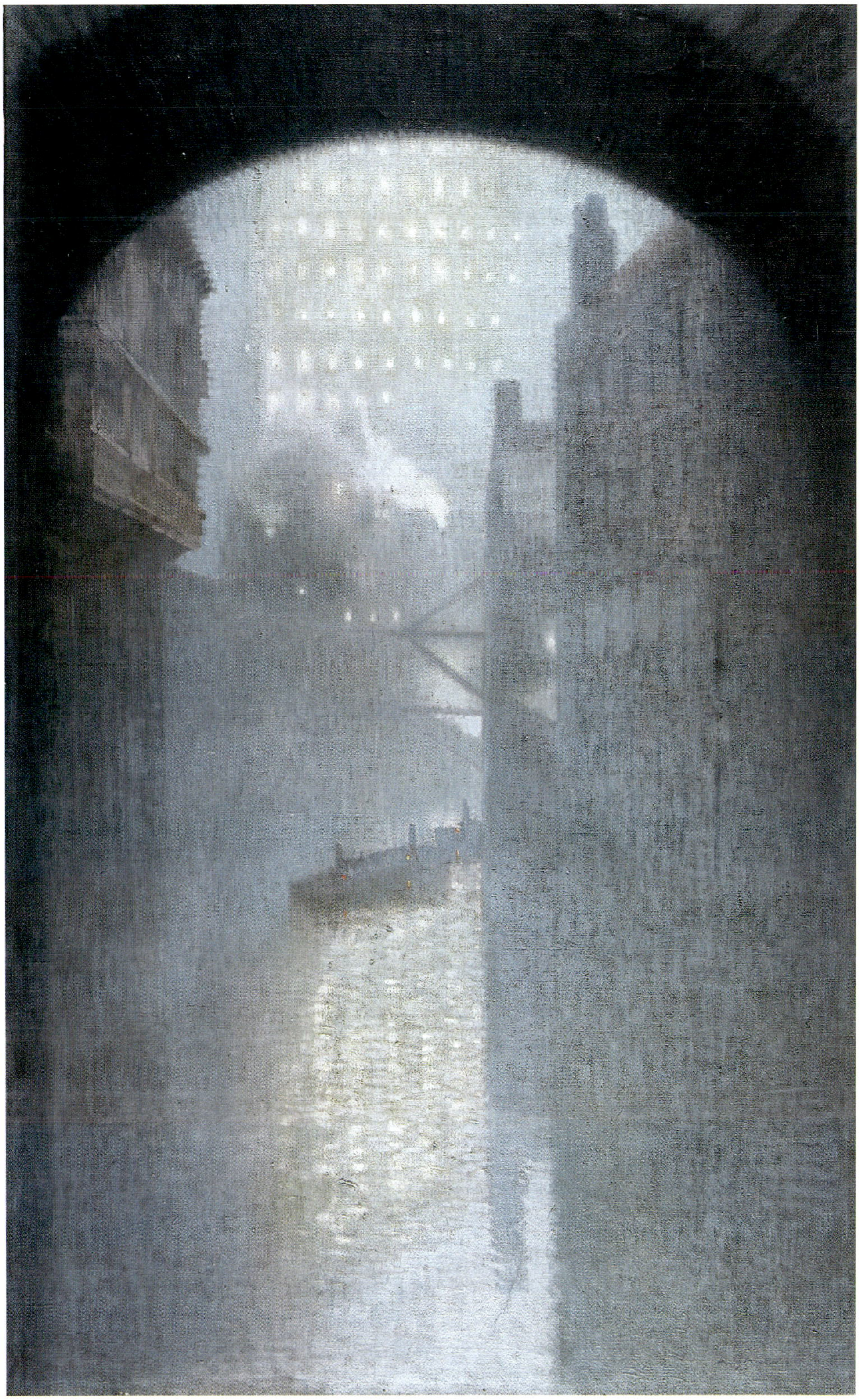

12 India House, Manchester, 1912

Oil on jute or linen, 142.4 x 86.1

Manchester Art Gallery

Manchester of industry and commerce. To the left of the picture, extended out over the river Medlock, is part of the Refuge Assurance building, now the *Palace Hotel*.

In the area surrounding the town centre of Manchester, the maps of the period show a jumble of industries and rivers and canals serving them, factories, loading bays, timber warehouses, foundries, cotton mills, allowing industry to dominate the environment completely, with, in addition, small workers' houses back-to-back, with windows on one side only; on the other hand, the middle classes and the petite bourgeoisie chose to live increasingly further out of the town, in the suburbs.

The painting 'The Irwell' (not illustrated) of 1913 exploits the poetic effects of the haze, using the industrial life of Manchester as a background canvas; in the background of this urban and industrial microcosm lies the cathedral, in profile, symbol of the Manchester of the Middle Ages, around which the city has grown chaotically.

The rivers (the Irwell, the Medlock, and the Irk) that wind through Manchester were a source of fascination for Valette, and responded to his curiosity for pictorial compositions located by water, surrounded by urban vistas of the industrial transformation.

13 *Manchester Street in Fog, dated on reverse 1909*
Oil on millboard, 15 x 23.5
Private collection

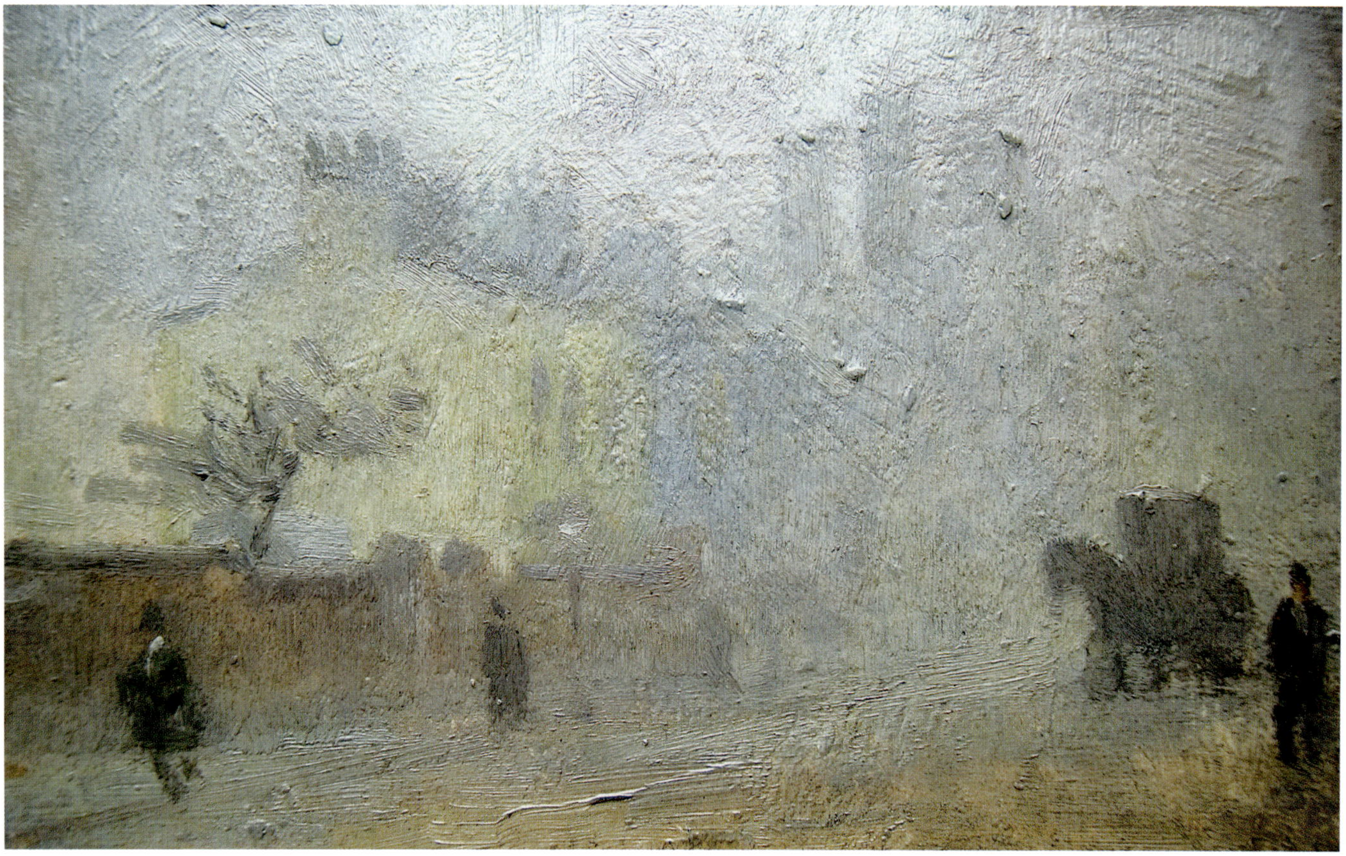

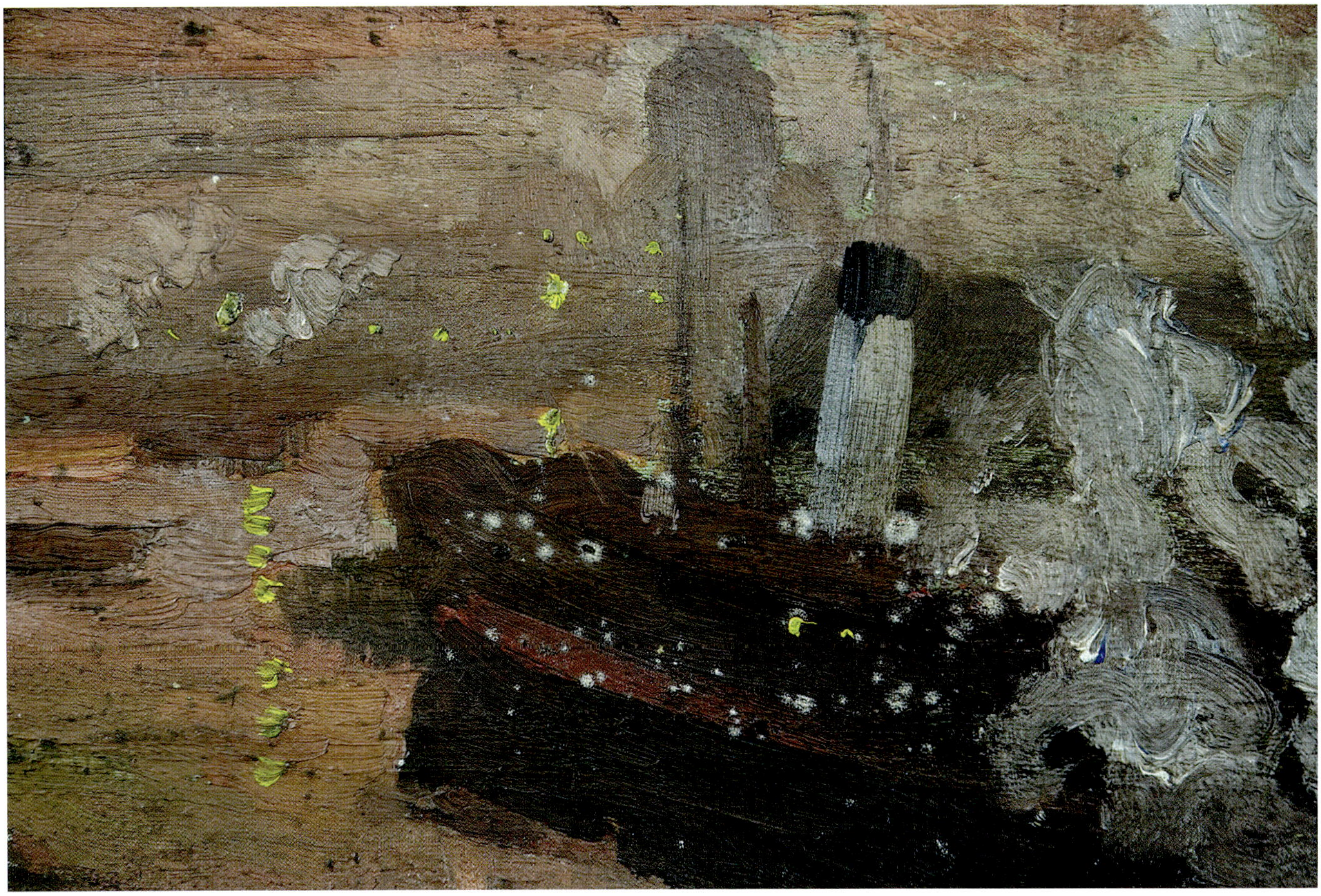

14 *Tugboat on Manchester Ship Canal*
Oil on board, 13.5 x 20
Private collection

While, as we have seen, the warehouses constituted the commercial arteries for the cotton trade in Manchester, the Royal Exchange was its heart. All the commercial transactions took place through it and a visitor would encounter a dense mass of nearly six thousand men engaged in discussion and in commercial and financial operations. There was also the Cotton Exchange, which in 1913 had more than 10,000 members. Buyers and sellers from all walks of life met there, and concluded numerous contracts in a short space of time while gathering information on the state of health of the various markets. The commercial importance of Manchester could also be measured in the number of operations performed by the 'Manchester Clearing House', which combined 12 local banks whose turnover was already in 1896 valued at £191 million.[16]

Manchester's economy was also on a significant scale in the field of insurance. Given the preponderance of Manchester in industry and engineering, it is not surprising that the city became a centre for the insurance of industrial risks. In the field of life insurance, the 'Refuge Assurance Company' whose building under construction appears in the canvas 'Oxford Road' (1910) (fig 10 page 18) by Valette, was the leader and figurehead in this sector.

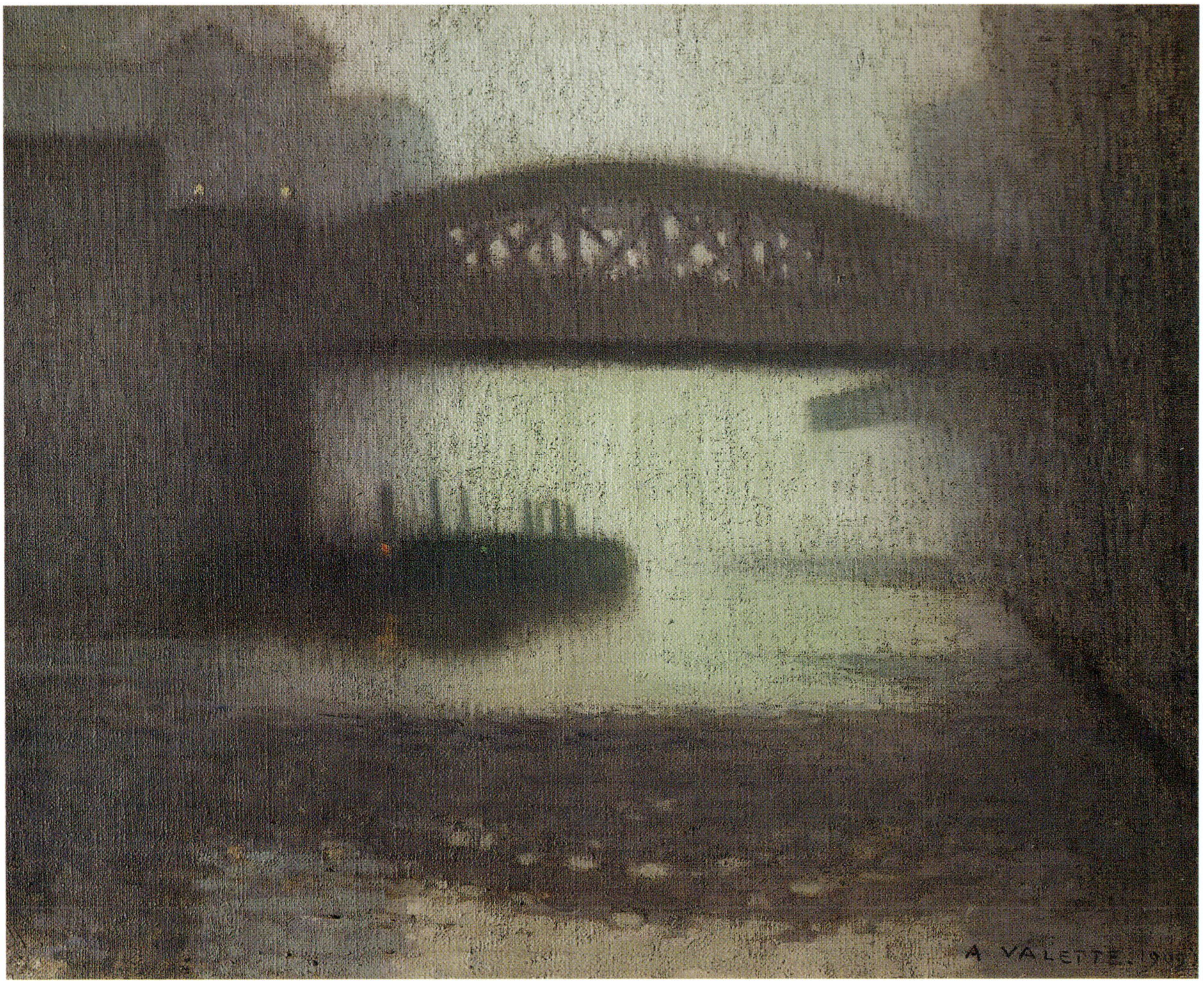

15 Windsor Bridge on the Irwell, 1909
Oil on jute, 50.4 x 61.1
Manchester Art Gallery

In the field of transport, from the mid-19th century, canals had lost their ascendancy to the railways, but in the 1890s one of the largest engineering projects was to restore the role of transport by water as a key aspect of the Manchester economy. This was to become a theme dear to Valette in many of his works. The Manchester authorities had commissioned the construction of the Manchester Ship Canal between 1887 and 1894. The canal was 35 miles long, linked Manchester to the sea and turned Manchester into the fourth largest maritime port in Great Britain. Its completion was of considerable significance for the reduction in the cost of the transport of goods, both raw materials and finished products.

A work of this magnitude which involved 75 steam shovels, 124 steam cranes and seven dredgers was a source of fascination to the people of the time. The

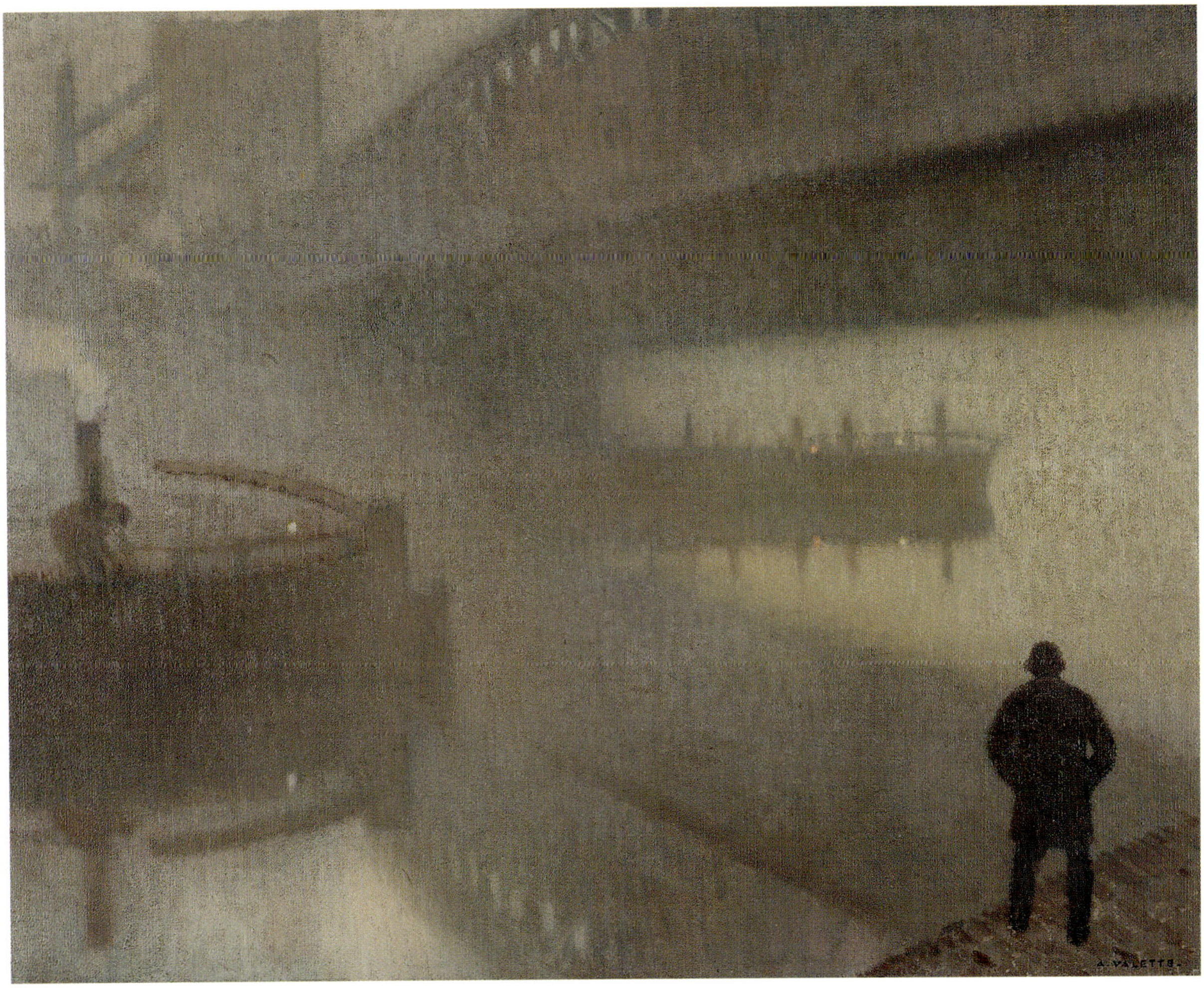

16 *Under Windsor Bridge on the Irwell, 1912*
Oil on linen or jute, 48.2 x 61
Manchester Art Gallery

canal was designed to be of the same depth as the Suez canal.[17] When the project was complete, Manchester had its own docks, the 'Manchester Docks', the 'Pomona Docks' and the 'Trafford Wharf'. Valette often set up his easel there and drew his inspiration from it. A painting of the Manchester Ship Canal dated 18 March 1908 (fig 89 page 86) is in fact the first known picture having industrial Manchester as its theme: Valette depicts the canal with cargo boats, barges, and in the background 'Trafford Wharf' with its warehouses, industrial buildings and grain elevator.

Valette was fascinated by bridges, factories, and the metallic structures overhanging the Manchester rivers and canals. 'Windsor Bridge on the Irwell' (fig 15 page 24) was painted in 1909, 'Under Windsor Bridge on the Irwell' (fig 16 page 25) was painted

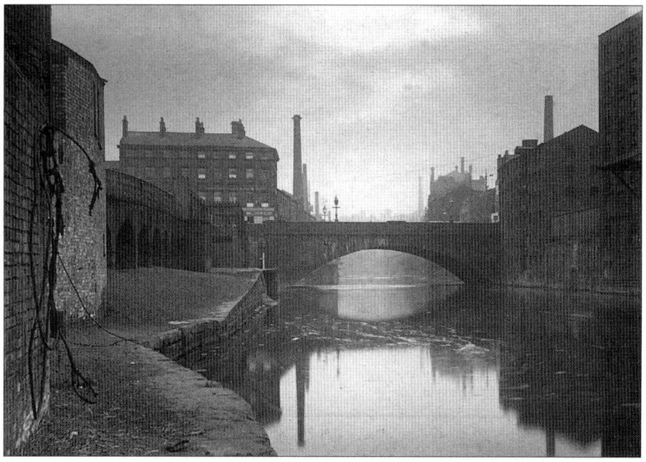

in 1912. In fact, both these paintings are of the Irwell Street Bridge, and were erroneously described as Windsor Bridge in the titles.

The painting 'Bailey Bridge' (fig 19 page 27) dated 1912 should be considered in parallel with the photograph of that scene taken in 1900 from the same vantage point (fig 17 page 26). We find all the elements that Valette was often to transcend: water, boats, the juxtaposition of industrial buildings with factory chimneys and structures such as bridges. The sky is obliterated by smoke, the water of the Irwell is dirty or malodorous, but this is the vector that carried the city's economy.

17 New Bailey Bridge Street, 1900
Manchester Archives and Local Studies

The cabs, many of them Hansom cabs named after their Mancunian inventor Joseph Aloysius Hansom, and horse-drawn omnibuses remained the normal means of transport for short journeys. We see them represented in Valette's pictures: 'Hansom Cab at All Saints' (1910) (fig 93 page 92), 'Old Cab at All Saints' (1911) (fig 94 page 93) and 'Albert Square' (1910) (fig 92 page 90). In 1893, the 385 omnibuses in Manchester required 3,583 horses to draw them. The streets of Manchester were not without their offensive smells. It was only from 1900 that the trams began to be electrified.

'Old Cab at All Saints' (fig 94 page 93) takes us to a part of the heart of Manchester that did not survive the bombings of the Second World War. The painting shows in the background the 'Registry Office' and one can also discern the silhouette of the church of All Saints, which was consecrated in 1820. The church was surrounded by a cemetery and was in the middle of the park of the same name. Very close to this was the Manchester Municipal School of Art where Valette taught, which would certainly have enabled him to work on the studies for his paintings in situ. So it was that Valette stayed in Manchester for the duration of the First World War.

'Albert Square' (1910) (fig 92 page 90) is the busy central square of Manchester. It is flanked on one side by the huge neo-gothic edifice of the Town Hall, built between 1867 and 1877 by Alfred Waterhouse. Valette's painting shows the statues of Prime Minister Gladstone, poised to harangue the passers-by, and of a local philanthropist, Oliver Heywood, as well as the monument to the Prince Consort Albert, husband of Queen Victoria. In the background, in profile, are the opulent premises of the Northern Assurance Company.

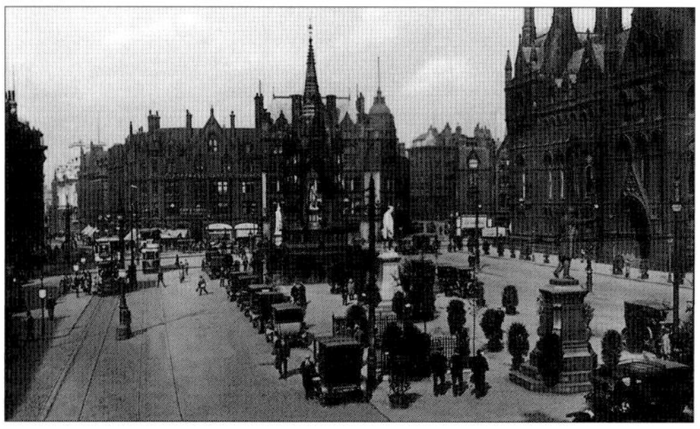

18 Albert Square, Manchester, 1910
Manchester Archives and Local Studies

Under the aegis of municipal public funds (the Manchester Corporation), the city sourced its drinking water from the Lake District and its sewerage network dated from the end of the 19th century. The benefits of the arrival of

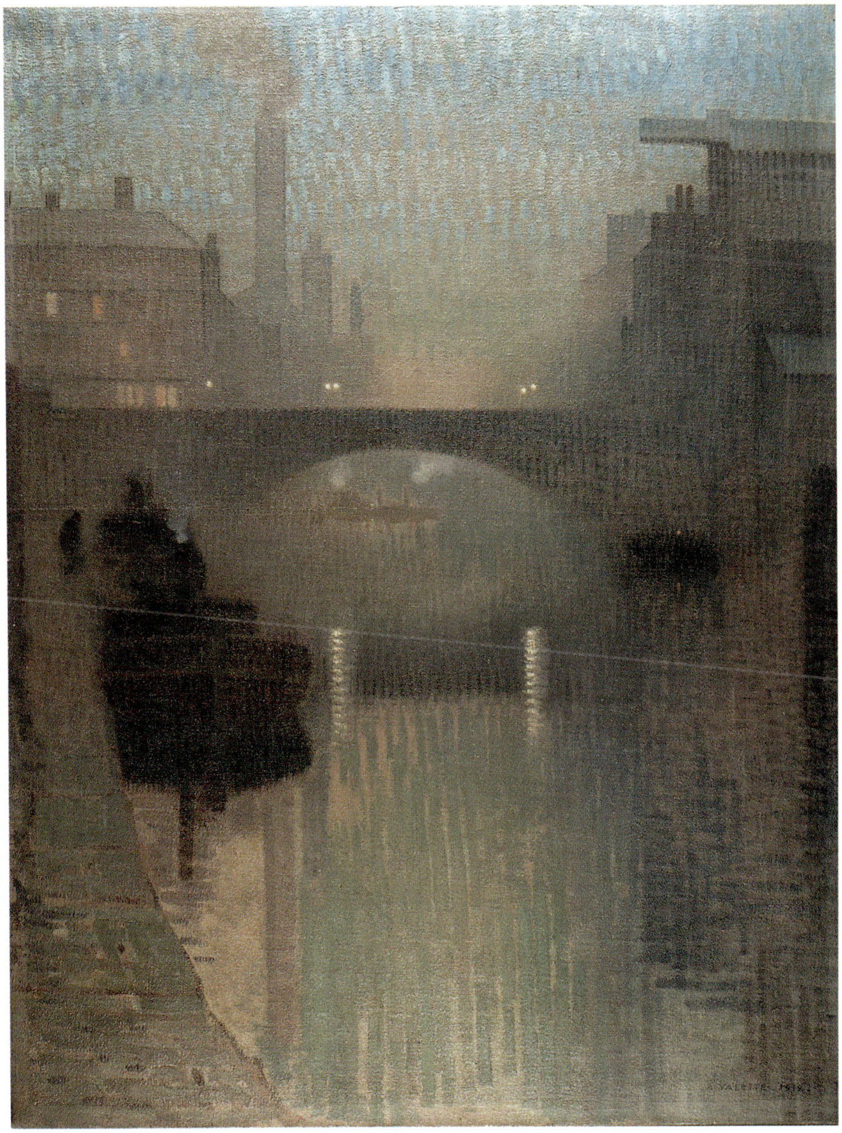

19 *Bailey Bridge, Manchester 1912*
Oil on jute, 155 x 115
Manchester Art Gallery

piped drinking water and of modern sanitation were many. The greatest benefit was undoubtedly the effect on public health, as Manchester had previously been prey to numerous epidemics and high levels of infant mortality. Before the building of the public sanitation sewer network, the Manchester rivers were open sewers and it was very onerous for industry to convert the contaminated water into the clean water required for chemical treatment processes for the manufacture of textiles. Hence industry benefited from access to less polluted river water which resulted in reduced manufacturing costs.

This undertaking of 'municipal socialism' was to extend to gas, electricity and the new electric trams, and also to the construction of houses. The Manchester Corporation also controlled public services ranging from hospitals to abattoirs, the Manchester

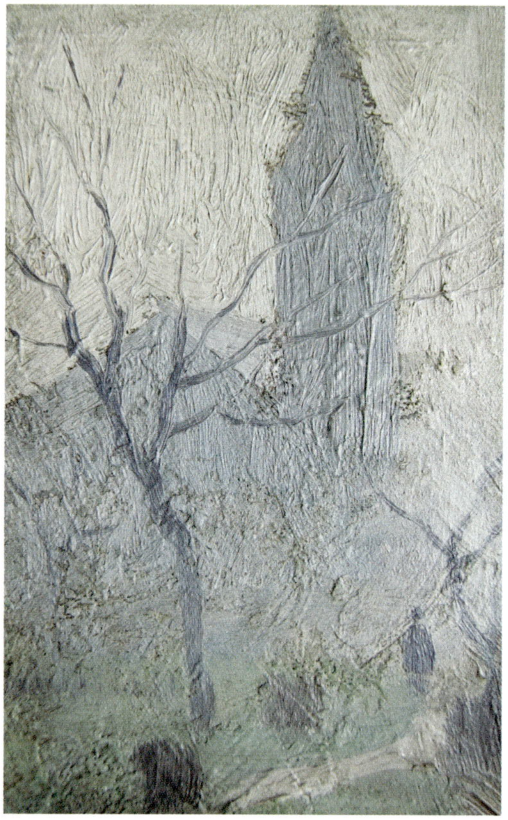

20 Churchyard, Manchester, dated on reverse 24 April 1915
Oil on millboard, 16 x 9.5
Private collection

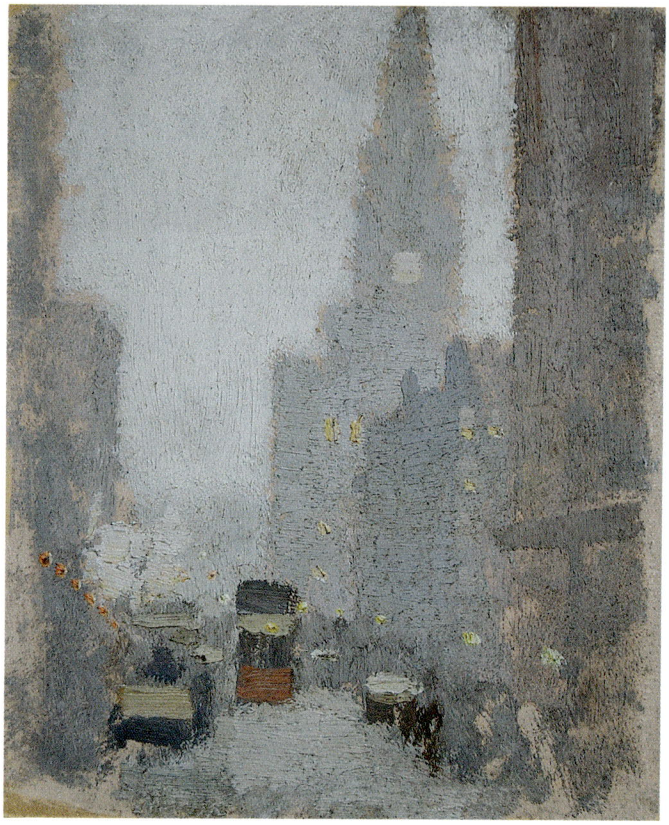

21 Manchester Town Hall from Mount Street
Oil on board, 16 x 12.7
Private collection

City Art Gallery (where Valette's paintings are currently exhibited),[18] libraries, parks, washhouses, publics baths and swimming pools. In 1909, the working week for tram workers, for example, was reduced to 54 hours and in 1918, the compulsory school age for children was raised to fourteen.[19] It can certainly be stated that, by the turn of the century, the city had become a much healthier place to live, even for the working-class population, which, little by little saw an improvement in the salubrity of the 'back-to-back' terraces, without garden or courtyard spaces, dating from the Victorian period, due to the fact that Manchester municipal authorities had started to demolish one in three houses, to provide ventilation between the houses and create an internal courtyard space.

Valette's different addresses in Manchester are known. In 1909, he had furnished rooms in the middle-class Plymouth Grove district, he then moved in 1910 to Clarendon Road in Chorlton-on-Medlock, and in 1917 to Herbert Street in Hulme, but it seems that, from 1918 to 1926, he lived and had his studio at 6 Nelson Street, in Chorlton-on-Medlock, at that time a district in the residential belt surrounding Manchester, where the middle classes tended to live. This residential district, as Valette knew it, no longer exists. It is now the site of the modern buildings of the University of

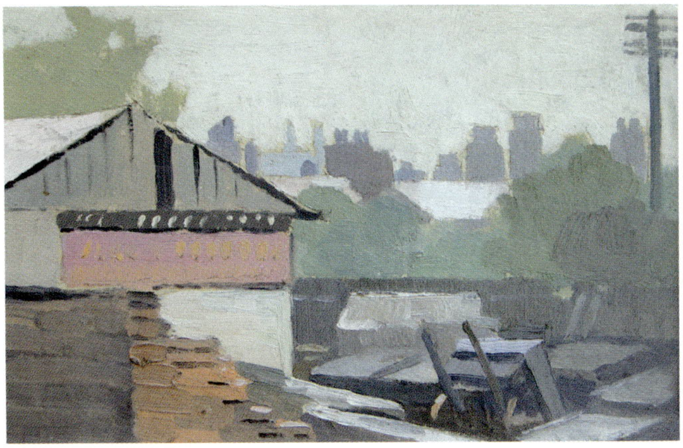

22 *Manchester Suburban View*
Oil on card 15.5 x 24
Private collection

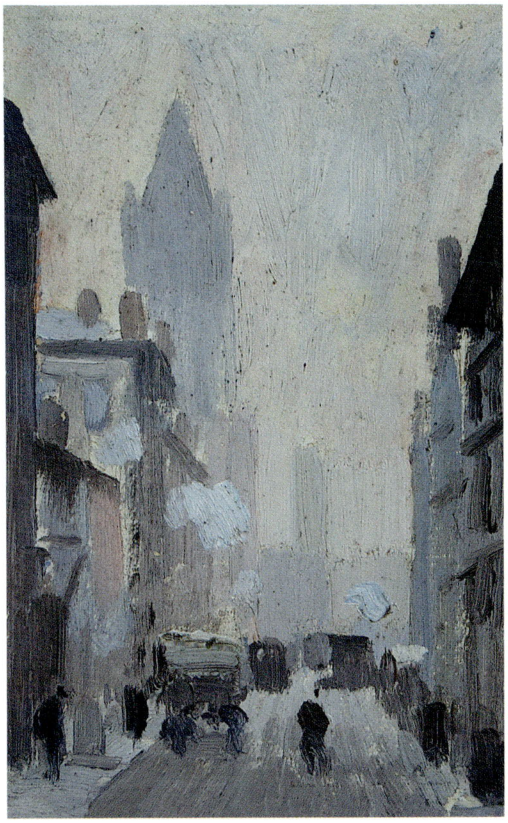

23 *Minshull Street with Old Magistrate's Court in the Distance*
Oil on board, 17.5 x 12.4
Private collection

Manchester and the complex of modern hospitals. Valette left a watercolour of Victoria Park, which was a residential park of elegant houses that had been built in the 19th century for the well-to-do who had abandoned the less than pleasant conditions of the centre of Manchester. In order to preserve the exclusivity of the locale, access to Victoria Park was through toll gates manned by uniformed keepers. It is most likely that Valette lived at 'Ellerslie' (fig 62 page 62) on Upper Park Road during the last years before he left Manchester in 1928.

Another particular feature of this city, as with Saint-Etienne, was that it was surrounded by an unspoilt and varied countryside that Valette also enjoyed depicting in his works. Valette was fascinated as much by the atmosphere of vitality and dynamism of the town as by the calm and tranquillity of the natural environment of the surrounding counties where he enjoyed staying for short holidays or weekends, very much as the Mancunians of the time were also wont to do. He also spent time at the elegant resorts of North Wales (fig 118 page 118), such as Llandudno (fig 24 page 30) and Anglesey, the mountains of the Lake District, the Shropshire Hills, the Derbyshire Peak District – magnificent regions where the residents of Manchester were accustomed to spend

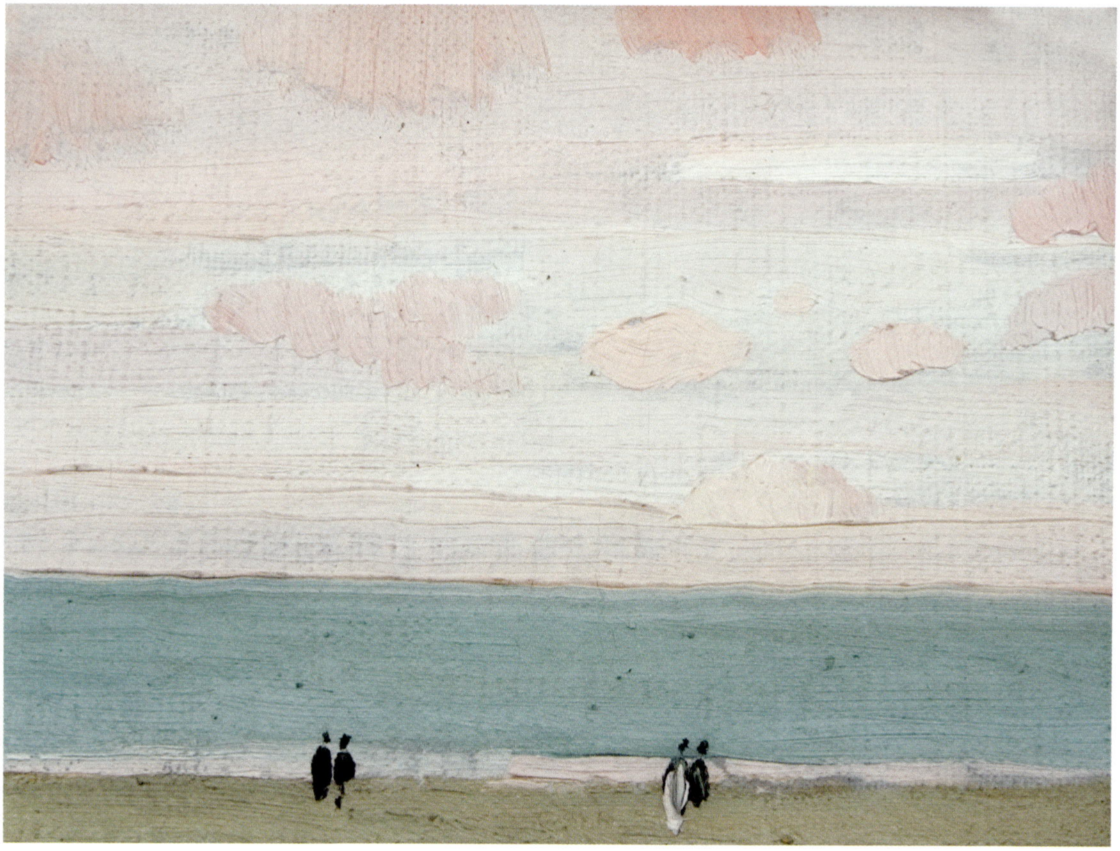

24 Llandudno
Oil on canvas, 12.5 x 16.5
Private collection

their spare time, and which he painted with great talent. There is evidence of Valette staying in Southport, one of the seaside resorts near Manchester, frequented by a distinguished class of person. It would seem therefore that Adolphe Valette extended his integration into his new existence even as far as adopting the same vacation habits as the local professional people.

Adolphe Valette's Arrival in Manchester

His first friendships, and first love, integration into a new artistic microcosm

Before establishing himself in Manchester, it seems that Valette's first destination in England was London, where, in 1904, he attended courses at the School of Art at Birkbeck College.[20]

In 1905, impressionism was at its height and the January exhibition organised by the gallery owner Paul Durand-Ruel at the Grafton Galleries in London constituted an unprecedented event, which established this movement in the English capital. Among the three hundred works presented, there were 59 Renoirs, 55 Monets, 49 Pissarros, 37 Sisleys, 35 Degas, 19 Manets, 13 Morisots, and 10 Cézannes.

It is not possible to confirm whether Valette was able to attend this exhibition, but it was undoubtedly with a strong imprint of this type of pictorial expression that he arrived, aged 28, in Manchester, in 1904.

One can only conjecture why Valette left London and went to Manchester. Similarly in France, he opted not to live in Paris, and perhaps he had set his heart on a city like Manchester, which was smaller than London, and where life would certainly be less pressured than in London. Did he perhaps meet someone in London who made a case for him to move to Manchester? This is entirely possible, but yet another enigma that will be difficult to resolve in the absence of documents and testimonies.

As we have seen previously, Valette, who was focused on the need to earn a living for himself, began work at the Norbury Natzio and Co Ltd printing company in Manchester. He painted portraits of young women posing as mannequins for clothing which were subsequently used as images for the printing of stock tickets. We have been able to view such a reproduction in a private collection. He also undertook interior décor work for private clients.

In parallel with this remunerated activity, he enrolled in evening classes at the Manchester Municipal School of Art in the Life Drawing and Engraving classes. Valette was already experienced in these disciplines from his years of study in France and had already applied them often in the context of his graphic design activities.

At the Manchester Municipal School of Art, he soon came into contact with other aspiring artists, such as Edgar Rowley Smart (fig 25 page 32), Elisabeth Orme-Colles and Margaret Nicholls. The arrival of Valette within this small group of young provincial English artists would most certainly have crystallised their aspirations. These Manchester artists would have been very aware of the pictorial movements of the time and of the impressionist exhibition in London in January 1905, but it was undoubtedly the arrival of Valette in their midst that motivated this small group. Valette arrived on the scene, with an aura of the charisma encompassing the impressionist movement, a synonym of the avant-garde; his immense talent confirmed that aura and he was immediately acknowledged by his new friends as an inspiring figure.

In 1912, with members of the Sandon Studios Society of Liverpool (E. C. Preston, J.H. McNair, and H.G. Smith) this small group founded an artistic association which they called the 'Society of Modern Artists' (in 1913, the association's name changed to the 'Society of Modern Painters').[21] This artistic group was founded with a common impetus to explore the various orientations in the development of contemporary art. Valette played a very important part in this, in echoing certain artistic trends in French art and in bringing an innovative freshness to the local artistic milieu.

These artists also felt the need to have a location specifically to themselves, which the Manchester Municipal School of Art did not provide for them. They often met at the Orme Buildings on Deansgate, where premises had been made available to them by Elisabeth Orme-Colles. They did not position themselves in opposition to the general public; on the contrary, they sought to build bridges directly with the public, insofar as the public subscribed to their artistic expression.

The names of Elisabeth Orme-Colles and E. Rowley Smart were thus often associated in this context with that of Valette, whether at the Municipal School of Art as students or as participants at the same exhibitions as Valette. It was undoubtedly within this group that Adolphe Valette encountered his first companions, formed his first friendships, received his first encouragements that were so vital to him, in more ways than one, in assuming the demanding status of artist but also as a foreigner in a new life, in a new city, dealing with a new language and new traditions. Edgar Rowley Smart played a considerable role in the founding of the 'Society of Modern Artists'. Rowley Smart initially enrolled on courses at the Manchester Municipal School of Art, and then subsequently withdrew from them as he criticised the School for its overly academic views; he went to study in Liverpool, was influenced by Augustus John and introduced the Liverpudlian element to the group. Rowley Smart was a great francophile and led a somewhat 'bohemian' existence, after the fashion of certain French painters that he admired. E. Rowley Smart also exhibited at the Manchester Academy of Fine Arts, as did Elisabeth Orme-Colles. Valette, on the other hand, never exhibited at these Spring Exhibitions at the Manchester Academy of Fine Arts.

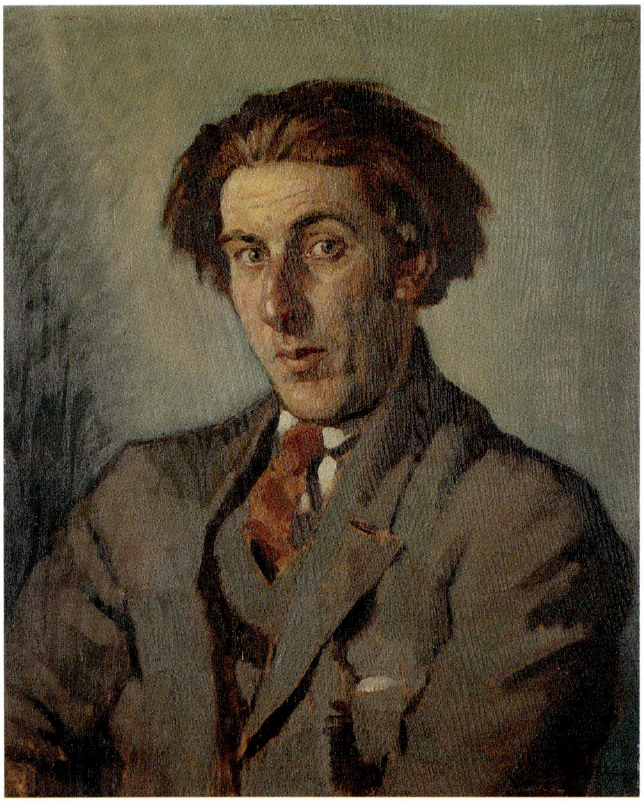

25 *Portrait of Rowley Smart, 1925*
Oil on panel, 66.3 x 55
Manchester Art Gallery

Rowley Smart and a number of others, including Bertram Nicholls (who had exhibited in 1905 with the New English Art Club, an association of artists influenced by impressionism), had also submitted their works for hanging at exhibitions at the Grosvenor Chambers on Deansgate in Manchester during the first decade of the century. We do not know if Valette was amongst them, but it would seem certain that he found affinities with these artists.

It was at this same period and context that Adolphe Valette made the acquaintance of a young Venezuelan woman, Gabriela da Bolivar, who was one of his students at the Manchester Municipal School of Art. Gabriela was a multi-talented intellectual woman, and one can imagine that her father, being a surgeon, had ensured that she had the benefit of a broad education. She did not hesitate, albeit in her early twenties, to present a lecture on her country of origin to the members of the Manchester Geographical Society,[22] even though she had lived only two years in her country of origin. Gabriela lived at

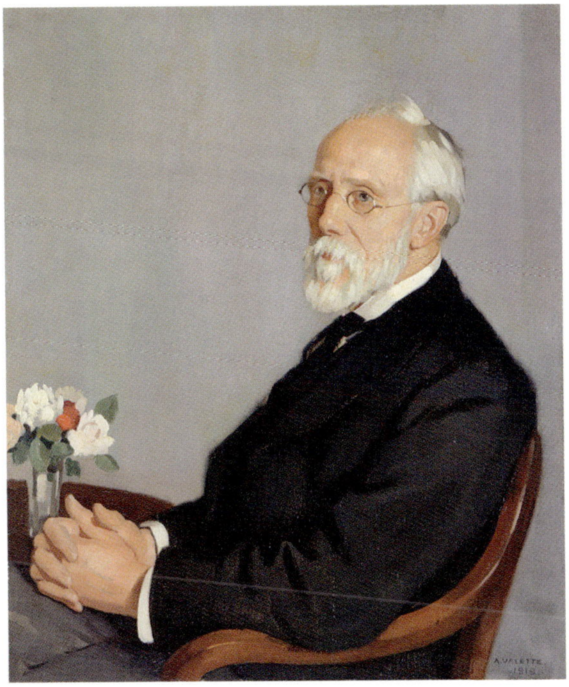

26 *Portrait of John Henry Reynolds, 1919*
Oil on canvas, 81.7 x 56.2
Manchester Art Gallery

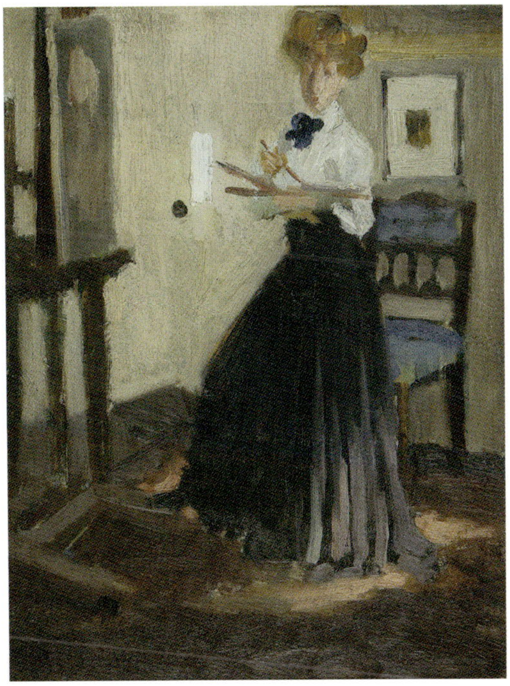

27 *Gabriela at the Easel*
Oil on board, 33 x 25
Sefton Samuels collection

25 Victoria Road in Pendleton; this was a sought-after district at the time. Gabriela's name never appeared amongst the distinctions and commendations awarded to the best students at the School and no work in her hand survives. However, Gabriela did exhibit at the annual exhibition of the Manchester Academy of Fine Arts in 1908 and in 1909, as a student at the Academy; the Academy did also in fact teach a number of courses. Gabriela exhibited a 'Portrait of a Girl' the first year and 'Pepita' the second.[23]

Other names have been associated with the new world in which Valette moved. The name of J. Millard, his colleague at the Manchester Municipal School of Art, often appears, for example, when they exhibited together in the same exhibitions in the Walker Art Gallery in Liverpool. Millard was a sculptor, who studied at the Ecole des Beaux-Arts in Paris and was very much influenced by these studies. He was known for his scintillating wit, sometimes tinged with causticity. He also naturally gravitated to the same circles as Valette in Manchester.

At the Manchester Municipal School of Art, Valette soon met J.H. Reynolds (fig 26 page 33), who was at that time director and secretary of the School[24] and principal of the Manchester College of Technology. They became friends and, later, in 1919 Valette painted his portrait.

Joseph Milner (fig 29 page 35) was also one of his friends from the earliest days, and attended the evening classes at the Manchester Municipal School of Art; they had started together as students in the Life Class. Milner was awarded numerous

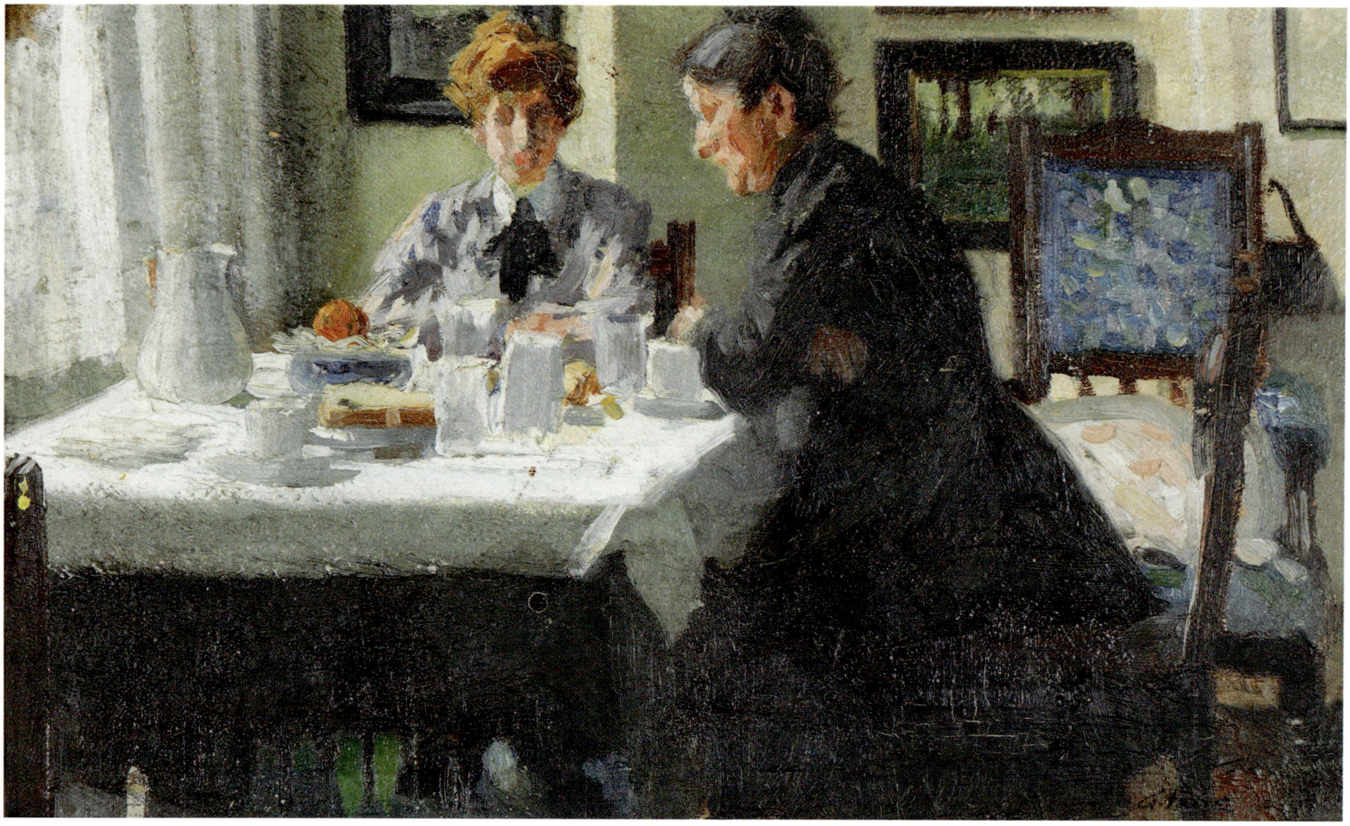

28 Gabriela and Madame Valette Mère
Oil on canvas on board, 21.5 x 35.8
Tib Lane Gallery

distinctions for his work at the Municipal School of Art by Valette who had by then become his teacher. Subsequently Valette dedicated a portrait of Milner, an art binder under his arm, with the caption 'A mon ami Milner' ['To my friend Milner'].

Despite the language barrier, Valette very quickly engaged with this small group of friends who essentially constituted the avant-garde of the Manchester art circles. Valette found in their company an artistic and professional satisfaction as well emotional happiness. This favourable climate was to contribute to his finding a personal sense of well-being and to the blossoming of his artistic personality.

'Mr Monsieur' – The Manchester Municipal School of Art

A Unanimously Appreciated Teacher

On his arrival in Manchester in 1904, Valette was, as we know, employed by the printing firm Norbury Natzio and Co Ltd.

Alongside this remunerated activity he also enrolled in evening classes at the Manchester Municipal School of Art, in the Life classes and Engraving classes. Valette, as we also know, had already mastered the technique of engraving from his studies in France and had also practised it in his previous commercial activities.

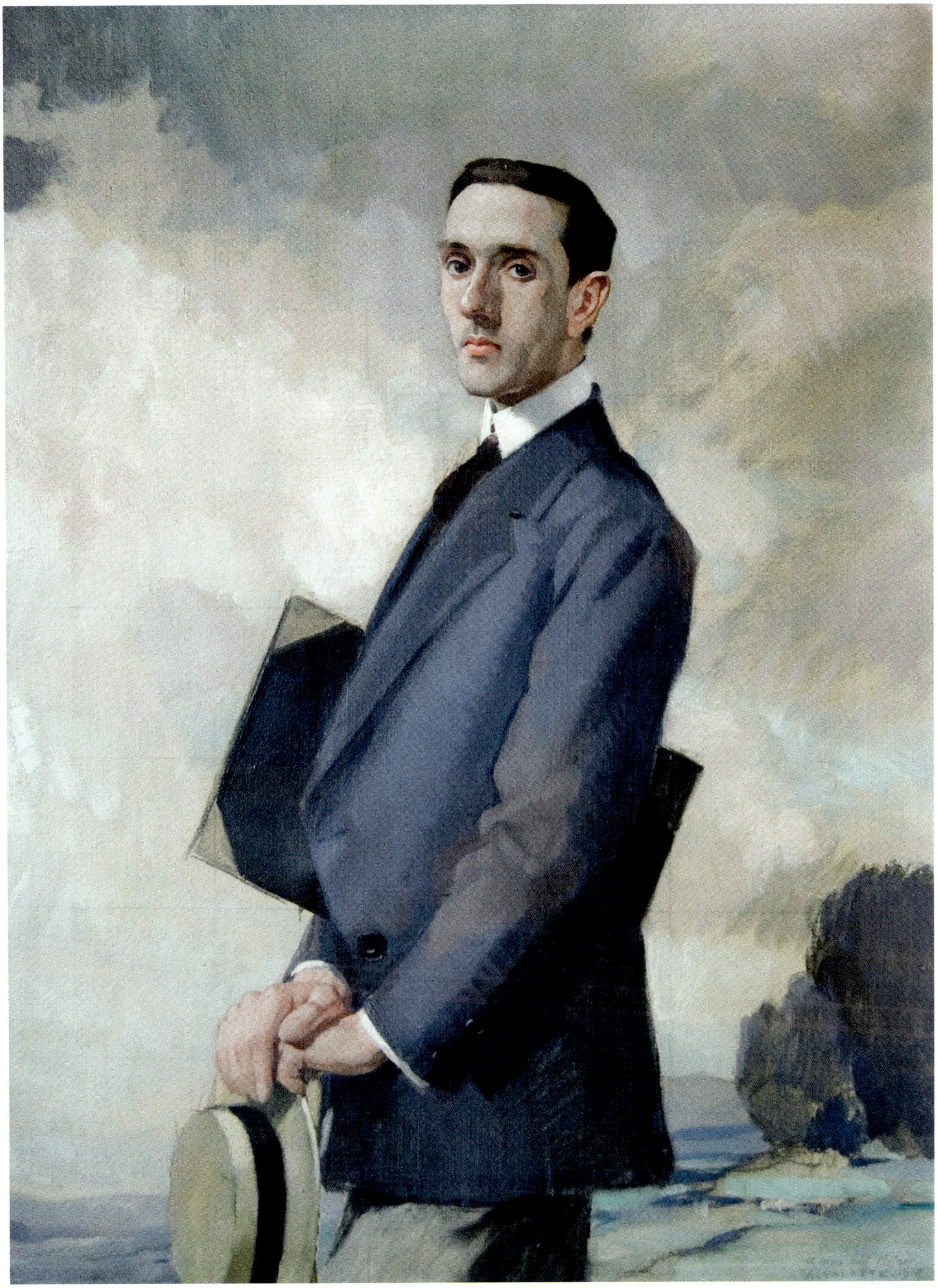

29 *Joseph Milner, 1918*

Oil on canvas over pencil, 76 x 56

Private collection

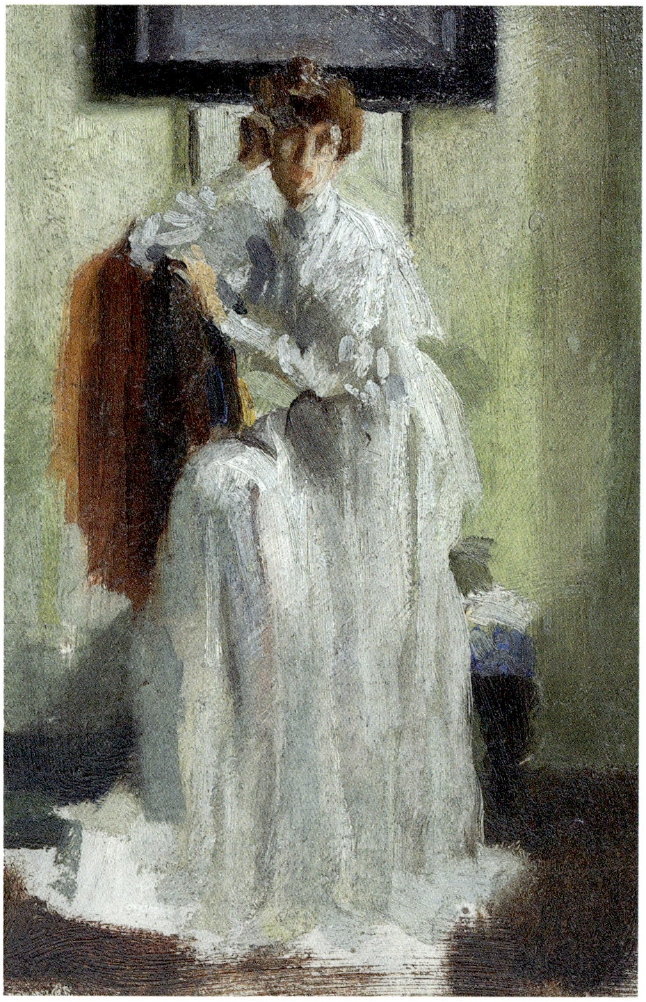

30 Gabriela seated, in a White Dress
Oil on board, 22.9 x 14.6
Tib Lane Gallery

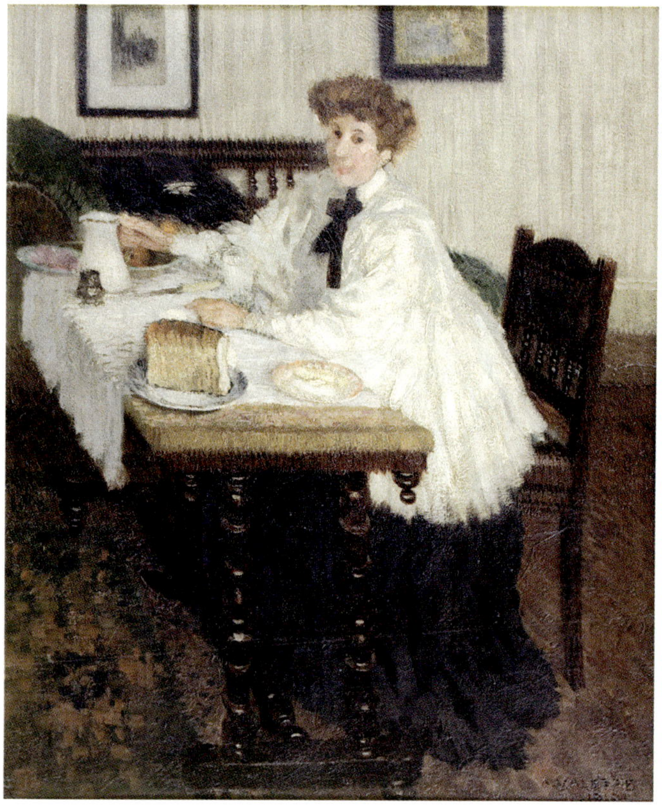

31 Gabriela assise à la Table du Petit Déjeuner, 1910
Oil on canvas, 81 x 65
Private collection

A black chalk drawing after a plaster cast of the Venus de Milo is confirmation of the presence of Valette at the Manchester Municipal School of Art, from 1905.[25] In fact the Art School had a vast hall containing casts retracing major works and styles in art history from the Antiquity (fig 33 page 37). Students reproduced these sculptures in the class on 'Drawing from the Antique'. This drawing of the Venus de Milo by Valette, which is of exceptional quality, represented a new, striking aspect of his remarkable talent, so much so that the headmaster of the School of Art, Richard Glazier, encouraged him to apply for the position of 'Master of Painting and Drawing'. His application was successful and, on 19 March 1906, Valette's name appeared for the first time in the minutes of the teachers' staff meeting. His appointment was from October 1906 with a salary of £225 a year.[26, 27] Valette accepted the position 'on his own condition that he should teach the pupils by actually painting with them.'[28] A classroom was assigned to Valette forthwith, in a school that had been enlarged and refurbished according to the design of its headmaster, Glazier, who focused his interest and efforts on art itself as the objective rather than merely on the administrative management of the school.[29] Glazier had formerly been a teacher of art at the Technical College in Manchester, which had been affiliated to the Municipal School of Art[30] and he was at pains to appoint only the best professionals as teachers. He probably also hoped to bestow a somewhat international flavour upon the school and would certainly have considered it necessary to surround himself with talented teachers reflecting the new artistic movements in France. Thus Valette and the sculptor J. Millard were recruited.[31] Millard, although born in Wigan, in Lancashire, had studied in Paris at the Ecole des Beaux-Arts under Injalbert and Alexandre Falguière. He was awarded the title of 'officier d'académie', a very important recognition conferred to honour an individual who had rendered services to the fine arts and to teaching. He had arrived at the Municipal School in Manchester in 1905,

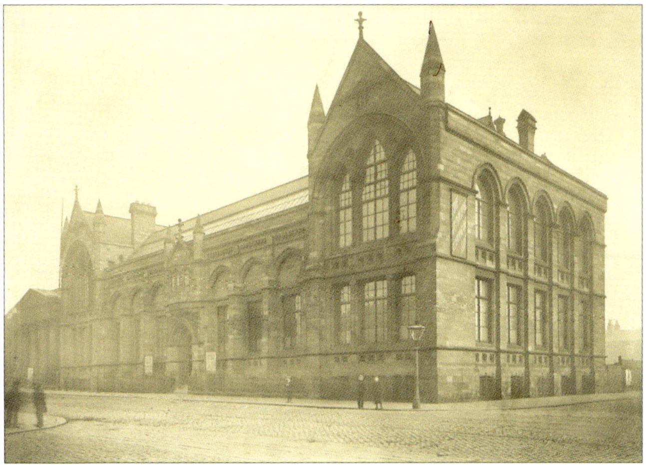

32 *The Municipal School of Art in Manchester, where Valette taught*
Manchester Metropolitan University Special Collections

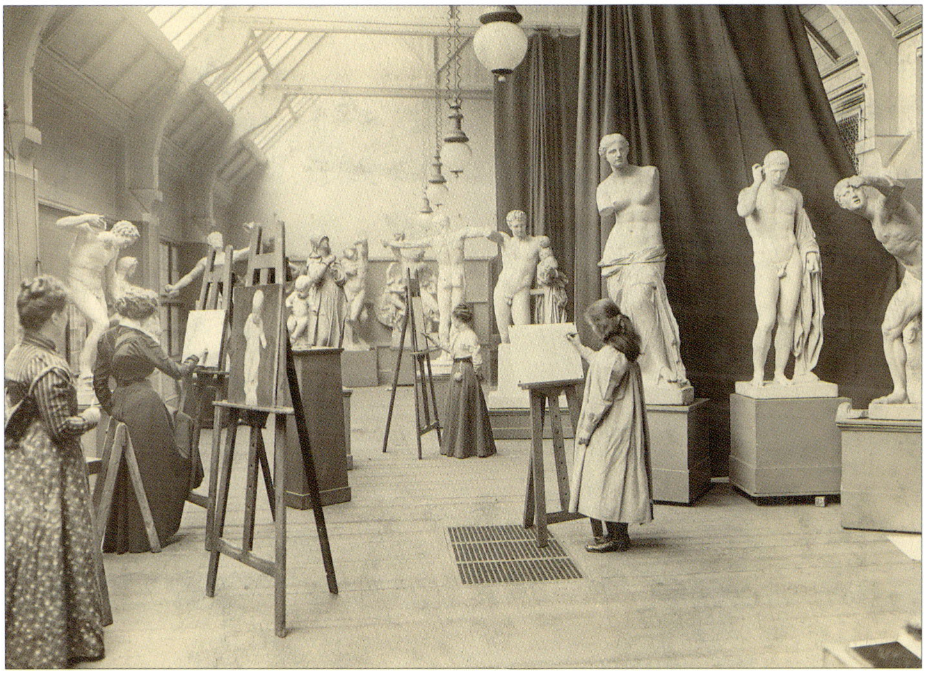

33 *Class of Drawing from the Antique, with cast of Venus de Milo*
Manchester Metropolitan University Special Collections

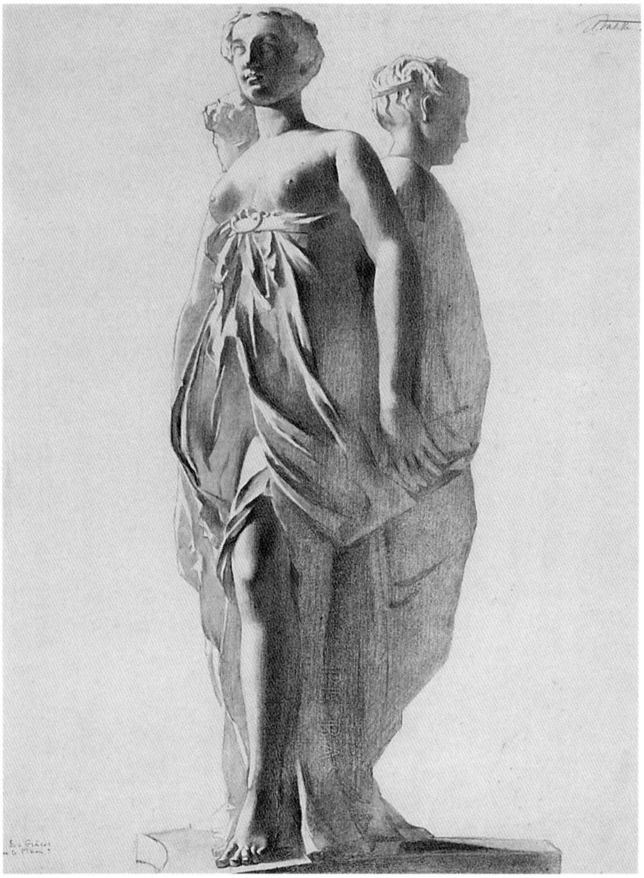

34 *Les Grâces de Pilon*

Black crayon and pencil on paper, 60.8 x 45.6

Manchester Art Gallery

and it is very likely that Valette sensed some affinities with Millard, given his knowledge of France.

The Municipal School of Art in Manchester also had a library and a museum, which were open to all, giving artists access to a full panorama of art history. The students liked to spend a few moments there before their classes in order to immerse themselves in the subject.

Valette, who had been affectionately nicknamed 'Mr Monsieur' by his students, brought with him the stimulus of his French experience, and the exhilarating knowledge of the French impressionists and of what was happening in the Parisian studios. He also brought his enthusiasm for the industrial landscapes of Northern England and their halos of drab, grey, gloomy, smoky colours.

Valette had a physiognomy that evoked the quintessence of the image of the impressionist painter. 'He looked like all the Impressionists rolled into one,' as one of his pupils described him, 'with a little black beard, black hair and a black cloak.'[32] Valette always dressed elegantly. 'He was very charming and very French.'[33]

He was much liked by his students who expressed to him their gratitude and affection for his direct and positive approach to teaching. 'One Valette drawing was worth three hours of talking,'[34] as Sam Rabin, one of his students, put it. As his knowledge of English was limited, he never indulged himself in long explanations, commentaries or diatribes, which were the norm for the teaching methods of the time, but he rather opted to teach by demonstration. He walked among his students, looking at their work, making them rework certain details, or made alterations to their canvases himself (fig 35 page 39). 'He used to do a little copy in the corner of your painting to show you what you'd done wrong,' as another of his students confirmed.[35] His rather approximate English and inaccurate pronunciation sometimes gave rise to plays on words and some surreal situations. For example, if he asked a student to 're-paint' something (from 'repeindre' in French), his bad pronunciation would suggest that he was asking the student to 'repent' for his painting. Even during his teaching time Valette sketched assiduously on any scraps of paper to hand. A small sketch of a cow suckling its calf has been found, on a sheet of paper originating from a note pad with the 'Municipal School of Art, Manchester' heading. This small sketch on this headed paper is the only one of its kind that has been preserved, but one can imagine that he would have produced hundreds like it (fig 36 page 39).

Valette's students bestowed upon him a respectful admiration and showed a genuine devotion to their teacher. They also conferred upon his personality an aura of romance and Parisian exoticism, by circulating all kinds of foolish rumours about an alleged life in Paris. In reality, our research with the Parisian artistic and academic institutions enables us to confirm with virtual certainty that Valette never lived or studied in Paris. He did, however, spend time there during some fairly long visits, when he immersed himself in impressionism and in other pictorial movements; on his return to Manchester, he brought back and shared his newly acquired experiences with his students. An etching of the Eglise St-Séverin (presented to the public in 1920) and two paintings survive as evidence of Valette being in Paris: 'Paris, le Jardin de l'Observatoire', an oil on board, dated 1907, 'Le Pont Neuf – La statue de Henri IV au Pont Neuf' (oil on card); there is also an unfinished watercolour of the Hotel de Ville with the pont St-Louis in the foreground.

Valette took his students on open-air study trips; a very attractive picture, 'Open Air Art Class, June 1906' (fig 37 page 40) shows a group of young artists with their easels positioned in a wood, in the open air. Painting in the open air was a new way of working, introduced by the impressionists. The Manchester Municipal School of Art was quick to recognise this and had established open-air painting classes as early as 1883.[36] At the time of Valette, outdoor painting trips took place in the city of Manchester itself for the 'Manchester sketches' for which Valette was to become famous, but also in the surrounding countryside, for example in Dunham Park, Alderley Edge, Prestbury, and Didsbury, but also the Bellevue zoo, which no longer exists.[37] In a portfolio of

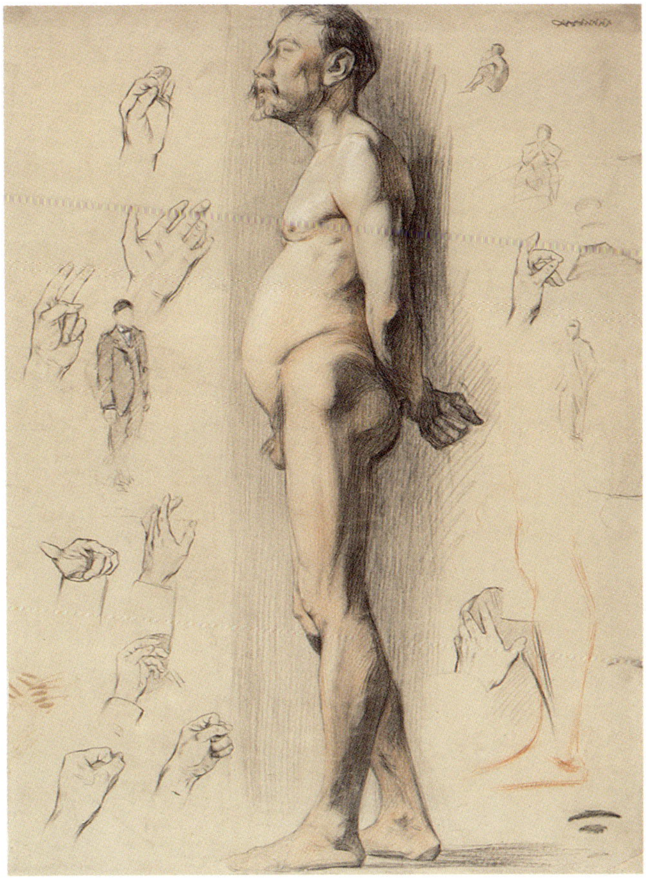

35 *Life Drawing of a Bearded Man*
Black, red and white chalk, 63.5 x 46.5
Manchester Art Gallery

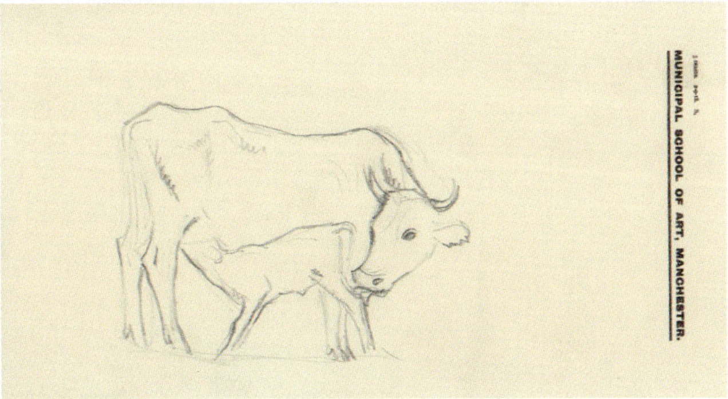

36 *Calf suckling Cow*
Sketch, pencil on paper with heading of the Municipal School of Art, Manchester
14.4 x 21.8
Private collection

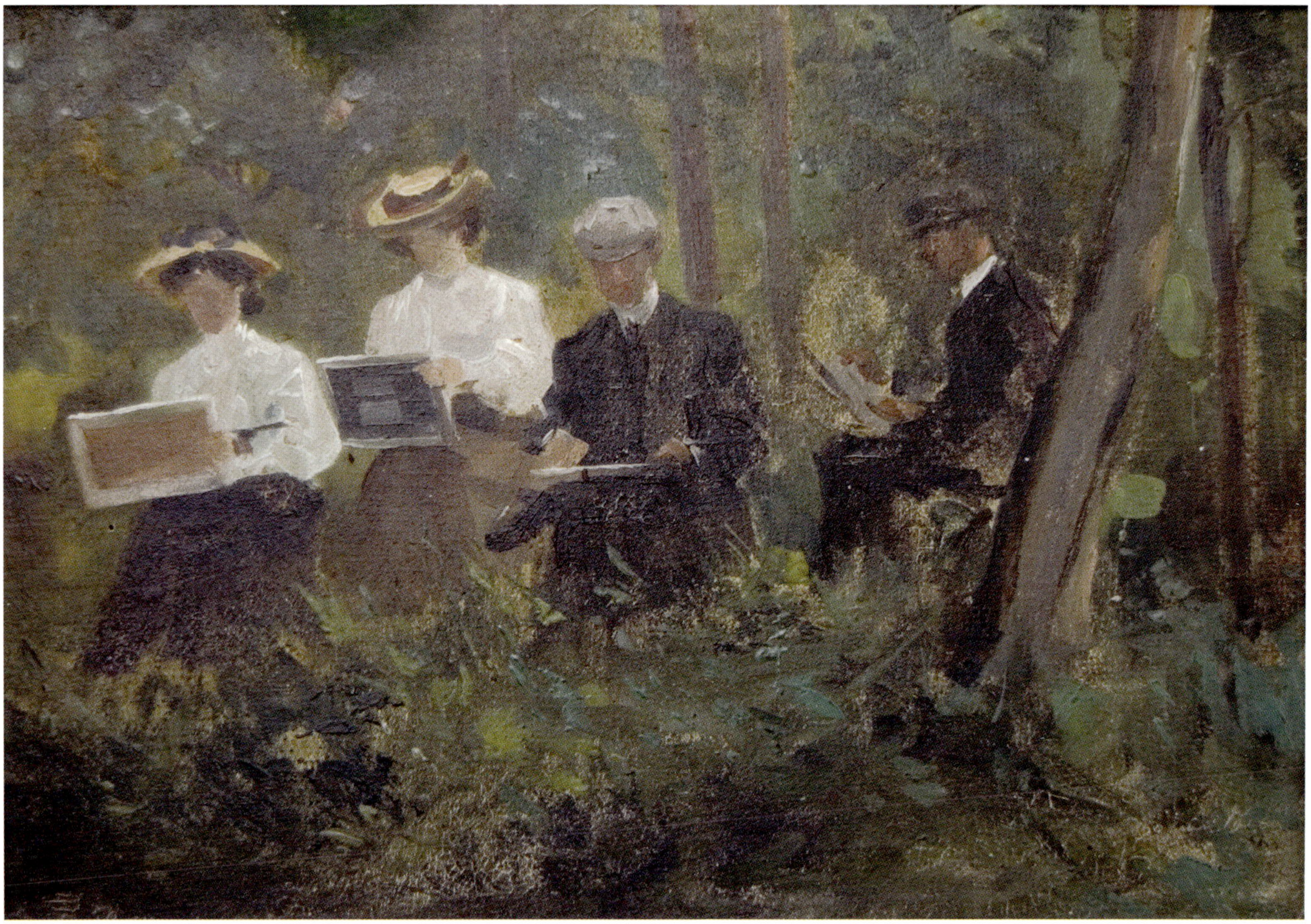

37 *Open Air Art Class, June 1906*
Oil on linen on board, 26.3 x 37.1
Private collection

two hundred or so sketches by Valette, we were astonished to find some drawings in Indian ink representing exotic animals; would they have been sketched on such an occasion? This will remain a mystery.

It has been said that Valette took some of his students to Paris; we know that 89 students from the School went to one of the Paris Exhibitions in the 1900s, but it has never been possible to establish with any certainty either the date of this trip or the presence of Valette amongst this group.[38] On the other hand, it has been clearly documented that Valette took part, with the other members of staff and students of the School, in representing the School at the Anglo-French exhibition that took place in London between May and October in 1908, to celebrate the fourth anniversary of the Entente Cordiale.[39] His French mother language would certainly have been an asset and he would have undoubtedly taken great pleasure in sharing his knowledge of France.

As we already know, it was at the Manchester Municipal School of Art that Adolphe Valette's sentimental destiny was determined. There he met one of his students, Gabriela da Bolivar, a young Venezuelan lady, and they soon became very close. Valette married Gabriela on 13 October 1909, when he was 32 and she was twenty-three. Gabriela was a young woman of relatively slight build but had a fine bearing. She soon became Valette's inspiring muse and he devoted a large number of sensitive paintings to her, portraying his attractive young wife in the elegant Edwardian clothes of the time. She can be seen in many interior scenes which are very intimate in character and which are reminiscent of the style of the school of Les Nabis.

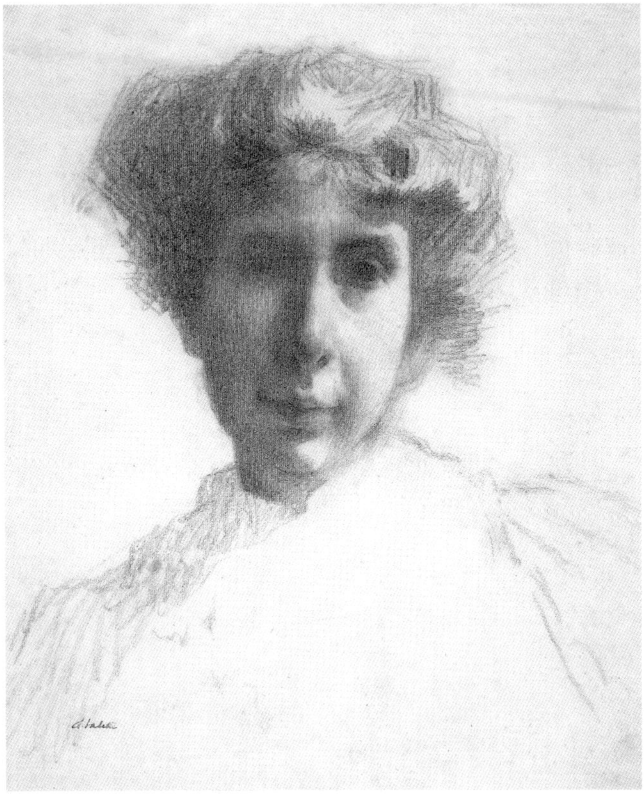

38 *Portrait of Gabriela*
Pencil on paper, 46.7 x 37.9
Tib Lane Gallery

He had an intense and very close relationship with Gabriela, combining the happiness of love and artistic closeness as well as the emotions and joys of being surrounded by a group of artistic common friends.

Their son Pierre Antoine Ferdinand Valette was born on 12 August 1910 and was very quickly nicknamed Peter or Tita; the love of his father is very clear from the numerous paintings of him as a child. Valette lovingly painted the world of his son, with his toys, sometimes with a hint of a Japanese style as was the fashion at the time. One has a sense that Tita was a happy, well-balanced child, surrounded by the love of his parents. Tita had the good fortune to have parents of such diverse origins, which must have provided him with an exceptional background. One can well imagine that these first years of marriage and the arrival of their son must have brought Gabriela and Adolphe Valette a burgeoning of the true happiness of a married couple. Very sadly, Gabriela had delicate health and died very young, aged only 36, on 13 March 1917; she died of pleurisy and pulmonary consumption, leaving behind her son Pierre, then aged six, and her widowed husband. Valette was overcome by immense grief at this loss.

At the Manchester Municipal School of Art, Valette was genuinely acknowledged as a wonderful teacher. We have numerous testimonies of Valette's qualities as a tutor. One of Valette's students, A.H. Knighton-Hammond, who did a great deal of lithography with Valette at the Manchester Municipal School of Art, recalls these privileged times:

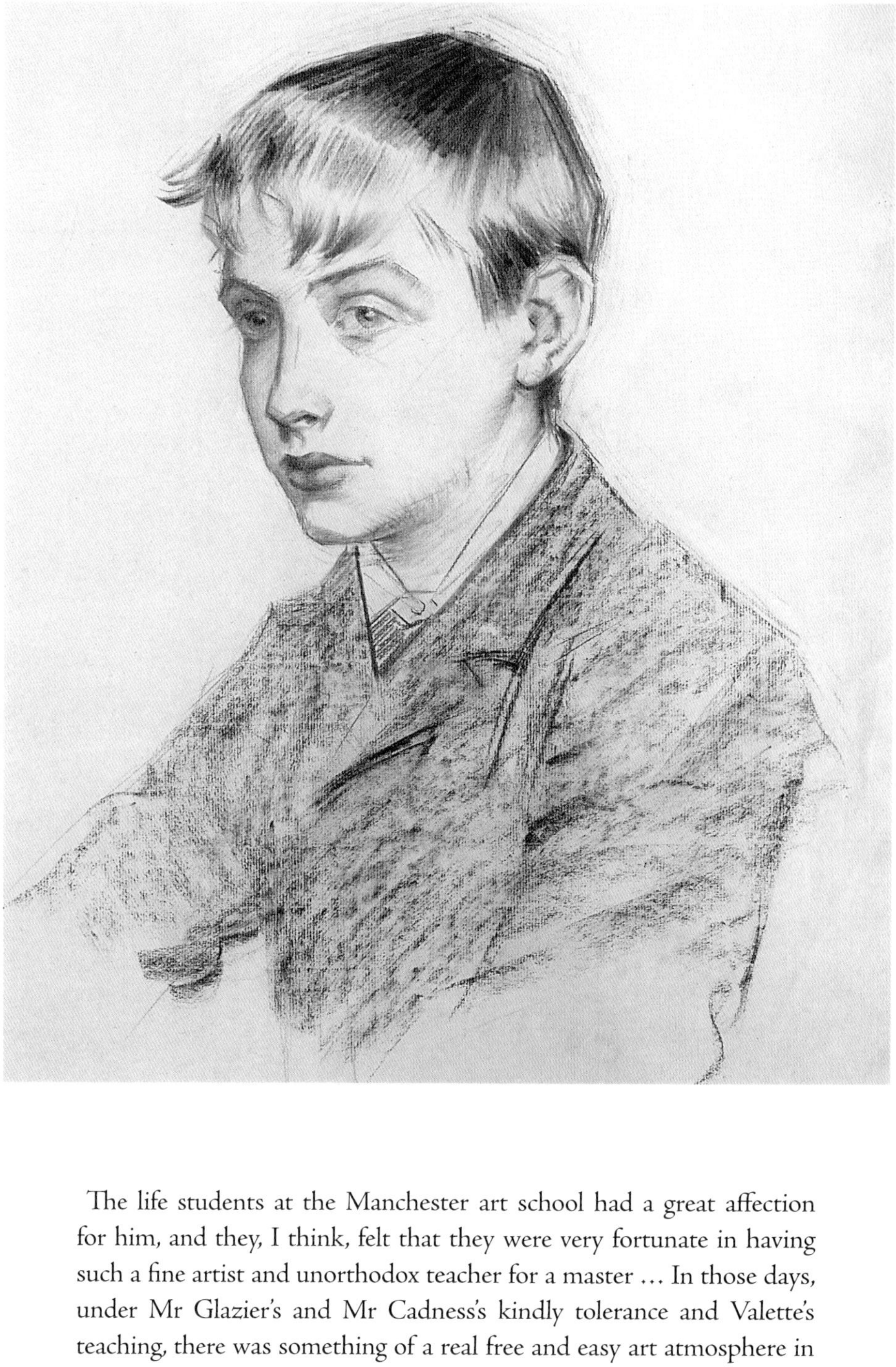

39 *Head of a Boy (Tita, the Artist's Son)*
Charcoal on paper, 57.5 x 42.5
Private collection

> The life students at the Manchester art school had a great affection for him, and they, I think, felt that they were very fortunate in having such a fine artist and unorthodox teacher for a master ... In those days, under Mr Glazier's and Mr Cadness's kindly tolerance and Valette's teaching, there was something of a real free and easy art atmosphere in the Manchester School of Art ...[40]

Similarly, Lawrence Haward, curator at the Manchester City Art Gallery when Valette died, also praised Valette's virtues as a fine teacher: '... a large number of students passed through his hands and largely profited by contact with him, for

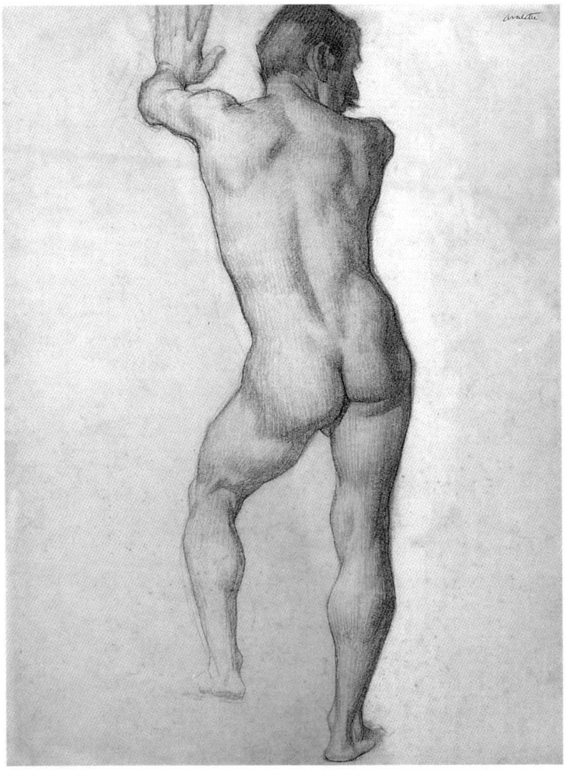

40 *Male Nude*
Charcoal on paper, 62 x 45.5
Private collection

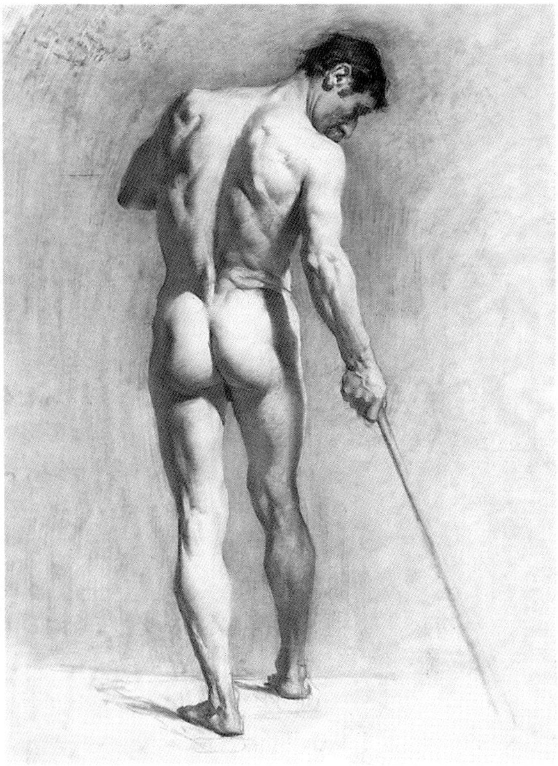

41 *Life Drawing of a Male Nude with a Cane*
Chalk on paper, 62.3 x 47.5
Manchester Art Gallery

he gave freely of his best and became a most stimulating influence … .'[41] There is a considerable list of English artists who attest to Valette's gifts as a teacher: David Ghilchik, Edgar Rowley Smart, John Bold, Emmanuel Levy, May Aimée Smith and the most famous, L.S. Lowry, who said, 'I owe so much to him, for it was he who first showed me the good drawings by the great masters … He was a real teacher, sir, a dedicated teacher. There aren't any more.'[42]

The Manchester Municipal School of Art, as was the case for all the establishments Valette had attended in France, fulfilled the dual needs, on the one hand of creative artists, but also of artist technicians destined for employment in industry. Another purpose of the Manchester Municipal School of Art was to provide an artistic training for teachers in primary or other schools seeking to include art in their general curriculum. The School also met the needs of these who simply wished to acquire an understanding of art as part of their wider education. At the time of Valette, the school had some 500 students, half of whom were enrolled in daytime classes and the other half in evening classes. The enrolment fee for an entire year of day classes was seven pounds and for the evening classes the fee was 15 shillings.[43]

The School Calendars published each year by the Municipal School of Art make it an easy matter to determine exactly what Valette's work and timetable consisted of.

Valette started his teaching career with the life classes. He had the title of 'Art Master' and he took the classes together with the headmaster, Richard Glazier.

The teaching took place in a room that had just been specially equipped for this type of teaching; the full length model, either nude or draped, would pose each week on Mondays, Tuesdays and Fridays, from 9.30 am to 12.30 pm, and from 1.30 pm to 4 pm; and from 7.25 pm to 9.30 pm, and also on Wednesdays from 9.00 am to 12.30 pm, and from 7.25 pm to 9.30 pm, and on Thursdays, from 7.25 pm to 9.30 pm.

In 1913, he was given three more classes: 'Drawing and Painting the Head from Life, which took place on Mondays from 9.00 am to 12 pm and from 1.30 pm to 4.00 pm; Drawing and Painting from the Antique Figure which took place every day and each evening in a studio containing a representative collection of casts of Greek, Roman, Renaissance and modern sculptures; the other additional course was an etching class which had already started on an informal basis in *c*.1909 when the School acquired a printing press.

In 1918, with the arrival of a new headmaster, Dawson, who gave the school a new academic configuration, further classes were added to Valette's timetable; the timetable for some of his classes overlapped and Valette had to move from one room to another to supervise them. This timetable filled the entire week, through all the available morning, afternoon and evening timetable slots; the only spare time being Wednesday afternoon. He had tenure for the following classes: Antique Figure Drawing and Painting from Casts of Grecian, Roman, Renaissance and Modern Sculpture; Life Drawing and Painting from the full length nude and costumed figure; Drawing Life from Memory, and Short Time Studies of Action; Drawing and Painting the Head from Life. In tandem with Cadness he also taught Draped Antique Figure, Exercises in preparation for Pictorial and Decorative Design and the Book Illustration and Poster Designing workshop. Naturally, he was still involved in the Etching and Lithography, Proof Printing in School Press workshop.

As we can see, the Manchester Municipal School of Art was focused both on pure art, as well as pragmatism and professional opportunities for the students; this was entirely in line with Valette's own career.

In May 1909, the Board of the School decided 'to establish an Etching Class under the direction of Mr Valette'[44] probably given the expertise that he had gathered in the course of his studies in France and his commercial career. An etching by Valette, 'Job Praying,' dated 1910 (fig 43 page 45), could well have been printed on the new press which had been acquired for the Etching Class, as the printing press was already in use well before the class was formally mentioned in the School Calendar of 1913. The press was kept in a common access room and was used frequently amongst others by Edgar Rowley Smart, Henri Vitofski and Sid Storiley. In 1918, a special room was allocated to the etching and lithography course. There is no evidence of prizes being awarded for etching and lithography, as they were considered to be practice exercises that had to be

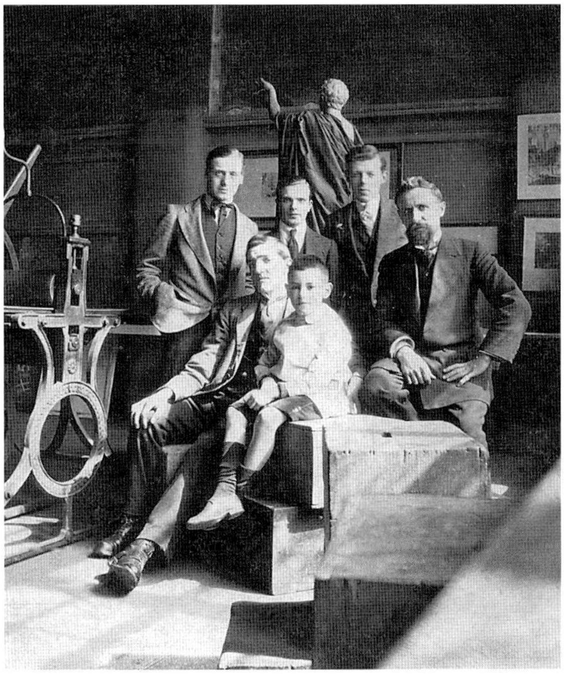

42 *Valette (right) with his etching class and the etching press*
Manchester Metropolitan University Special Collections

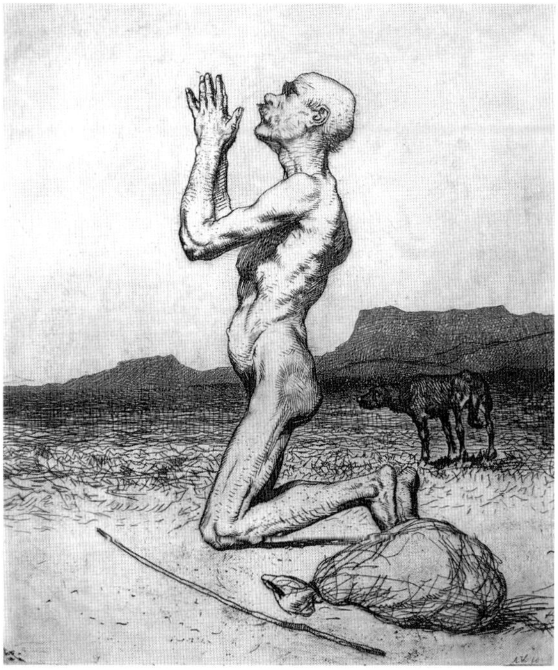

43 *Job Praying, 1910*
Etching on paper, 19.5 x 15
Private collection

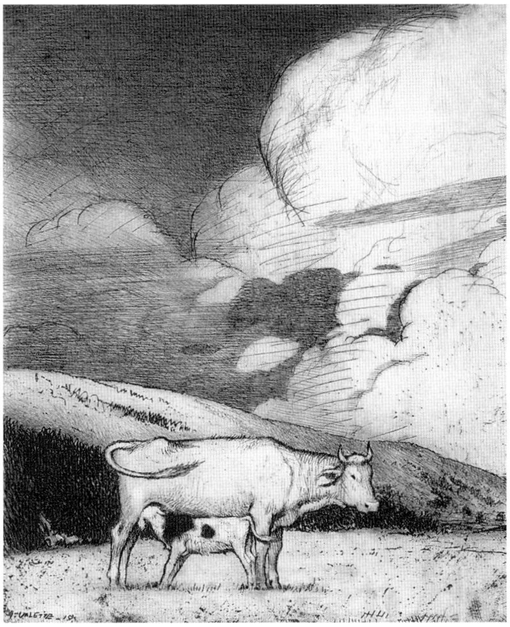

44 *Cow and Calf, 1919*
Etching on paper, 28 x 24.2
Private collection

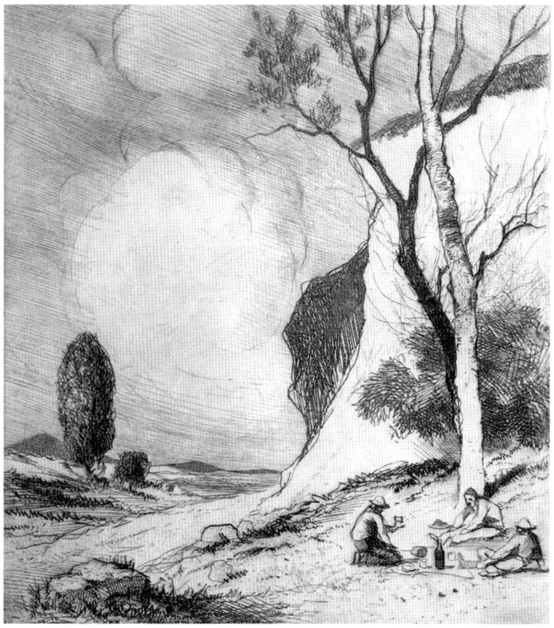

45 *The Picnic*
Etching on paper, 15 x 12.6
Private collection

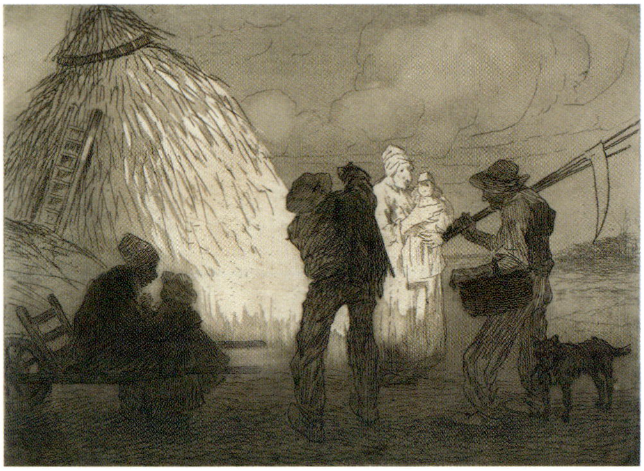

46 *Peasants going Home*
Etching, 13.1 x 18
Tib Lane Gallery

supplemented by related studies in drawing etc. Examples of sketches have survived where we can see how Valette prepared his lithographs: he drew the finest detail in pencil on paper, before proceeding to the engraving work.

The Manchester Municipal School of Art building was continually enlarged and improved, due to the constant efforts of the headmaster Glazier who was at pains to provide his students and teachers with good working conditions; unfortunately, the premises for the Life Room, although newly designed by Glazier, were severely criticised by its users: there was a ventilation and heating problem which meant that it was not a healthy place to use. Valette suffered from these poor working conditions and after the 15 years during which he spent long hours there, his health began to show the effects of it. But more of this later.

Not without a considerable struggle, Glazier managed to ensure that the objects and structural items of the building were not requisitioned for the war effort. In 1915,

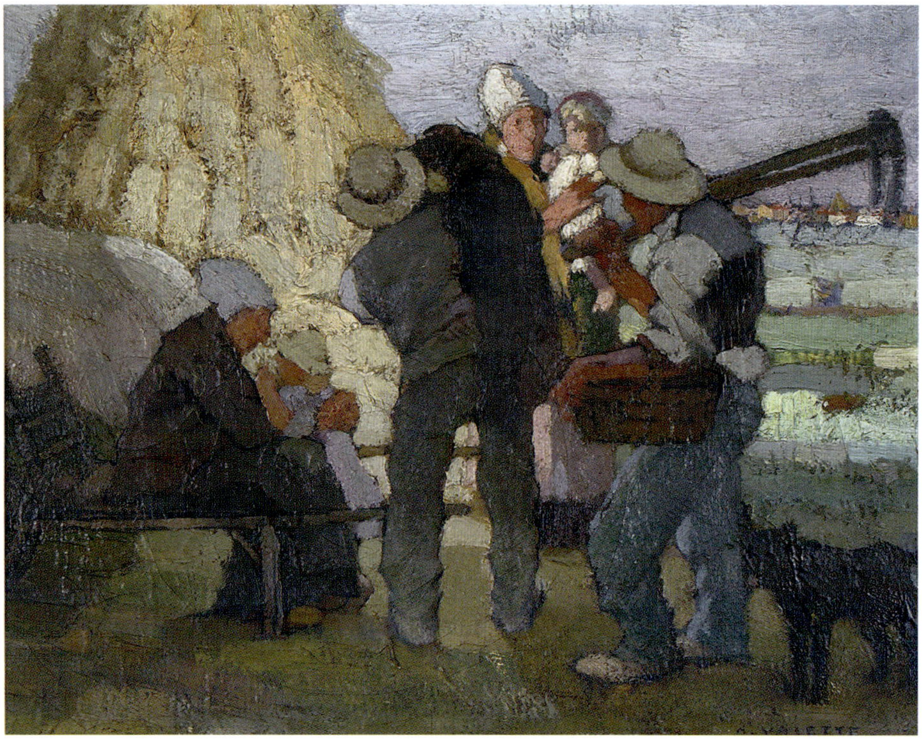

47 *Peasants going Home*
Oil on canvas, 30 x 38
Sefton Samuels collection

a report of the Studies Committee of the same year noted 'a Roll of Honour was begun of the names of those men who felt that Kitchener's need was greater than the School's.'[45] These were students of the School who fell in action in the First World War.

Valette himself demonstrated a very distinct gratitude to the assistance offered by England to France in the 1914-18 war, as is attested by a sombre commemorative painting in homage to the British dead, which he painted in 1919, 'England called, they answered' (fig 48 page 47). The Manchester Municipal School of Art recommended that all students in the School's advanced classes who served in the armed forces should be given an Associateship of the School, an award that hitherto had only very rarely been conferred upon students.[46]

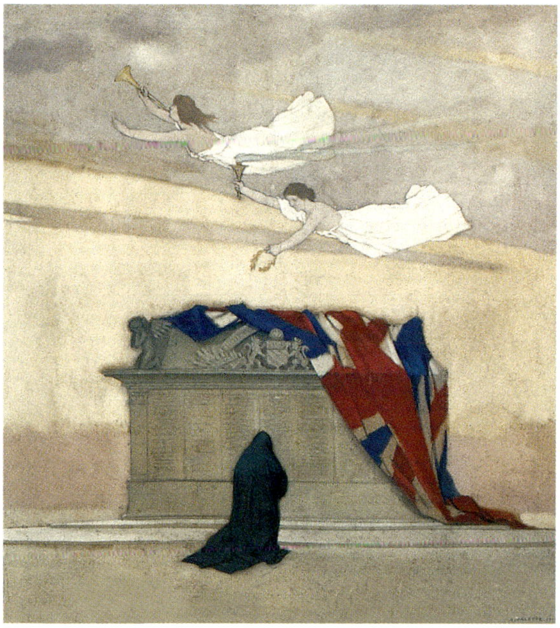

48 *England called, they answered, 1919*
Oil on canvas, 121 x 110
Mairie de Blacé collection

As one will recall, during the early years of his teaching post at the Manchester Municipal School of Art, Valette only dealt with the advanced Life Drawing class: to enter this class, students had a year of instruction in drawing and elementary geometrical forms, as well as the effects of light and in studies based on casts and antique sculptures. Students, therefore, considered it an achievement and an honour to be able to join Valette's life class.

For these classes, Valette would determine the model's pose, which could remain the same all week, and then students chose their location in the studio and their angle of view. Valette himself would position his easel where he could find room; on other occasions, he would stay in his personal place and only re-emerge half an hour before the end of the class. The students enjoyed previewing their teacher's work, before setting to work themselves. Josephine Duddle, one of Valette's students, confirms this: 'I went first to have a look at the masterly Impressionist painting of the model which Monsieur Valette was painting. How fortunate we were to have such a tutor!'[47]

The absence of a rigid discipline was appreciated by his students. Although men and women were not permitted to draw female models while seated side by side in the same class, Glazier and Valette were very relaxed about the age at which male students could join the Life class.

Most of the models were of Italian origin, such as Valente who was a circus professional, and the Pachito sisters; the name of Louise Gunnery recurred very frequently as a female model (fig 50 page 49); some also worked in the Manchester theatres. There was also Mr Aeronson, 'Old Julian' (fig 117 page 117) who was also a model at the Salford Royal Technical Institute and who worked at the Life classes but also for drawings 'in costume' and who would pose, either draped as a leading light at the bar, or dressed as a monk, a fisherman, a peasant or a Bedouin. It would appear that he had 'quite a character and had the gift of being able to match his facial expression to suit the occasion.'[48] This particular circle – of artists and models – was a small but very well-tempered microcosm, one which was even experienced by the somewhat austere and timid L.S. Lowry who attended Valette's classes for over ten years.[49]

Valette was indeed an extraordinary teacher. He excelled in all fields of art and his work, which was of an exceptional quality, created a stimulating vortex in this provincial school and a high standard to which the students at the Manchester Municipal School of Art could aspire.

Valette's Exhibitions in Northern England

A number of years after his arrival in England, Valette took part in art exhibitions. It was in fact Liverpool that was first to see his art and the most significant of his compositions. Valette took part in the Autumn Exhibitions of the Walker Art Gallery. These shows were a great success in the North of England and enabled local authorities and private art collectors to acquire representative contemporary canvases. The first question that springs to mind must be, why exactly Valette did not exhibit first in Manchester? There are a number of possible reasons for this. Firstly, let us consider what artistic events existed in Manchester. Manchester had the Academy of Fine Arts which organised an exhibition each year in February in the Manchester City Art Gallery. When reading the names of those who took part, it is clear that this was very much a local show (which, furthermore, was specified in the regulations which restricted admission to artists from the Manchester region and those who had lived there for at least twelve months) and there are no names of particular repute amongst them. Many of Valette's students exhibited there, including Gabriela, before her marriage to Valette. One can therefore imagine that Valette did not see himself showing his own works alongside those of his students. He was undoubtedly keen to find a show that was a better match for the calibre of his talent and was more cosmopolitan.

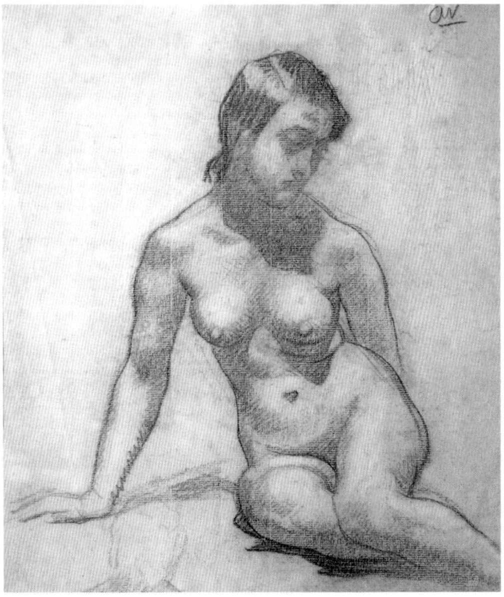

49 *Nude Study Drawing*
Charcoal on paper, 33.2 x 28.4
Private collection

His choice was, therefore, for the Autumn Exhibition in Liverpool. This was an event which had existed since 1867 and from 1877 took place at the Walker Art Gallery. The exhibition was more highly rated and much more prestigious than the one in Manchester; the big names in English painting of the time took part and rubbed shoulders with international artists. This exhibition also had a certain reputation in France, and French participants were able to send their works there by submitting them to the gallery owner Pottier in Paris, who would assume responsibility for taking

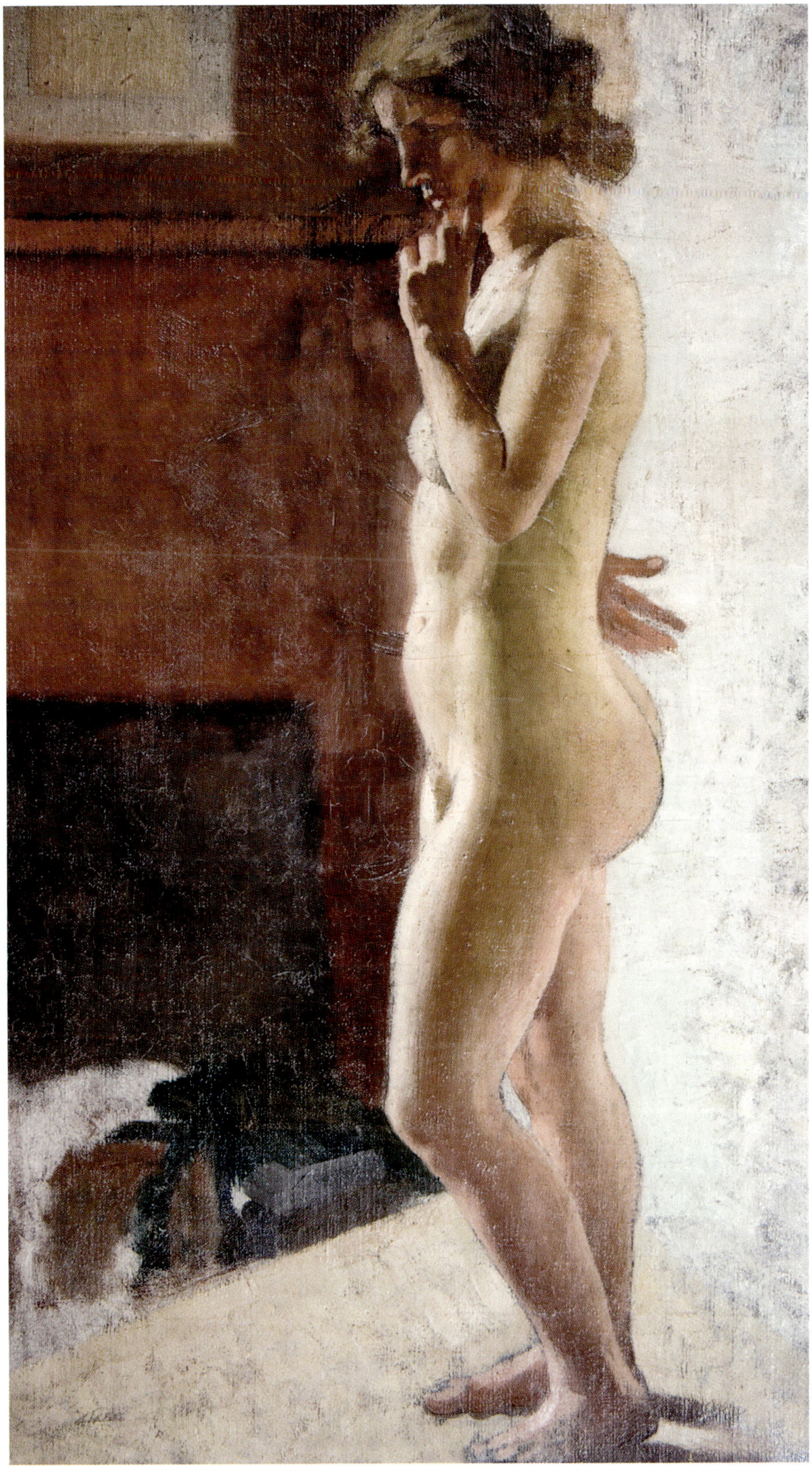

50 *Standing Nude (Louise Gunnery)*

Oil on board, 80 x 50

Private collection

them to Liverpool. The Liverpool exhibition had aspirations of being something of a Northern England counterpart to the Royal Academy Exhibition in London. During the years when Valette exhibited there, the British artists included Arnesby Brown, J. Farquharson, Lord Leighton, W. Orpen, Russell Flint, Charles Shannon, John Lavery, Wilson P. Steer, Sir L. Alma-Tadema, Anning Bell, Britton Riviere and many others.

The continental artists had their own room entirely to themselves. The presence of artists from the Belgian school is also noteworthy (Emile Claus, Leon Frederic, and Victor Gilsoul), as well as the Dutch, Swedes and many other nationalities.

Among the French participants were names such as Henri Le Sidaner, Lhermitte and E.L. Gillot. Henri Le Sidaner worked in London in 1907 and in 1908; he combined a pictorial technique, derived from both Monet and the neo-impressionists, with a delicate sense of intimist poetry. Lhermitte was a painter and engraver, a realist artist whose style was sometimes tinged with impressionism. Gillot frequently painted the sea and in London experienced the revelation of Turner, from whom he borrowed the luminous mists, in the context of scenes from industrial life. In 1910, the Royal Court invited him to paint the coronation of George V and the naval review that followed it. He travelled extensively in the Anglo-Saxon countries.

In 1909, in Liverpool, Valette exhibited four works including 'Windsor Bridge'. In 1910, six works, including 'Oxford Road'; comparing the Gillot painting exhibited that year, the 'Alkali Works, Northwich', and 'Oxford Road' by Valette, a critic remarked that these pictures were 'The only two attempts in the exhibition … to find material for the painter in industrial England'.[50] In 1911, Valette showed 'Albert Square' and two more works in 1912. Next to the large canvases that were emblematic of his work, his other contributions to the exhibition were almost all dry-point engravings, lithographs or aquatints, reminiscences of his initial training. All these works were offered for sale and, on reading the catalogues, one realises that the prices asked by Valette were in quite a high bracket in relation to the average prices for works at the exhibition, which gives an indication of his rightful assessment of the potential of these unique canvases. Unfortunately, no buyers were forthcoming. We will see later that Valette had to settle for much reduced amounts when he finally sold them in 1928 to the Manchester City Art Gallery.

In 1912, the year Valette last exhibited in Liverpool, he held his first exhibition in Manchester with the 'Society of Modern Artists', this group of artist friends whose acquaintance he had made on his arrival in Manchester and with whom he had laid the foundations for this association. Valette again submitted his 'Oxford Road' as well as six other works; the following year, the association had changed its name and now appeared under the denomination of the 'Society of Modern Painters' and Valette submitted seven works for its October 1913 exhibition, including 'The Irwell'.

The painters of the 'Society of Modern Artists' held their first exhibition in September 1912, the year of the creation of their association, in the 'Orme Buildings', at St Mary's Parsonage, on Deansgate, probably in a family-owned building in which Elisabeth Orme-Colles had space at her disposal that she was able to use as she

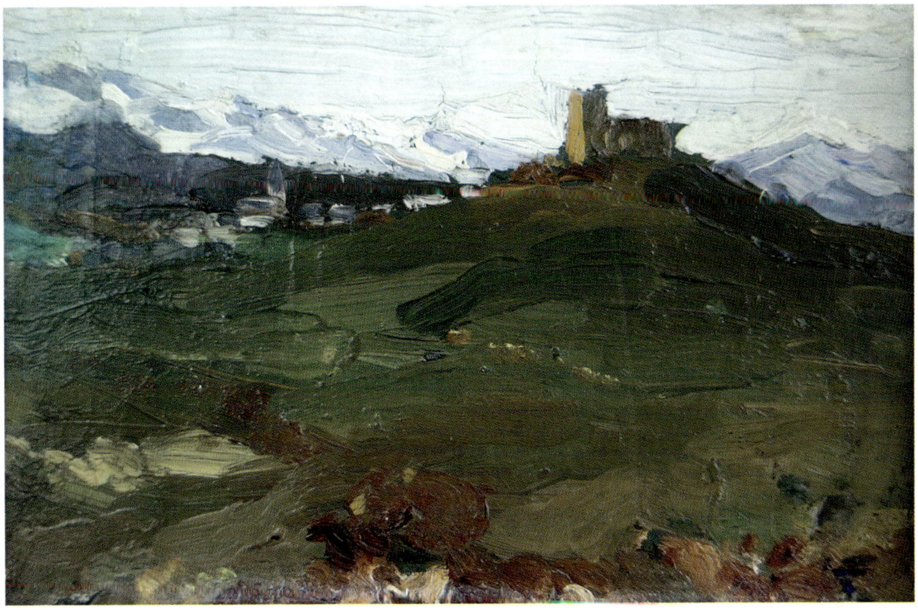

51 *French Alps, Early Landscape*
Oil on board 10.7 x 15.2
Private collection

pleased, for herself and for her friends. This studio offered a sufficiently large space in which to hang the pictures and the rooms were large enough to be able to view the paintings in comfort. Elisabeth Orme-Colles and Edgar Rowley Smart, another of Valette's friends, had already given courses there on Life Drawing over a period of two years so that many artists and art enthusiasts were already familiar with the location.[51]

The first exhibition was extremely well-received by the people of Manchester and the local press. Reports of the exhibition emphasised the different types of paintings that were exhibited. This diversity did indeed match the intentions of the association, which were for each artist 'to express their individual way of seeing with their new Freedom, rather than to represent one school of painting.'[52]

The critics homed in on Valette straight away: 'What seems to us the most complete achievement in the exhibition, however, is a small landscape, without title, by Mr Valette (No. 45). This is a Manchester view of canal or river crossed by a heavy iron bridge, with barges grouped on the left of the composition, and a man leading a horse along the towing-path to the right. The skilful use of the unpromising masses in the design, the sympathetic treatment of the figures, and, above all, the extreme delicacy of atmospheric effect make this one of the best interpretations of our city landscape that we have seen at any time.'[53] This description was not only laudatory in the extreme but will also arouse the art historian or collector dormant in each of us, as, based on the description of this picture, one will realise that it has been lost, unless it is in a hitherto unknown private collection.

The paintings by Valette's friends were equally reviewed by the press, but with more restrained praise: 'By Miss E. Orme-Colles there are several portraits, that one of 'Mrs T.M. Young' and the large picture of an interior with a figure of a lady being very pleasant in colour and arrangement. The artist's sense of structure is not strong; however, her very real feeling for colour is seen best in a number of pastels, of which 'Globe Thistles' and 'St-Mary's Gardens, Manchester' are among the best. The landscapes of Miss M.S. Nicholls, again, are best in colour, this being always harmonious. ... Mr E. Rowley Smart, another Manchester artist, shows pictures of widely varying subjects, from figure compositions in the modern German manner to etchings, drawings, and paintings of Manchester streets and watercolour landscapes. On the whole we like these etchings and watercolours best, along with an open-air portrait, 'Under the Branches'. They show the artist's ability better than others, because in them he seems less determined than usual to himself, or, in other words, less determined to insist on carrying out his preconceived idea whatever his subject-matter may be able to suggest for itself.'[54]

In 1913, the 'Society of Modern Painters' again subjected itself to the evaluation of the public and Valette was once again noticed for his Manchester scenes ('The Irwell', 'Dover Street', 'Swinton Bridge', 'Whitworth Institute', 'Trafford Bridge') and his pastels ('Point de Salles', 'Aiguille de Varens' and 'Vallée de l'Arve'), wrongly identified by the reviewers as 'Swiss pastels', as in fact they are of French Alpine landscapes.[55]

With the 1913 exhibition, the critics were somewhat more forthcoming with information on the creeds of this group that Valette had co-founded with his colleagues. As we have not found documents authored or signed by any of the members of the group, we must base our information on what is reflected by the critique. The *Manchester Guardian* reviewer, who is constructive and receptive to innovation, tells us that the works presented at the exhibition belong to 'what is known as Post-Impressionist, with an occasional overflow into Cubism and other enthusiasms even newer'.[56] The *Manchester Guardian* corespondent summarises their philosophy in these terms: 'Painting that is a direct reproduction of nature – as that of the nineteenth century was, for the most part – may succeed pretty well in its aim, with hardly any expression of either thought or feeling on the part of the painter. Surely it is a reasonable thing to argue that the painter's thought and feeling are of more importance than any objective realism. The greatest men, of course, have always fashioned nature to their own ends. But it is possible to carry logic further than this; and, as the scientific logic of the Renaissance led to the most complete imitations of nature, with little else in the picture, so the opposite train of thought would lead to an entire banishment of nature and to the attempt of the artist to express himself by symbols of form and colour as abstract as those of mathematics; and the second logical conclusion is at least as reasonable as the first.'[57]

For other reviewers less partial to the avant-garde, the exhibition was a truly traumatic experience: they referred to 'Wild Beast Art in Manchester',[58] which recalls the same terms used in Paris by the critic in relation to the Fauves ['wild beasts'] painters; one journalist refers to 'violent and barbaric colour'; The exhibition was a bombshell and above all dominated by the cubist paintings of Karl Hagedorn, 'Rhythmical Expressions in Line and Colour' and the highly coloured and 'kaleidoscopic' pictures by Arbuthnot.[59]

It is also reported that the exhibitions were of a very friendly character and 'ended up with a fancy-dress dance which was a great success', with people dressing up as a 'Cézanne, Gauguin, or a Van Gogh'.[60]

All of this conveys Valette's openness of spirit, his enjoyment of being light-hearted and of being associated with the innovation of new artistic movements, and indeed why not shake up somewhat the conformist and conservative ethos that prevailed at the time in Manchester?

Valette spent the time of the 1914-18 war in Great Britain and was very much affected by the events of the time. In 1915, Valette submitted a work for the 'Manchester War Fund Art Exhibition'.

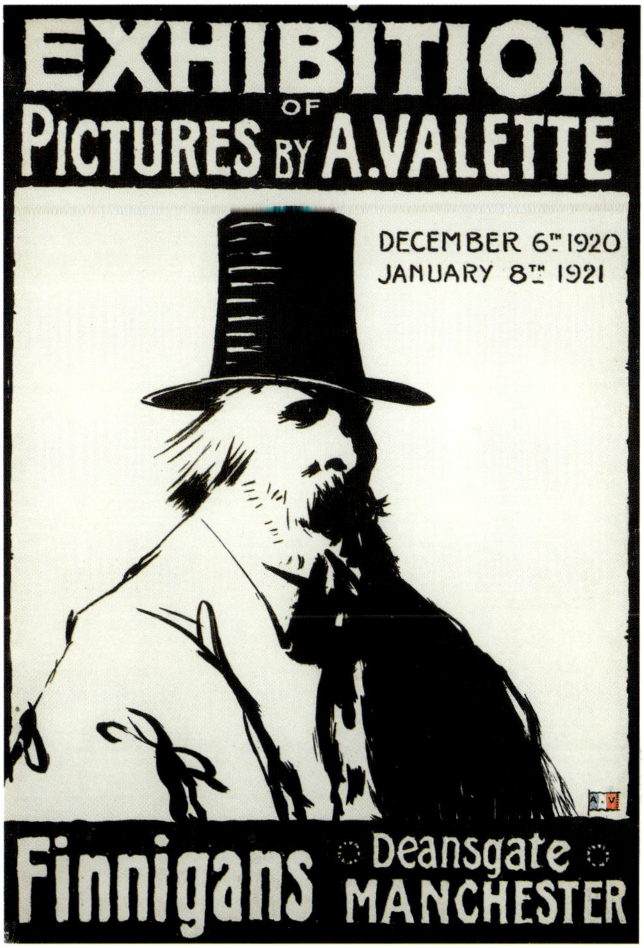

52 *Exhibition of Pictures by A. Valette*
Finnigans, Deansgate, Manchester, 6th December 1920-8th January 1921, Print
Tib Lane Gallery

In 1918 he mounted a solo exhibition at the Finnigans Showrooms, a large, elegant shop on one of the main streets of Manchester. It was here that Valette won the significant recognition of the public, who enthusiastically purchased the majority of the works exhibited. He presented a 100 oils and pastels, 22 watercolours and 15 engravings. He had the pleasure of spontaneous assistance volunteered by his students in the mounting of this exhibition. Valette reintroduced certain atmospheric pictures of Manchester that had already been exhibited in Liverpool, as well as of the English countryside and coastal scenes, and we note the significant presence of agrarian and pastoral subjects executed in the Beaujolais region or during his visits to the French Alps. The reviews were excellent. The *Manchester Guardian* considered that this was 'one of the most distinguished single-artist exhibitions that has been seen in Manchester for a good many years'.[61] The *Manchester Evening News* also commented: 'One is impressed not merely by the marked individuality of the artist and his freedom from the trammels of any school or cult, but also by the facility with which he works both in oil and water and the vigour of treatment of subject, whether landscape, portrait, or impressionist study'.[62] The *City News* also enjoyed the exhibition and highlighted the duality of Valette who liked to paint the Manchester fog but preferred the sun ('more of a lover of sunshine') in France.[63]

The list of pictures exhibited as listed in the catalogue of the 1918 solo exhibition (*see* Summary of Documented Exhibitions by Valette during his Lifetime, page133) includes compositions intended for use in decoration, such as 'Baigneuses (Décoration)', 'Ceiling for a Ballroom', 'Le Soir (Décoration)', 'Sketch for Decoration', 'Au Bord de la mer (Décoration)', 'Les Bûcherons (Décoration)', which shows that Valette was active in this field.

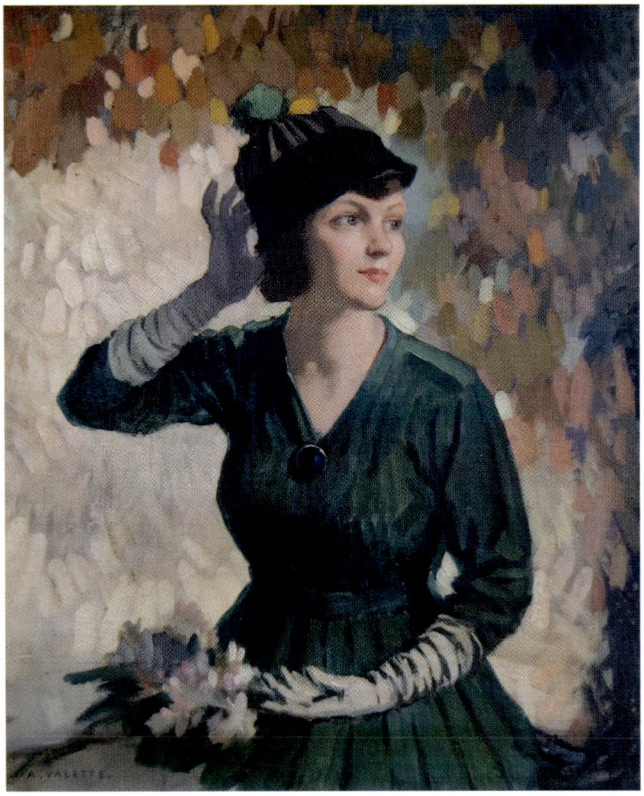

53 *Young Woman in a Green Dress and Gloves*
Oil on canvas, 60 x 49
Private collection

Given the huge success of the exhibition, a similar event was repeated in December 1920 with a show of similar themes and works offered for sale. Valette also designed the poster for the exhibition in which he portrayed himself very humorously (fig 52 page 53). Yet again the reviews acclaimed the exhibition as a great success; the overwhelming majority of the reviews were laudatory but the *Manchester Guardian* journalist, perhaps with justification, did voice some small reservations about the portraits: 'One would sacrifice a little of the facility and surface brilliance for rather greater mystery and depth ....'. Astonishingly, and counter to the verdict of posterity, the same critic expressed reservations about his 'atmospheric gradations' which 'he does not see in depth, but in surfaces, and, it must be said, he does not always escape the accompanying danger of choosing for representation chiefly the surface aspects of things.'[64] In this aspect, the judgement of posterity has subsequently revised this hasty commentary.

In the 1920 exhibition there were numerous portraits, which had either been executed for friends, or for commissions and loaned by their owners for the duration of the exhibition. The commissioned portraits fell into the category of work that artists very often agree to do, often for purely remunerative reasons and in so doing necessarily renounce a significant element of their inspiration. However, the fact that Valette included them in one of his key exhibitions would indicate that he did not see in them any sense of a betrayal of his art. An enthusiast for the work of Valette will however appreciate these paintings, which, while they are indeed very conventional, are nonetheless remarkable.

Valette had the opportunity to show other aspects of his multiple talent on other occasions at the Finnigans Galleries in Manchester, as evidenced by the 'Design for

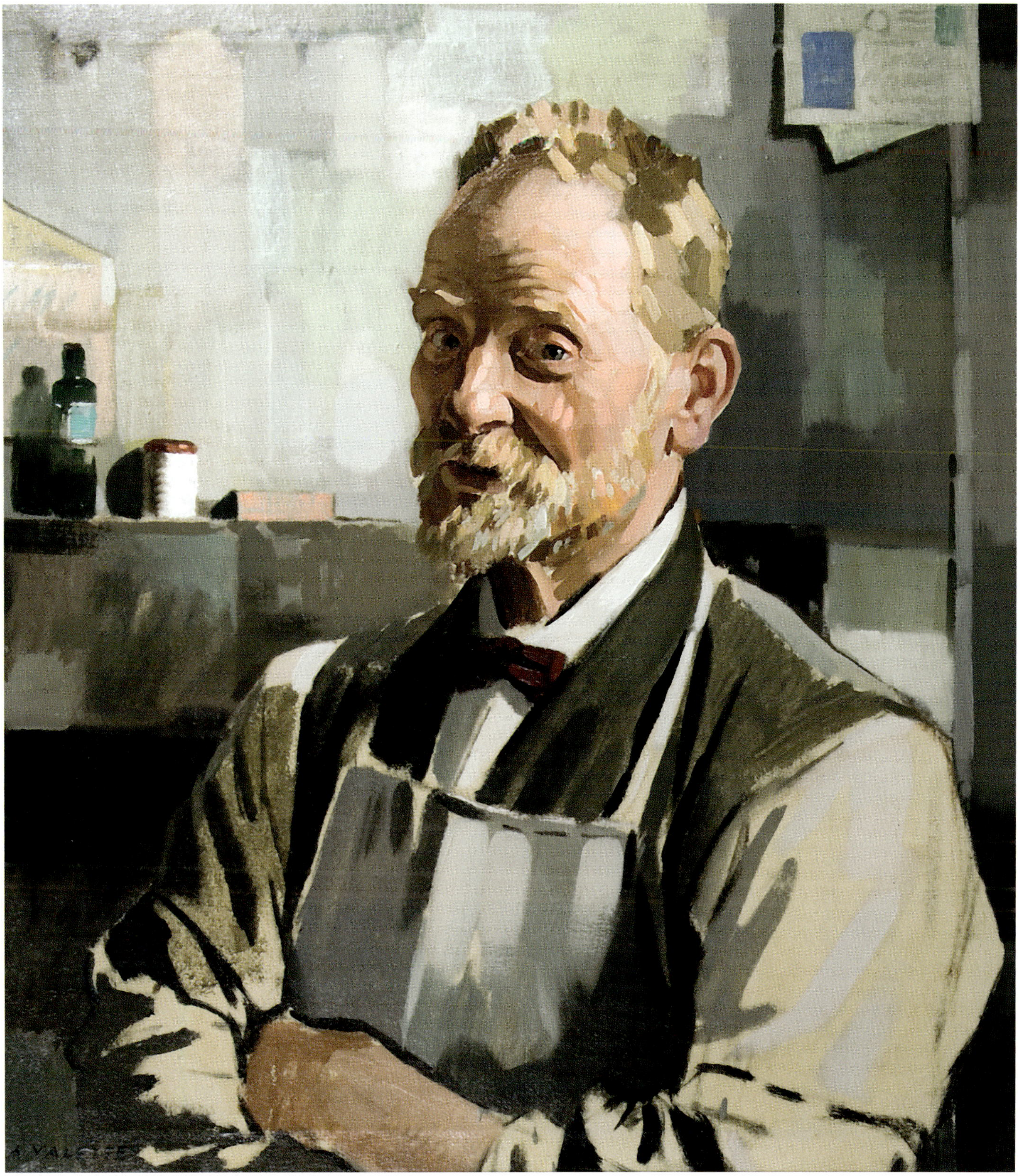

54 *Robert Carruthers*
Oil on canvas, 71.5 x 61
Private collection

an Exhibition of Colour Prints,' illustrated here (fig 55 page 56): namely the creation of posters. Unfortunately, we have been unable to ascertain the date or circumstances of the exhibition associated with the illustration. For an art lover or art historian, the task of cataloguing an artist's ancillary, more minor activities is always very difficult, since, by definition, these are unsigned works which were also carried out to meet commercial imperatives.

In 1924, 1925, 1926 and 1929, Valette continued to submit his works for hanging at the exhibitions organised by the 'Society of Modern Painters.' This association, that he had co-founded a good decade earlier and which at the time showed what was the most 'cutting edge' in Manchester, did evolve over time which moderated the temperaments of its members, and which, while it did present accomplished pictures, did not truly reflect the avant-garde of turmoil of the latest movements of the 1920s.

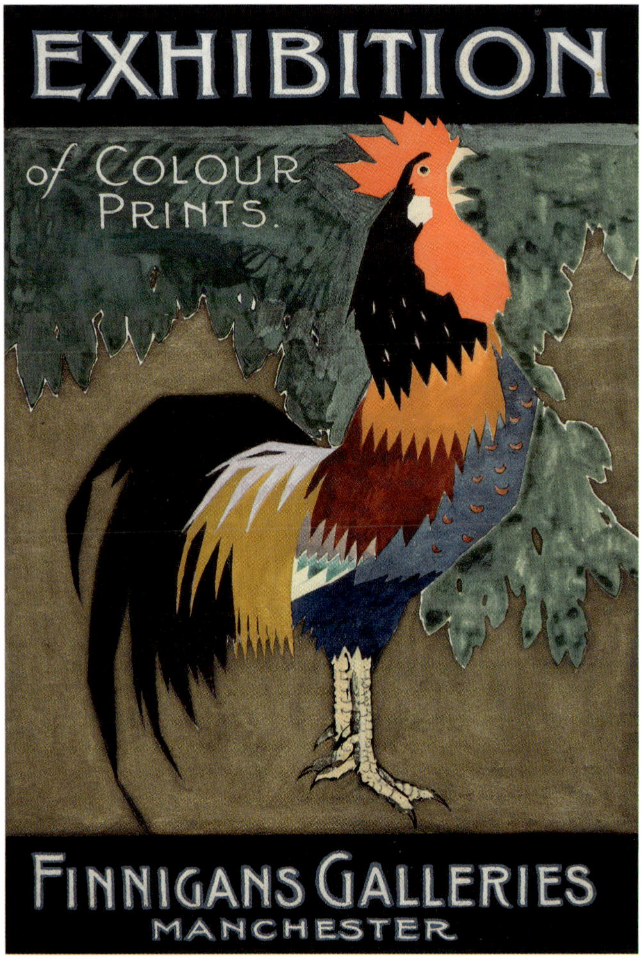

55 *Design for an Exhibition of Colour Prints, Finnigans Galleries, Manchester*
Watercolour and mixed media, 39 x 26
Tib Lane Gallery

The Last Decade in Manchester

Happiness regained, re-marriage, professional successes but health and family worries

In 1918, following the sudden death at the age 66 of the headmaster of the Manchester Municipal School of Art Richard Glazier, his deputy, Henry Cadness continued in the role in a caretaker capacity until the appointment in October of the following year of R.A. Dawson. Cadness had already introduced a more disciplinarian style of management in the School, recommending that 'male students under 18 years of age should not be admitted to the class for drawing from the nude female model.'[65] For the academic year 1919-20, Dawson arrived in Manchester from Belfast in Northern Ireland and soon picked up the pace with these new authoritarian measures: he introduced drastic changes in the approach to discipline at the school. He banned coffee and cigarette breaks, and commented with cynicism on the transgressions of the tutors, particularly in respect of their lack of punctuality.[66]

This new regime was certainly far from being to Valette's taste, but the most pressing issue for him at that time was his failing health. Valette suffered from the overheated atmosphere in the Life class room in the School of Art in Manchester, as well as from the debilitating

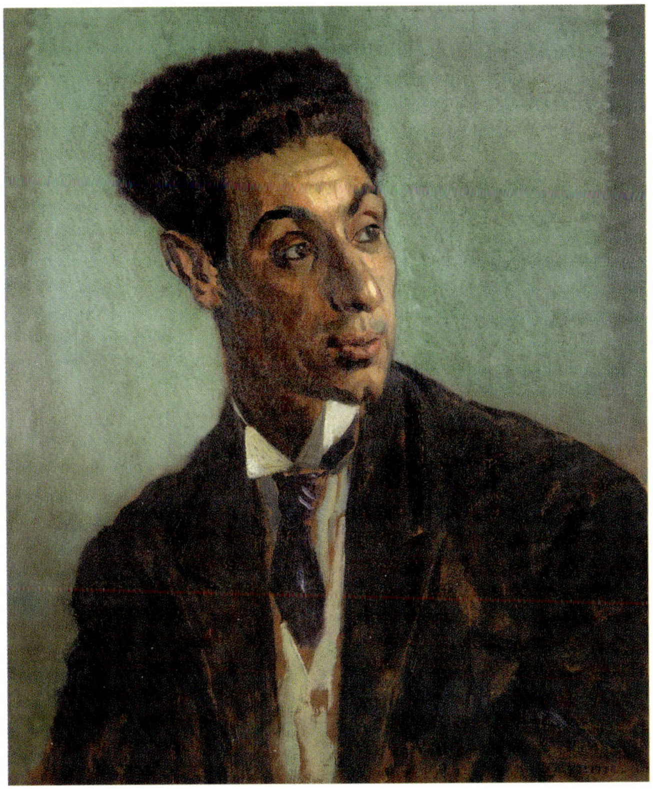

56 *Portrait of A Loutfi*
Oil on board, 64 x 53
Private collection

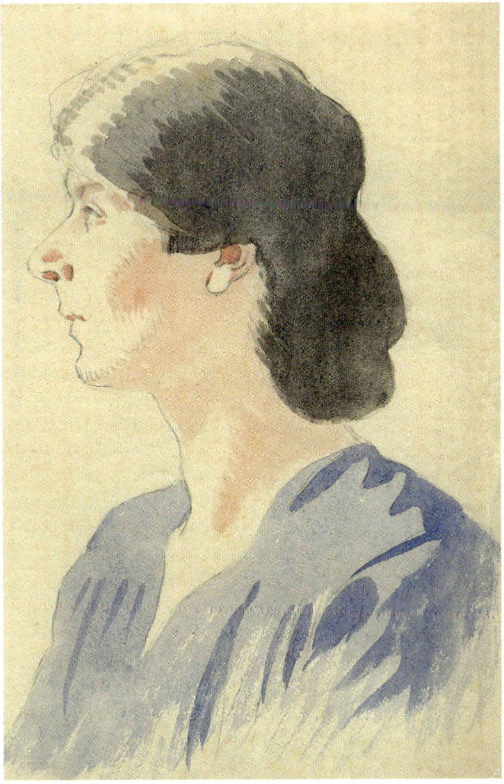

57 *Portrait of Andrée*
Pencil and watercolour on paper, 38.2 x 27.2
Private collection

effects of a number of surgical operations. Consequently he was absent from his classes for most of 1919 due to ill health. He took advantage of the summer holidays to rest at his house in Blaceret, where, never far from something to draw, he produced a large number of sketches, as he was accustomed to do each year during his summer retreat to the Beaujolais region.

On his return to England, in Chorlton on Medlock, on 3 October 1919, he married (Hélène) Andrée Pallez, whom he had met in Manchester, where she was teaching French at the University of Manchester. She was a Protestant, which would have differentiated her, given that the vast majority of French people were Roman Catholic. She began her career in Manchester at the commencement of the University academic year of 1917-18 as a 'temporary assistant lecturer'; the following year she was confirmed in her role with a promotion to 'special assistant lecturer'. Andrée continued to progress very rapidly and was appointed 'lecturer' a few months before their marriage.[67] At the time of their marriage, Valette was 42 and Andrée 31; she was the daughter of a Captain in the French army. Like Gabriela, Andrée was an intellectual and she had a great admiration for her husband's work. Andrée Valette spent a large part of her academic career on the study of the life and works of Victor Hugo. She was

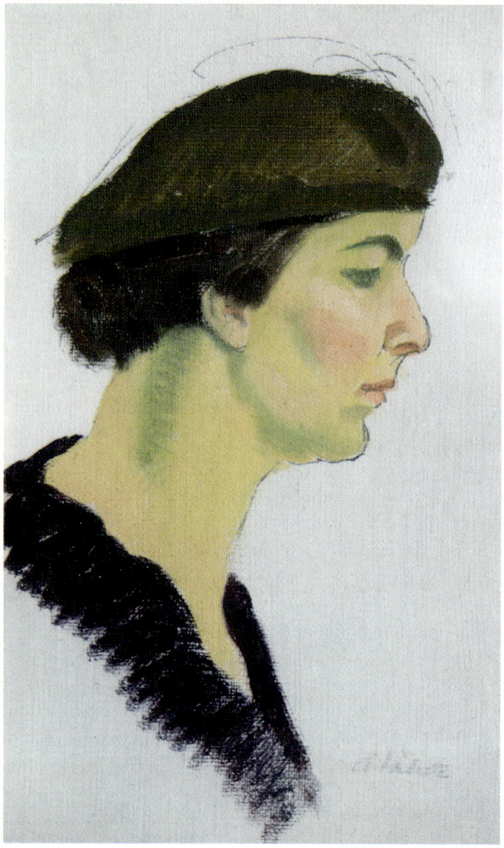

58 *Andrée with Beret*
Oil on canvas on board, 23.5 x 14.5
Private collection

thoroughly bilingual, and had a love for English literature, with Henry James and Malcolm Lowry being among her favourite writers.[68]

Andrée was a cultivated and intelligent individual, who spoke English almost without any foreign accent, she was ambitious for herself and for her husband and had the exceptional merit of taking in hand Adolphe's career whose artistic stature she immediately discerned. Andrée encouraged Valette to exhibit, and to take control of his career despite the health problems he was beginning to experience. Andrée and Adolphe shared a love of art and literature, and also walking and travelling – they were an adventurous couple by the standards of the period. We know very little about the relationship between Andrée and her stepson, Tita. There are few paintings portraying Andrée, which is understandable, given that she was engaged throughout the day with her occupations as a teacher at the University and thus had very little time to sit as a model for her husband. When Andrée is painted in a picture she often has serious, solemn features, which are in fact less flattering than the few photos we have found of her.

Valette continued to practise his art as much as he could. He received fulsomely enthusiastic reviews following two major exhibitions in Manchester in 1918 and 1920 at the 'Finnigans Showrooms' on Deansgate, and was from that time held in great reverence at the Manchester Municipal School of Art, so much so that he was appointed 'Principal Master of Painting' by the new headmaster in October 1920.

Despite this promotion, Valette did not occupy the position long, and in December 1920 his name no longer appeared among the ranks of tutors. His illness persisted and his general health was not good; reference was made with increasing frequency in the School's minutes to the fact that the premises of the 'Life Room' had become stifling and unhealthy. It is also possible that the numerous changes initiated by Dawson in the internal management of classes had precipitated his departure. Henry Cadness, the assistant headmaster, who had had a long career with the School, also took his retirement at this point. The successor to Valette's post at the Municipal School of Art was Albert W. Dodd.

It would seem obvious that Valette wished to lighten his timetable in order to have more time for commercial work, which, given his increasing fame, would certainly provide him with a greater income than would a teacher's salary.

After a period of convalescence at Church Stretton in Shropshire (fig 59 page 59) and in France in Blacé as well as a number of months in Paris, Valette returned to Manchester in 1921; he took on two part-time teaching positions, one as 'Instructor in Drawing' in the faculty of architecture at the University of Manchester and the other at the Municipal School of Art in Bolton, where he taught the Life class until his resignation in September 1927. In Bolton he was visited by his former pupil L.S. Lowry.[69]

It was a perfectly logical step for Valette to teach in Bolton, as the headmaster of the School was one of Valette's former students, Ernest Hartley. Hartley had won a second-class prize in Valette's Life class at the Manchester Municipal School of Art in 1907-8, and had been awarded an 'associateship' of the School in 1908-9, which was its highest distinction; he had also been awarded one of its travelling scholarships, the 'Procter Memorial'. What would be more natural, therefore, than to recruit his former teacher? Although teaching the Life class in Bolton, Valette must have been delighted by the existence at the school of an 'Open Air Studio', with a south-west aspect, which 'extends down to the River Croal, and the Manchester Bolton and Bury Canal, thus affording great opportunity for "Sky and Atmospheric effects" in Landscape Painting.'[70]

59 *At Church Stretton, 1919*
Watercolour on paper, 23.5 x 32
Private collection

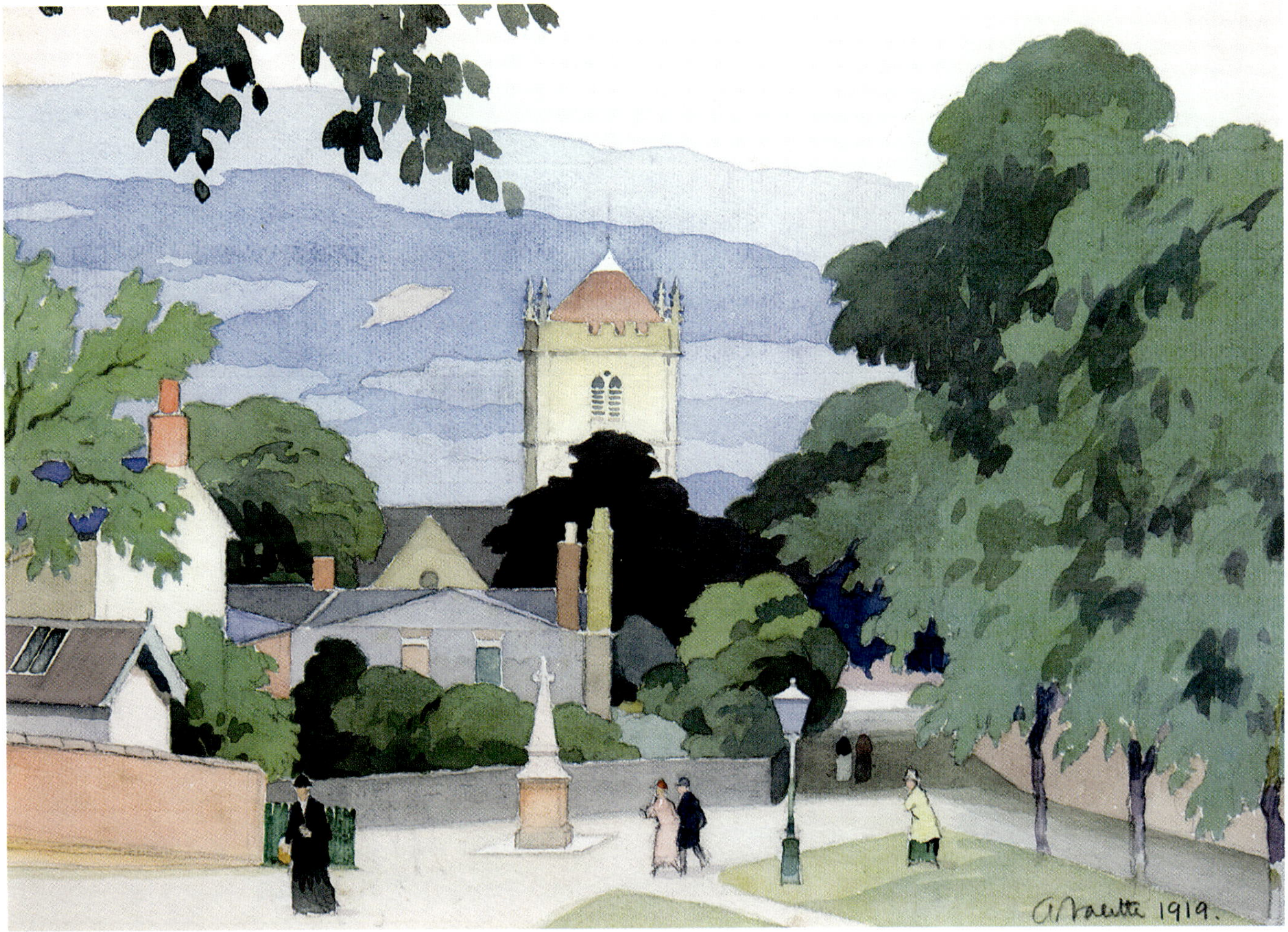

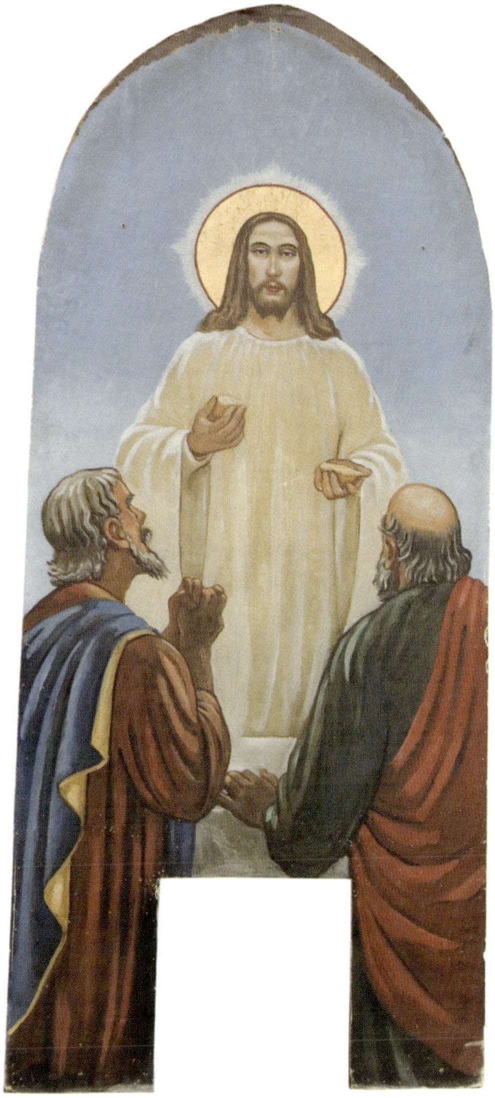

60 *The Breaking of the Bread, St Luke 24*
Oil on canvas on wood panel, 162 x 70.5
Our Lady Star of the Sea, St Annes-on-Sea, Lancashire

Valette's other part-time position was at the University of Manchester. Here too, the excellent credit he had with his former colleagues paid dividends. The head of the Department of Architecture was Professor Dickie, who had been his colleague since 1912 at the Manchester Municipal School of Art. Valette started at the University of Manchester for the academic session 1922/23 with the title of 'part-time Instructor in Drawing', then in 1927/28 he became 'Special Instructor in Life Drawing'; in December 1927, this post was reconfirmed for a period of three years with effect from September 1928, which shows that he was very much appreciated, but we now know that he did not complete his term of office due to the death of his mother in Blacé and the need to take care of his handicapped sister.[71]

Valette supplemented his income with paintings for churches (St Anne's-on-Sea, Werneth, Royton, Denton, Glossop, and Wardle) and for private houses and public buildings in the North of England.

The traces of some of these frescoes have survived, for example those done for the church of Our Lady Star of the Sea in St Annes-on-Sea, one of the Lancashire seaside resorts (fig 60 page 60). These frescoes were in the form of a fairly monumental triptych: a reproduction of the design for this triptych was published in the *Journal of Decorative Art* in 1921. It was well reviewed: 'Strong colour and a fairly free use of gold has been introduced and the effect is extremely decorative. Mr Valette's drawings is strong, and his treatment broad. Visitors to the Lancashire seaside town should make a point of inspecting this interesting example of ecclesiastical decoration.'[72]

In the vestry of the church, there is a photograph taken in the 1950's of the visit of the Bishop of Lancaster, and the panels by Valette are clearly visible behind the high altar. In the meantime, the panels by Valette have been removed. We have recently been able to locate the central panel, which is still in the possession of the church but unfortunately the two side panels of praying angels could not be found. The central panel depicts the story of the 'Breaking of the Bread' on the road to Emmaus, with the risen Jesus breaking and blessing the bread before his disciple Cleopas and a companion (The Gospel according to St Luke, chapter 24).

One can appreciate that the commissioned work, especially for ecclesiastical subjects like this one, imposes constraints on the scope of the painter's expression, who must remain within the bound of the subject commissioned. Nonetheless, Valette's technique and talent are very much in evidence.

At the Anglican Church of St John in Werneth, nine panels were also exhibited. The ninth panel represents a young soldier from the First World War who 'kneels in awe to pray before a visionary manifestation, in which Christ appears crucified on the cross-shaped antlers of a white deer, which stands on the summit of a heather-covered mountain.'[73] This, as in the painting 'England called, they answered' (fig 48 page 47), is another testimony to Valette's interest in iconographic scenes relating to the First World War.

He also worked again in the commercial sector, which in fact he had never entirely abandoned; he had remained active in this field, executing textile designs for a calico printing firm[74] and for instance, amongst the rare surviving examples of this type of work, a banner for the Shakespeare tercentenary for the Stockport Garrick Society,

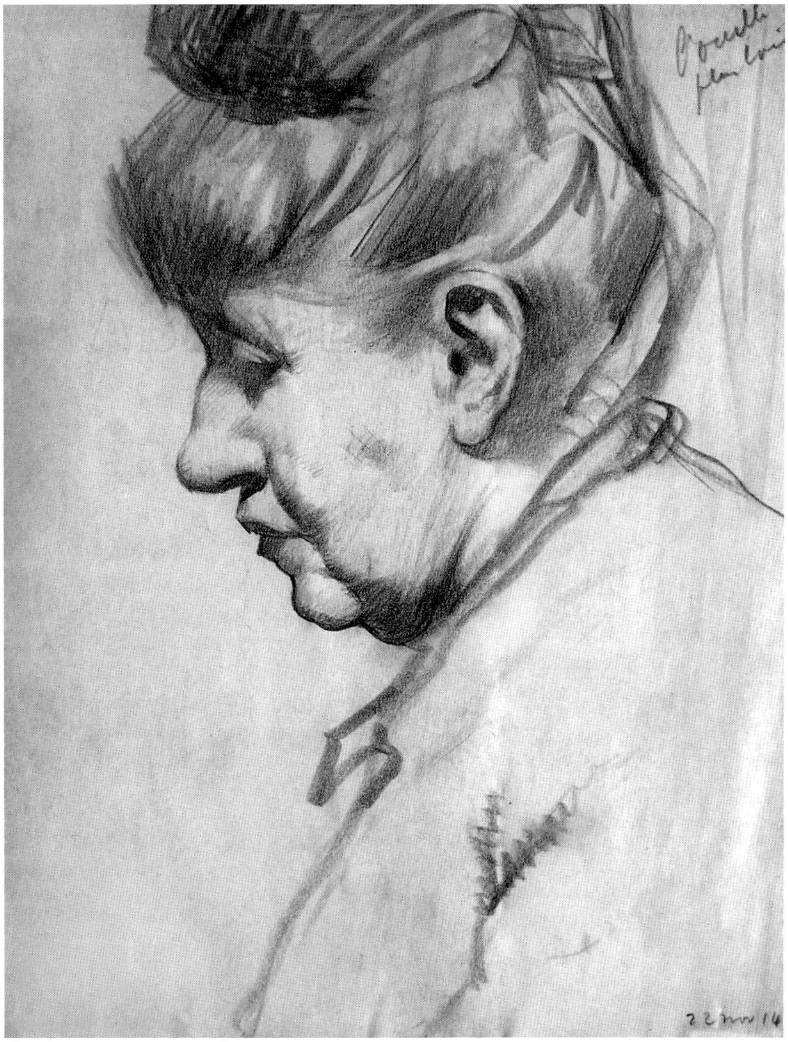

61 Portrait of the Artist's Mother, 22 Nov 1914
Drawing on paper, 24.8 x 19.2
Private collection

an amateur theatre company. The theatre company still owns this work which can be seen at the theatre.

Valette left Manchester in June 1928. His departure is described by François Feuillée, a writer and friend of the artist, in a journal article entitled 'Well-known Artist's Farewell': Very few passengers on the London Express recognised a quietly dressed figure stepping into a first-class carriage a week ago. With characteristic modesty, begging his friends to abandon their idea of a farewell dinner at the *Midland Hotel*, followed by a boisterous send-off, Monsieur Adolphe Valette bade adieu to the smoky city where, for two decades he has been the beacon and inspiring guide to all true artists. It is difficult to estimate the extent of our loss.'[75]

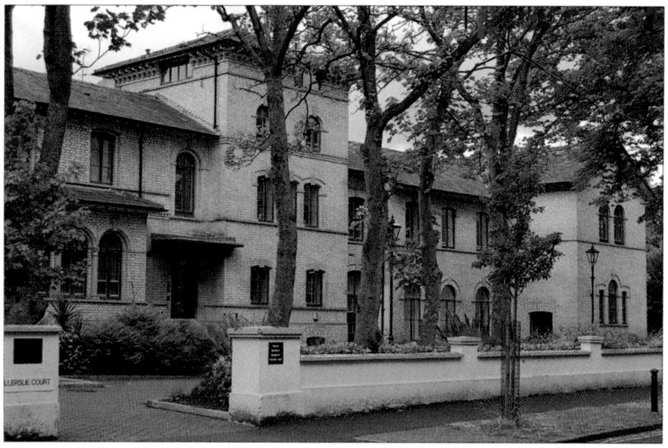

62 *'Ellerslie', a residential building in Victoria Park, probably Valette's last address in Manchester. The old façade has been preserved.*

More than anything else, his departure from Manchester and return to France was precipitated by the death of his mother and the fact that his sister Louise, who suffered from a mental handicap and had hitherto lived with his mother in Blacé, was now on her own.

Valette returned to Manchester in 1932 for four months and again the following year. Having been unable to find most of his former students, who had not achieved the success he had hoped they would, his brief visit of 1933 was tinged with sadness and disappointment.[76] Valette did not return to Manchester after this. In a postcard that he sent from Blacé, on 22 May 1939, to Lawrence Haward, curator of the Manchester City Art Gallery, Valette refers to the possibility of a further visit to Manchester, which 'might give me the opportunity and the pleasure of having a good look round the Gallery.'[77] The Manchester City Art Gallery had acquired several of his works in 1928, due to the encouragement of one of Valette's devoted students, Charles Holmes. This wish to return to Manchester remained unfulfilled; on 3 September, Britain and France declared war on Germany and Valette spent the war years in Blacé until his death in 1942.

3 *The Return to France*

Retirement to Blacé, a tranquil painting style,
the foundation of an artistic society, travels, exhibitions

The Return to his Homeland

In 1928, having left Manchester in June, Adolphe Valette moved permanently to Blacé, to his house in the hamlet of Blaceret, in the Beaujolais region. His mother had died at the beginning of the year and she was buried in the cemetery of Villefranche-sur-Saône. Valette became the owner of the house following the cessation of the joint ownership between his brothers and sister.

The origins of the house can be traced back to 1812; at that time it was surrounded by land of over a hectare, planted with alfalfa with some land as a meadow and orchard; as with most such houses, it was built in adobe, and sheltered from the north winds. This was a simple wine-grower's house with its own cellar and wine fermentation vessels in the ground-floor room and with the living room and bedroom on the first floor. The house was initially lived in by Adolphe Valette's mother who was by then widowed. She had sold the land, and lived there in the house with her daughter Louise who was mentally handicapped. A judgement by the Tribunal Civil had pronounced Louise an 'Incapable majeure' [legally incompetent adult]. Louise was what is referred

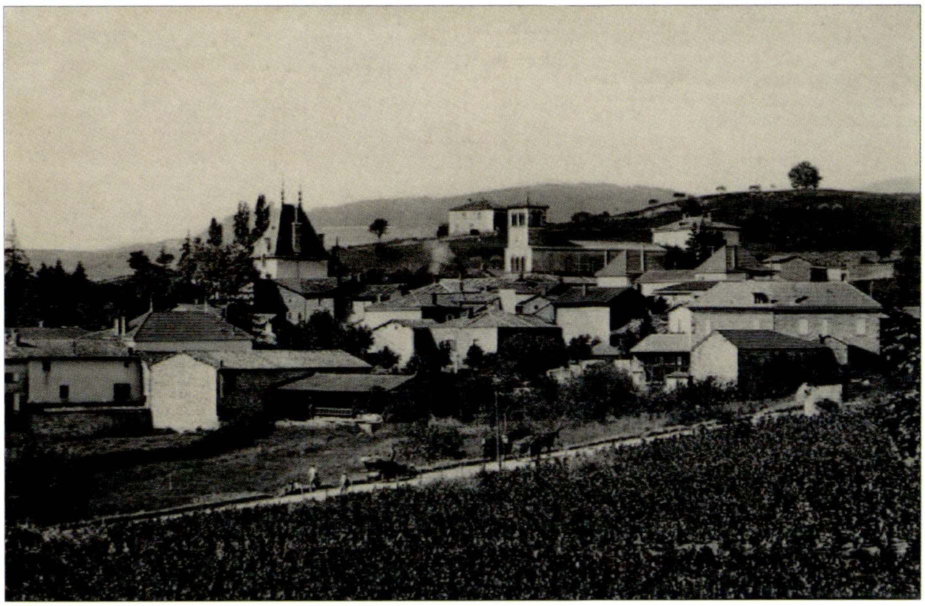

63 *View of the village of Blacé in the Beaujolais, where Valette retired in 1928*

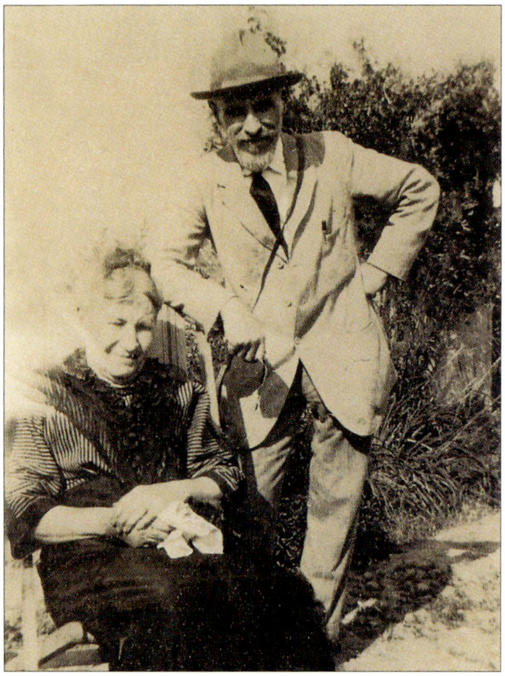

64 *Photo of Valette and his mother*
Private collection

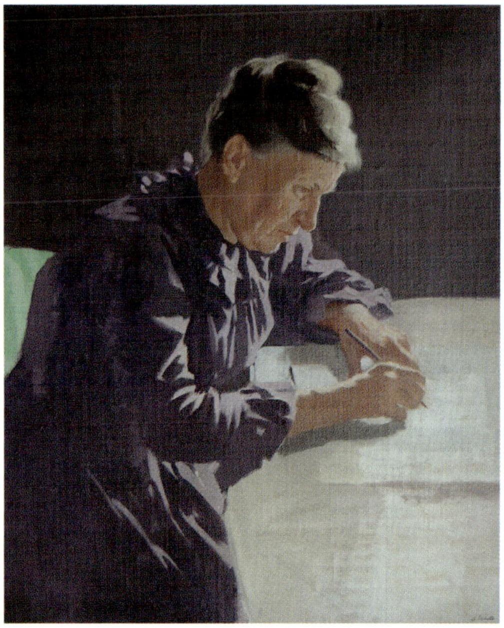

65 *Madame Valette, the Artist's Mother*
Oil on canvas, 70 x 57
Private collection

to as a mentally retarded person, and she was often seen going for walks wearing a large number of jingling medals. We believe that this was one of the reasons that led to Valette's return to Blacé: after his mother died, someone had to look after Louise.

Already, back in 1909, Madeleine had adapted the hayloft as a one-room apartment; perhaps this was to enable her son to visit and to provide a degree of independence. After Madeleine's death, the house thus went to her son Adolphe. He later converted the wine fermentation room into his painting studio and the attic into a storage place for his works which he was continuing to send to Manchester.

Adolphe Valette had already spent many holidays in the house in Blaceret, while he was still living in Manchester. In fact the calendar of academic vacations at the Manchester School of Art enabled him to spend many weeks there, at Easter, Whitsun and in the summer. From June 1928, he occupied the house permanently, although his second wife, Andrée, was still a lecturer in French in Manchester which she continued to be until the academic year 1937/38.[1] She then taught at the University of Oxford, at Somerville College, one of the first colleges in England to take women; Andrée only joined her husband during her own academic vacations.

In 1929, on 9 July, Valette experienced the great sadness of the loss of his only son Pierre, who died in Manchester at the age of 18, suffering from acute tubercular meningitis. This was a cruel blow for this man who had already had more than his fair share of suffering, such as the premature death of his first wife Gabriela. Pierre, whose name had been anglicised to 'Peter' and who also retained his childhood nickname Tita, was, at the time of his death, an apprentice in the British merchant marine. Rather curiously, there are differing accounts of Tita's death. It has been suggested that he died in a submarine accident; it was also suggested that he died during a trip to Calcutta. However, the Manchester coroner's registers are specific as to the causes of death which are, according to British practice, certified by a doctor. It was in fact one of his maternal cousins who notified the Registry Office of his death. One may be surprised that it was not Andrée Valette who notified the Registry Office of Peter's death, even though Andrée was still a lecturer at the University of Manchester at this time.

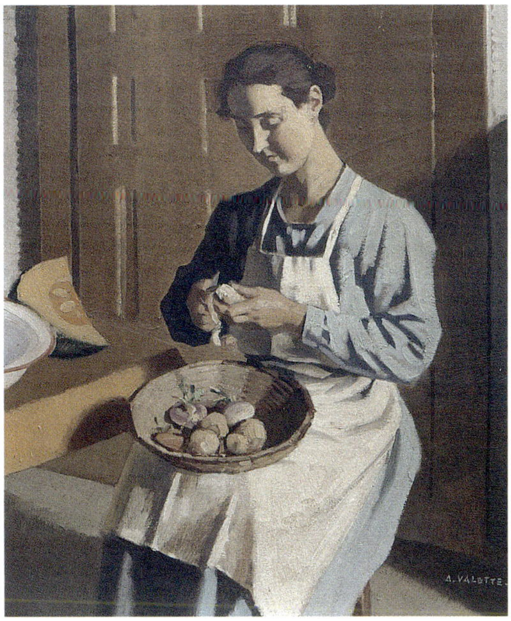

66 *La Ménagère*
Oil on board, 62.5 x 52
Private collection

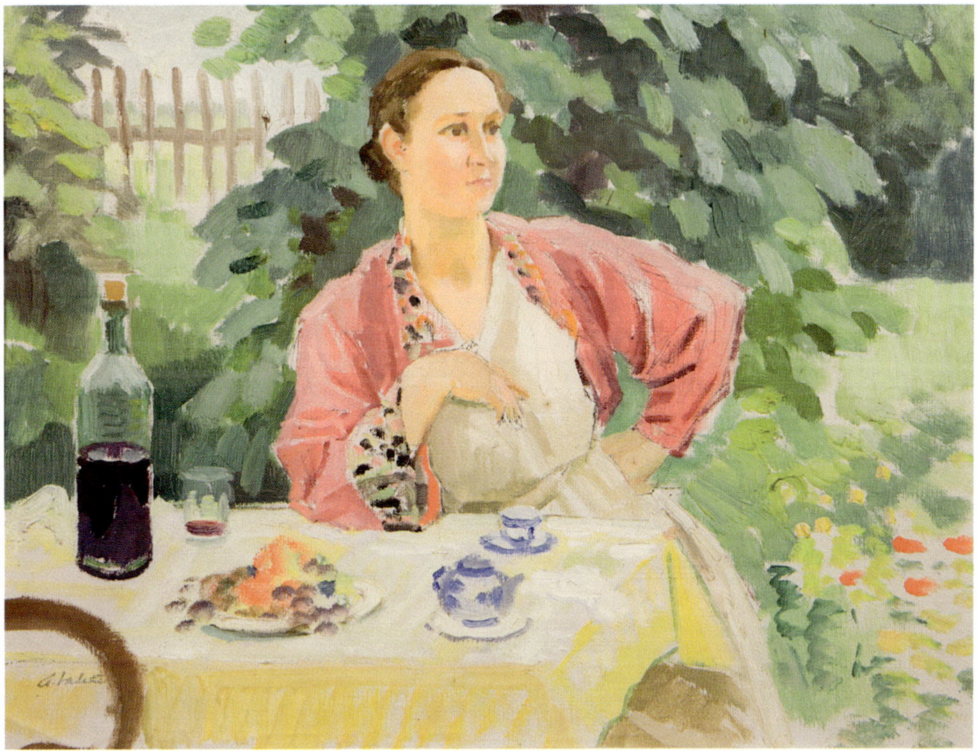

67 *In the Garden*
Oil on canvas, 31 x 39.5
Private collection

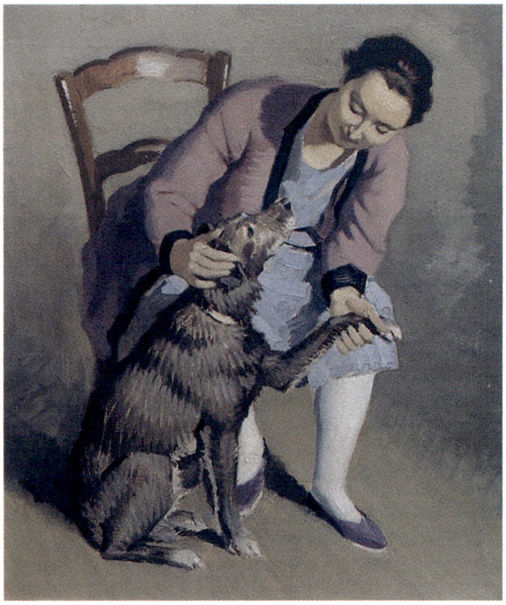

68 Le Chien Malade
Oil on board, 63.5 x 52.5
Private collection

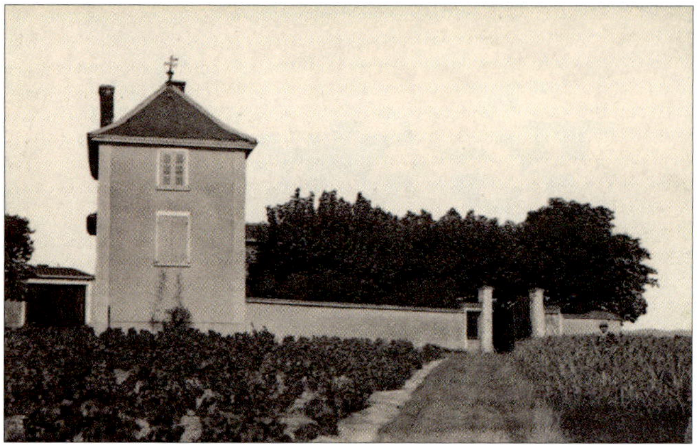

69 Blaceret, le Château Bleu
Valette lived very close to this house, and painted it often.

In Blaceret, Valette's day-to-day requirements were managed by his housekeeper Maria Lafond, who also became his model and inspiration as his muse for the last twenty years of his life.

Maria was a young woman from the same hamlet, and Adolphe Valette was a friend of her parents; Maria lived with her mother who had been widowed. The simple domestic life in Blaceret inspired many of Valette's paintings: Maria sewing, Maria about her household tasks (fig 66 page 65), Maria in the garden (fig 67 page 65), Maria with the sick dog (fig 68 page 66). In the absence of his wife Andrée who had remained in England, Valette particularly valued the domestic help Maria provided for him; they established a relationship based on mutual consideration and respect. From the correspondence she sent to her mother, it transpires that Maria accompanied Valette on his painting trips to some interesting locations and landscapes. These travels lasted weeks at a time and Maria was very pleased to discover these locations in conjunction with her housekeeping duties. Valette valued her company 'to share his enthusiasm' at the sites they visited.[2]

Maria was married late in life, in 1940, to a native of Lyon, Mr Desdier, who had been the owner for some years of a cottage in the same road as Adolphe Valette and Maria Lafond. Mr Desdier had a business in Lyon producing

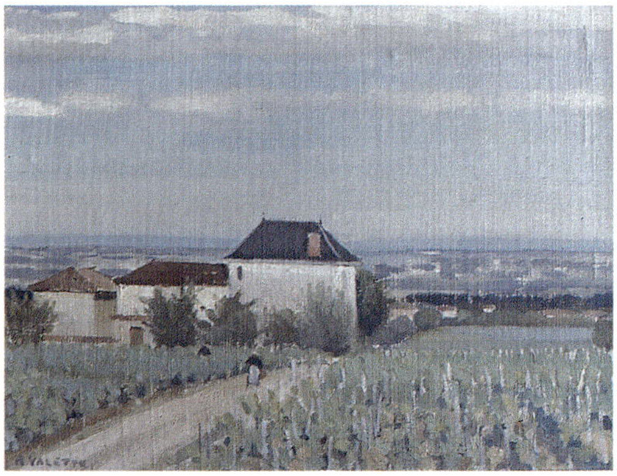

70 Le Château Bleu
Oil on canvas on board, 31 x 40
Private collection

71 *Paysage Beaujolais avec une Voiture*

Oil on board, 37 x 49

Private collection

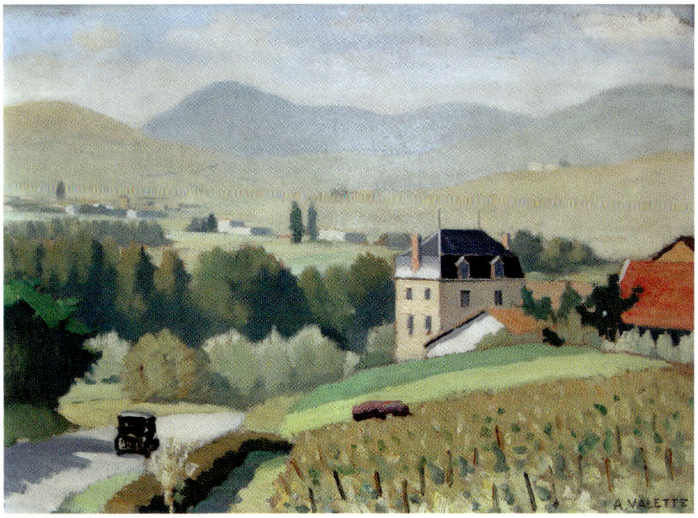

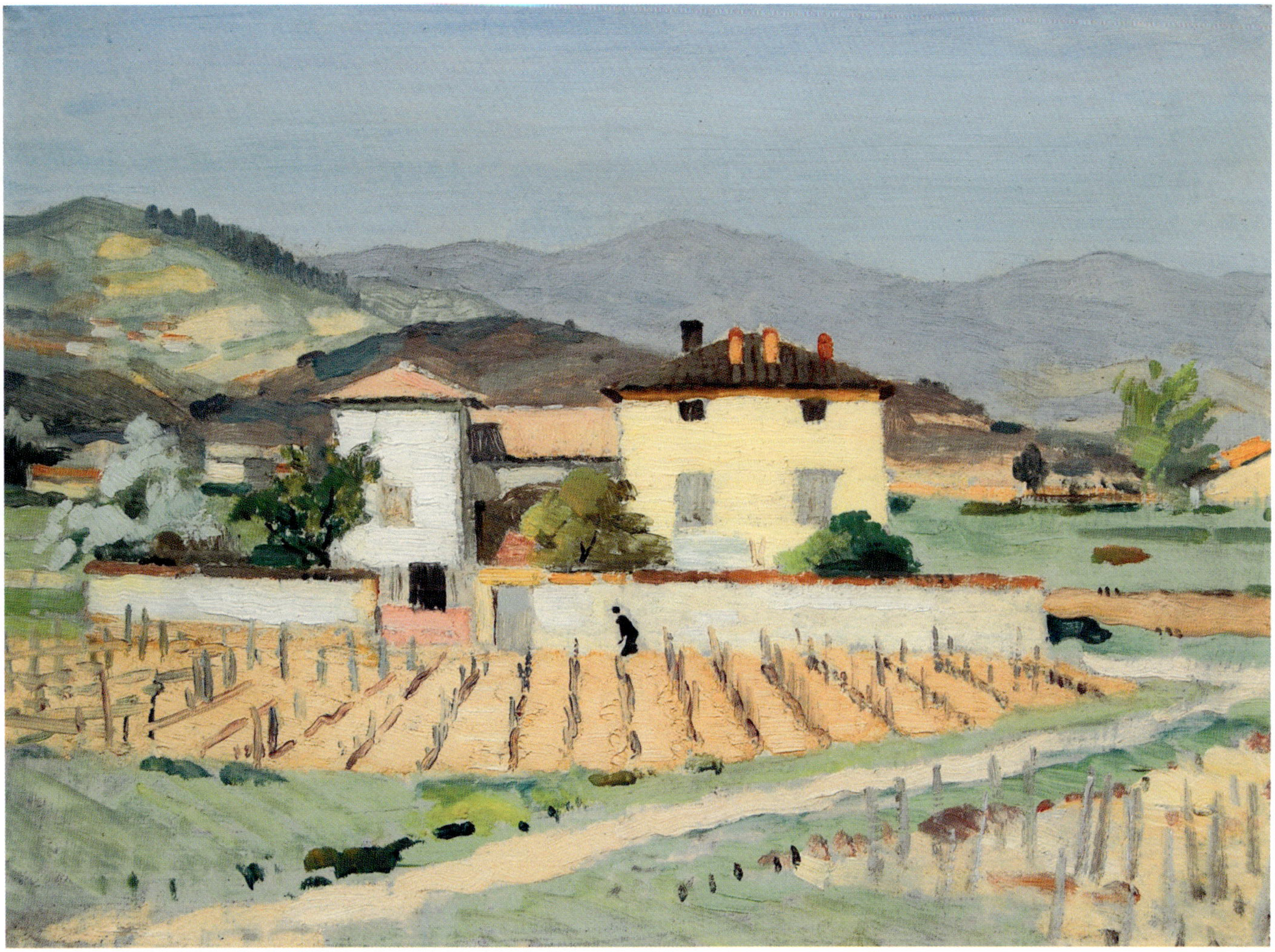

72 *La Ferme Sanlaville*

Oil on canvas on board, 32.5 x 43

Private collection

wooden moulding components for metal foundries and he provided Valette with numerous wooden frames for his pictures.

Other than the travels, Valette also enjoyed painting the simplicity of agrarian nature during his retirement in Blacé. There is a whole series of paintings of the neighbouring farms and landscapes, and of his neighbours, such as the Sanlaville family (fig 72 page 67), for example, who provided Valette with eggs and milk, who in return allowed them to use the telephone, the only one in the hamlet. His life was punctuated by small-scale human events, involving the simple joys of the peasant environment in which he revelled. He chatted with shepherds and goatherds, with harvest workers, and lived in the symbiosis of the cycle of agriculture and the production of wine.

Artistic Societies and Exhibitions

However, Valette did not neglect the social and commercial contingencies of his art and frequented the artistic circles of Saint-Etienne and Lyon.

He was an active member of the Société des Arts du Forez. This artistic society in Saint-Etienne was founded in 1902 by a group of former students of the Ecole Régionale des Beaux-Arts that Valette attended from 1891 to 1895. It was Jean Dablin, Valette's former teacher, who became director of the art school a few years later, who was the catalyst behind the formation of this society. From the outset, it generated a steady flow of support and interest among the town's public authorities. The object of the association was to offer a means of expression to the former students and to enable them to continue to exhibit their works (painting, sculpture, engraving, industrial draughtsmanship) at the various salons that were organised each year. The statutes also specify that, at this annual exhibition, prize-winning artists from the Paris Salons would be specially invited, with a view to providing a stimulus for the local Saint-Etienne artists. While he was living in England, Valette remained a member of this association; this enabled him to retain contact with his birthplace. Once back in France, Valette became an active member of the Committee and exhibited his own works alongside artists such as van Dongen and Puvis de Chavannes.

In 1930, with ten or so other artists, including the fauvist Jean Puy, Valette founded the Association des Artistes Foréziens which included amongst others Paul Signac as one of its honorary members. The objective the Association des Artistes Foréziens set itself was to expose the Saint-Etienne public to some of the new trends in modern art. In its statutes, we also find the interesting concept of offering its members moral support as well as its 'effective support within the limitations of an equitably mutuality' ['concours effectif dans la limite d'une juste mutualité'] and of course the organisation of events associated with the fine arts. This materialised in the form of a Salon de Printemps (Spring Exhibition), which was to be the annual counterpart of the Salon d'Automne of the Société des Arts du Forez, of which Valette was also a member.

One may observe certain points of convergence between Jean Puy and Adolphe Valette. They were the same age and came from the same region. Puy was born in Roanne in 1876. It is also more than likely that the two men met at the time of their studies in Lyon, as they both frequented the studio of Tony Tollet. From an artistic

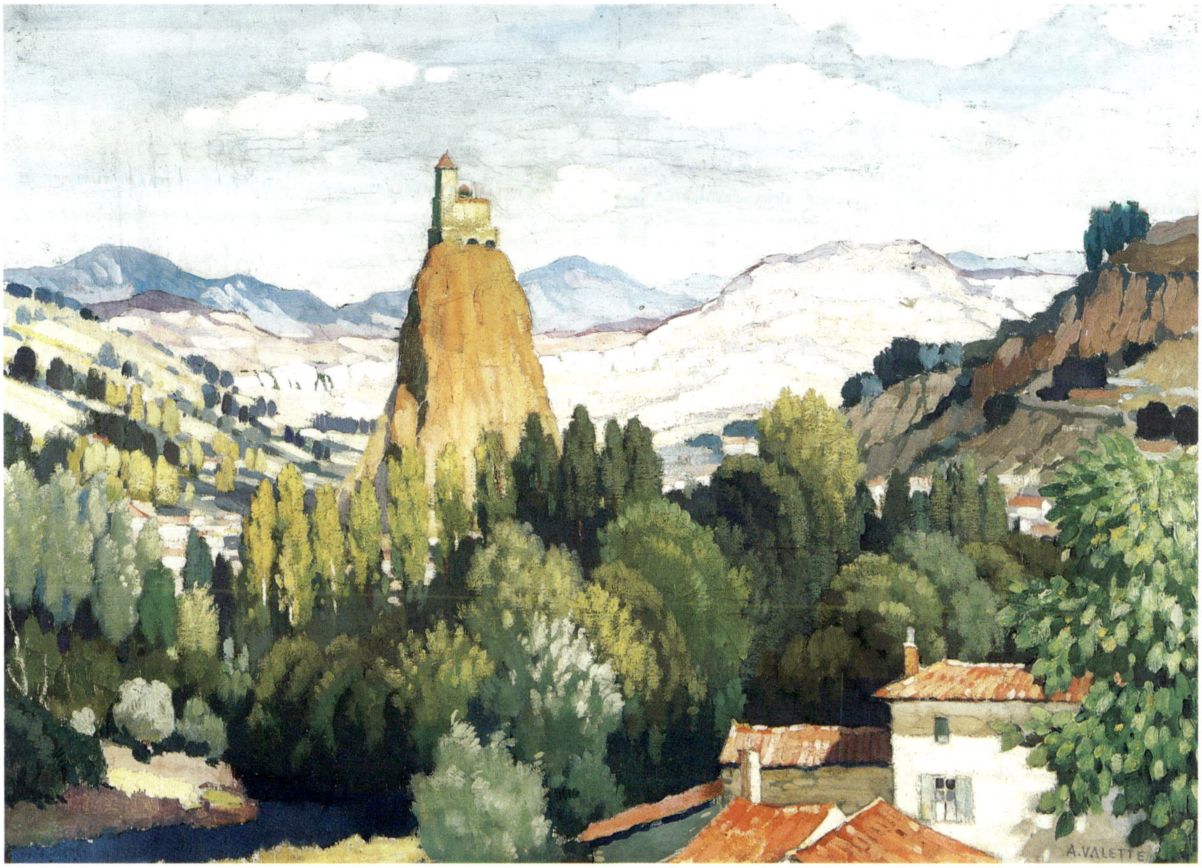

73 *Rocher St-Michel au Puy*
Oil on canvas, 57 x 98
Musée d'Art Moderne de Saint-Etienne Métropole

point of view, both Jean Puy and Adolphe Valette were a step back from the most extremist of their co-religionists and, towards the end of their lives, opted to plough their own respective furrows at a distance from any artistic excesses.

The Salon of the Association des Artistes Foréziens attained a certain stature: in 1930, 186 works were exhibited including a watercolour by Paul Signac 'Suresne', a canvas by Jean Puy 'En Bretagne', and two works by Pierre Combet-Descombes.

Adolphe Valette submitted five canvases including: 'Le Turban Rose', 'L'Eglise (Rochetaillée)' and the 'Ruines représentant les Restes d'un Château Fort'. In 1931, a canvas by Valette even had the distinction of being selected as an illustration in an article in the 'Région Illustrée', a local journal of high artistic standing: this was 'Devant la Maison' which represented a woman seated (most probably Maria Lafond) on a bench in front of a house with a dog playing in front of her, a tree and a fence. The critic found that 'Mr Valette distinguishes himself with a deliberately cold colouring, but which is not without charm. His drawing is dry perhaps, but precise. There is no mannerism, and

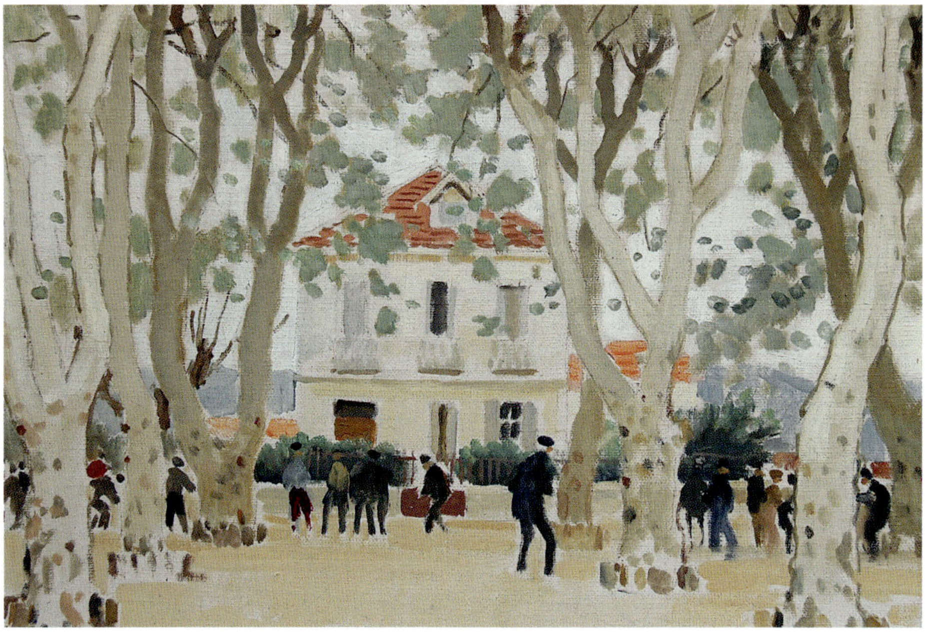

74 *Place des Lices, Saint-Tropez*
Oil on canvas on board, 30.7 x 40.1
Private collection

all is simplicity.' ['M. Valette se distingue par une coloration volontairement froide, mais qui n'est pas sans charme. Son dessin est sec peut-être, mais précis. Sa manière, toute de simplicité'].[3] The following year, in 1932, Valette exhibited four paintings, 'Paysanne et ses Chèvres', 'Rochetaillée', 'St-Julien', 'Vieille Maison': the critical appraisal of Valette's works was similar: 'Valette's works are notable due to personal approach, reducing the colours of the landscape to a few essential tones and by producing decorative effects, albeit a little dry.' ['Les oeuvres de Valette se font remarquer par un procédé personnel, réduisant les couleurs des paysages à quelques tons essentiels et produisant des effets décoratifs, mais un peu secs'].[4] Valette was further cited amongst those regional artists who had made a significant impact at the sixth Salon de Printemps at Easter 1935.

On the reverse of some of Valette's works, exhibition labels testify to this day to their presence at these salons.

In 1931, he had a personal exhibition at the Galerie Livet, rue de la Loire (now rue Georges-Teyssier) in Saint-Etienne, which at that time was Saint-Etienne's major private art gallery. This gallery had opened in 1874, and highly regarded regional painters such as François-Auguste Ravier, Emile Noirot, and Charles Beauverie were among the first artists to be represented.

From 1929, Valette regularly sent a large number of his works to the Salons of the Société Lyonnaise des Beaux-Arts. This association, founded on 12 November 1887, originated from the merger of two societies: the society of the 'Amis des Arts' and the society of 'Artistes Lyonnais'. Its first salon took place on 16 February 1888, in place Bellecour, in a fine, vast wooden construction, which had to be dismantled and re-assembled each year until 1903. During his studies in Lyon from 1895 to 1899, Valette would thus have been able to visit this society's salons, which were open not only to paintings, but also exhibited drawings, watercolours, pastels, miniatures, enamels, faïences, porcelain, stained glass cartoons and stained glass works, sculpture, engravings, lithography and architectural work.

When he retired to Blacé, each year, between 1929 and 1940, Valette sent a number of works to this Salon, which was by this time established on the quai de Bondy. He selected them according to the criteria of a fairly conventional Lyon public, to the extent that amongst them were a number of paintings of bouquets of flowers and local scenes and landscapes, all works liable to find buyers among the visitors to the Salon. Alongside certain more minor works, there was however the magnificent 'Esthera' which he submitted in 1931, the 'Turban Rose' in 1932, which he never managed to sell, and some nudes in 1937. In the first catalogues of these Salons d'Automne, Valette is presented as a pupil of Tony Tollet, who was very well known in Lyon, a Prix de Rome laureate, and a painter mainly of technically very respectable portraits but whose conformity is undeniable. This reference 'pupil of' subsequently disappeared, probably as Valette did not necessarily see this affiliation as an altogether positive reflection.

Valette was also an artist member of the 'Société des Artistes Lyonnais', founded in 1901, which gathered together artists from Lyon or from the département as well as artists originating from Lyon but now living in Paris. He sent his works to this salon between 1936 and 1942. They were exhibited (like those of the Société Lyonnaise des

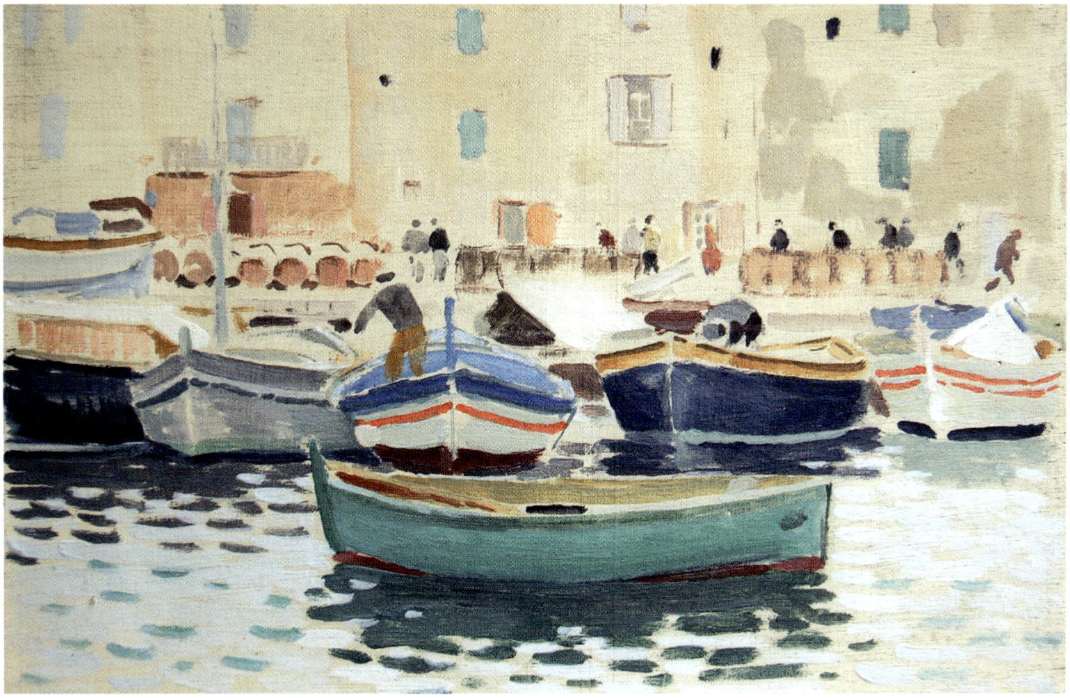

75 *Saint-Tropez*
Oil on board, 24 x 32.5
Private collection

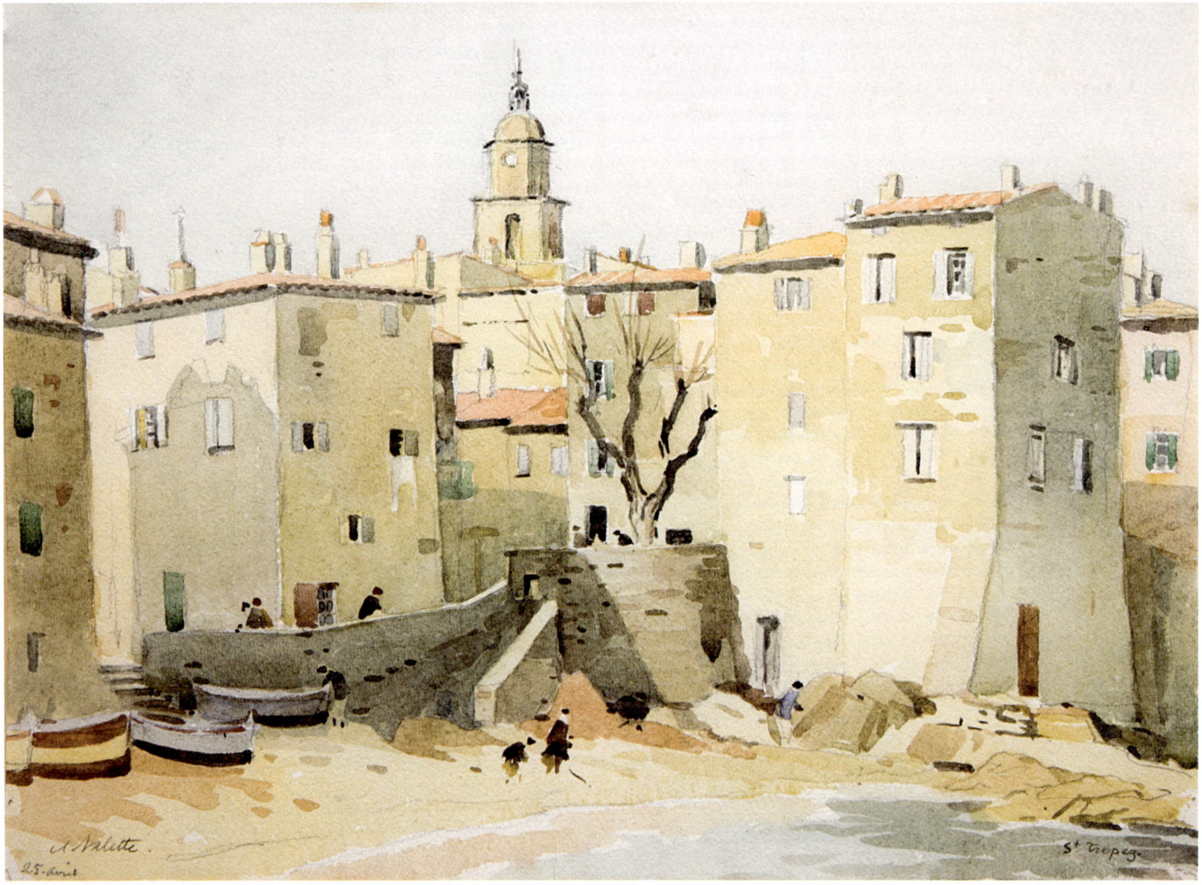

76 *Saint-Tropez, 25 avril*
Pencil and watercolour on paper, 28 x 37.5
Private collection

Beaux-Arts) on the quai de Bondy, in the Palais Municipal des Expositions during the 'Salons d'Automne'.

Here, too, Valette sent scenes of day-to-day life that he had captured in the Beaujolais region ('Basse-cour', 'Tête de Femme', 'La Ménagère' (fig 66 page 65), but in both these salons, there were also English subjects (Burrington Hall, Herefordshire and Arundel's Farm).

It was also during his retirement at Blacé that Valette began to enjoy a degree of recognition amongst the French art galleries, two of which purchased works by him.

The Saint-Etienne art gallery (Musée d'Art Moderne de Saint-Etienne Métropole), in his birthplace, was the first French art gallery to recognise his talent and in 1929 purchased a canvas of the Rocher Saint-Michel au Puy (fig 73 page 69). In 1943 this same art gallery made a posthumous purchase of a very intense portrait of the artist's mother (fig 1 page 2). The Ecole Nationale Supérieure des Arts et Industries Textiles in Roubaix purchased his 'Portrait de Femme' on 22 June 1937, but unfortunately this work has disappeared from the collections.

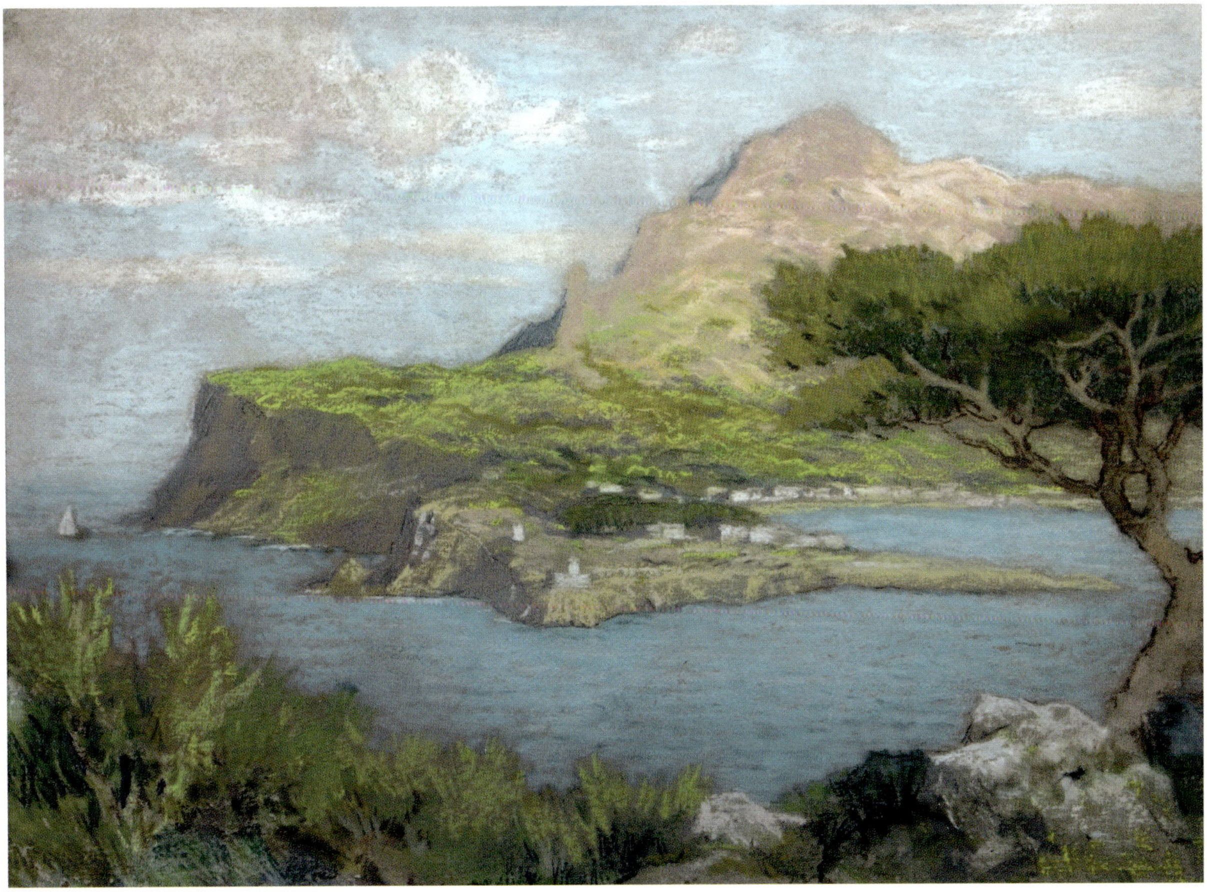

77 *Puerto Pollensa*
Pastel on board, 47.3 x 63.4
Private collection

Travels

Valette made Blacé a base for numerous trips to the south: he took his easel to Sisteron, Antibes, Saint-Paul de Vence, Grimaud, Bandol, Sospel, and to the Alps and the Pyrenees. He was a prolific and remarkable painter of Saint-Tropez which he painted in various ways, sometimes with a discreet pointillism derived from Paul Signac and Derain (fig 75 page 71). Saint-Tropez was, at the time, a fishing village which was difficult to access, which around the turn of the 19th century became a meeting place and inspiration for young artists.

It was Paul Signac who discovered the village in 1892 when looking for a mooring for his yacht. He fell in love with the place, so much so that he purchased a house 'La Hune', which soon became a rallying point for a whole generation of innovative artists: Van Rysselberghe, Matisse, Manguin, Marquet, Camoin, Puy, Kisling, Cross, Luce, Dufy, Bonnard, Picabia etc … Saint-Tropez should also be mentioned in the context of the writer Colette who received various writers at her villa 'La Treille Muscate'.

This village thus benefited from an immense aura and soon became a compulsory place of pilgrimage for a whole set of the French intelligentsia with whom the Valette couple could identify.

They also travelled to the Balearics, bringing back pastels, watercolours, and oil paintings from Puerto Pollensa (fig 77 page 73), Formentor and Valldemosa. One can well imagine that Andrée and Adolphe would have enjoyed the idea of following in the footsteps of the writer George Sand and musician Fryderyk Chopin who spent the winter of 1838-9 in Valldemosa. George Sand described this stay in the book 'Un Hiver à Majorque' ['A Winter in Majorca'].

When Andrée and Adolphe Valette set off on these 'sketching holidays', they often took their car. They sometimes rented a house in situ such as at Vernoux, in 1931. They would stay for a while to enable Valette to complete some excellent paintings of views of the region (Viviers, Saint-Montant). Maria Lafond, who accompanied them, reports back to her mother in a letter that 'Mr Valette has worked well, the

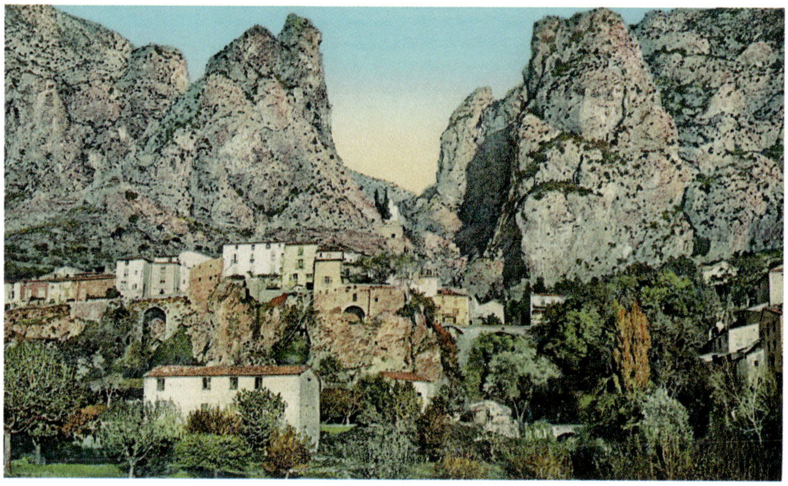

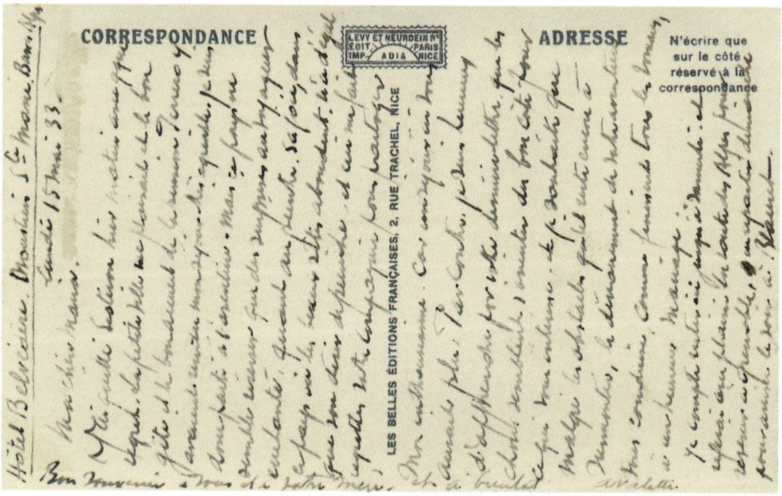

78 Postcard of Moustiers-Sainte-Marie, sent by Valette on 15 May 1933 to his housekeeper in the Beaujolais, Maria Lafond. This is one of the rare surviving documents written by Valette.

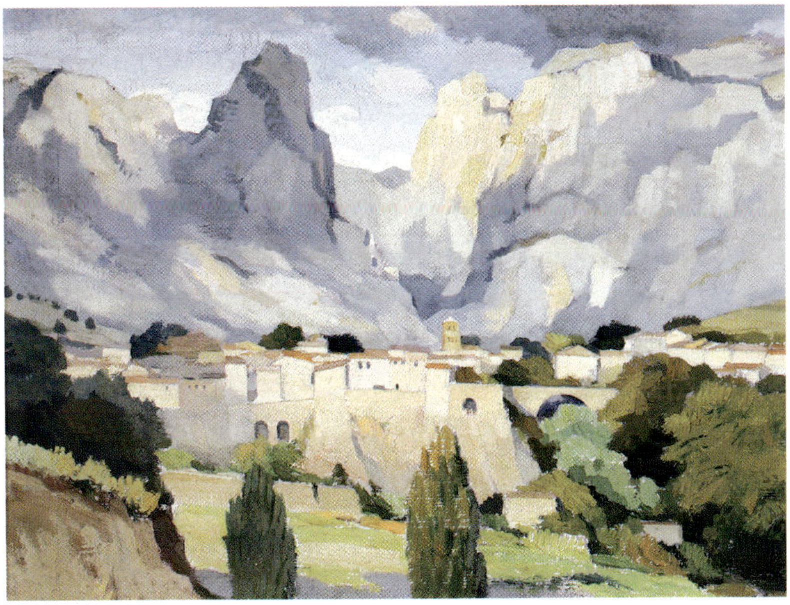

79 *Moustiers-Sainte-Marie*
Oil on board, 46 x 58
Sefton Samuels collection

countryside pleases him greatly.' ['Monsieur Valette a bien travaillé, le pays lui plaît beaucoup.'][5]

Sometimes he would set off on his own, for example as in 1933, when he stopped off at Sisteron and Moustiers-Sainte-Marie. At Moustiers, he described himself as an 'enchanted traveller' ['voyageur enchanté'] and expressed 'his joy at being a painter' ['joie en tant que peintre'], and that 'there is an abundance of good sites' ['les beaux sites abondent'].[6] During this trip he also travelled via Grenoble.

In 1935, he was staying and painting in Sospel, a medieval village close to the Italian border astride a rushing river and with a mountainous background.

The Valettes loved mountain and hill walking which they did at the time in England in the Shropshire Hills and in the Lake District, as well as in France, in the Pyrenees or in the Alps; it was also clear that they had a liking for the elegant, fashionable resorts such as Deauville, Anglesey and Llandudno.

During these trips there was the opportunity for Valette to set up his easel in the open air and to paint numerous watercolours that he sold very easily in England and which provided him with a degree of financial return, unlike his canvases which he always found more difficult to sell. These watercolours were sometimes executed with a few brushstrokes in situ, while others were more intricate, with a pencil line drawing before the addition of colour. He devoted himself to this type of painting with considerable enjoyment until the end of his life. Exhausted and with failing health, he found in it a distraction that was less demanding than oil painting. These watercolours have an informative character in relation to the places he frequented during his trips and enable us to follow him, as with an Ariadne's thread, on the route of his many travels.

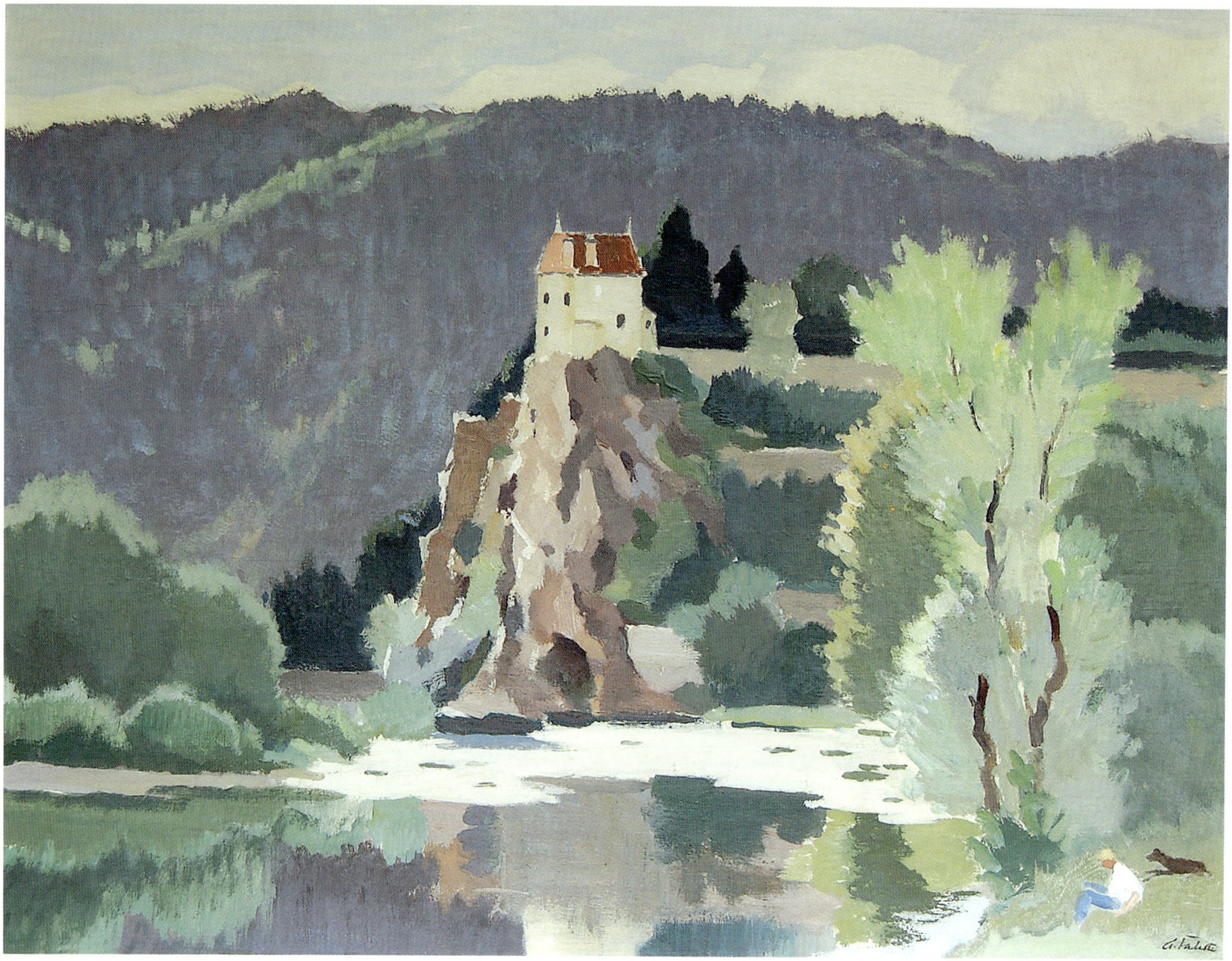

80 *Château de Lavoute*
Oil on board, 46 x 59.5
Private collection

His Last Days

During the war, Valette stayed at his house in Blacé and endured adversities during the German occupation of France. Amongst other things he was a victim of the 'faux-maquis', bandits who stole and pilfered in the French countryside. These brigands stole his valuable jerry cans of petrol that he had kept for use with his car and motorcycle.

Blacé was at the time in the Free Zone (the southern regions of France, still administered by the French during the German occupation), but even so there were significant restrictions of all kinds. For example, in the first two years of the war, wine growers had to uproot their vines in order to plant cereal crops and potatoes to meet food requirements.

At the beginning of the 1940s he managed to make a painting trip to Beaumes-de-Venise and Bormes-les-Mimosas.

During the war years Valette's health deteriorated and he was taken to hospital in Lyon in April 1942. He died there on 18 April at the age of 65 after a long renal illness;[7] the commune of Blacé has the record of his death. He was initially buried in Lyon on 21 April that year, in communal land, in the Guillotière Nouveau cemetery. However, his remains were exhumed on 13 May 1943 to be taken to the cemetery of Villefranche-sur-Saône where he lies to this day, next to his mother Madeleine, who had died in 1928, in a family tomb with a perpetual concession purchased by his wife Andrée. The news of his death only reached Manchester in August 1942. The *Manchester Guardian* published a sensitive résumé of the parameters of his life and his art: 'Valette was a shy and sensitive man whose sensibility made life often difficult for him, though it served him well as a painter. A series of pictures of street scenes in Manchester showed that he had nothing to learn in rendering the atmosphere of the industrial North.'[8]

Sixty years on, in Blacé, he is remembered by the country people as a courteous and affable man, living each moment of his existence for his art, as evidenced by the numerous notebooks and jotter pads filled with little sketches and outlines of animals of the countryside and farmyard. His neighbours remember him walking the country in jodhpurs, with a cap, and positioning his easel in farm courtyards or in fields.

His wife Andrée spent the war years with him in Blacé. Andrée, who was a lecturer in French at Manchester University and then at Somerville College, Oxford, was an intelligent and highly cultivated woman. In the house at Blacé, she was frequently working on the correspondence that she had with highly reputed English and French poets, writers and artists.

After she was widowed in 1942, Andrée kept on the house in Blacé and stayed there very frequently. She preserved the artistic heritage of her husband remarkably well and long after his death she continued to perpetuate her husband's oeuvre. Andrée Valette created an artist's stamp carrying her husband's signature, so as to authenticate the countless unsigned works that Adolphe Valette had left behind when he died. She continued to sell these works little by little during the 30 years following his death.

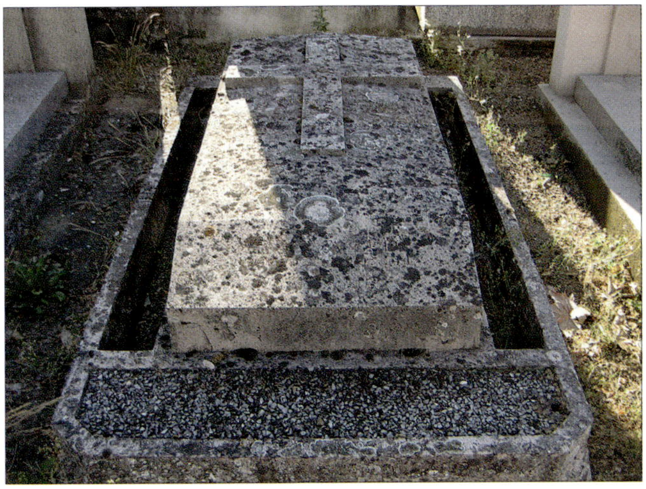

81 *The tomb of Adolphe Valette in the cemetery of Villefranche-sur-Saône*

In 1943, Andrée Valette organised a retrospective exhibition of her deceased husband's works in Villefranche-sur-Saône. In Spring 1945, three works by Valette were exhibited at the Exposition Rétrospective des Peintres Foréziens, organised by the Amis du Musée de Saint-Etienne: a 'Paysage avec Chèvres' ['landscape with goats'] depicting 'a woman draped in a pittoresque old red shawl, supporting herself on the smooth trunk of a silver birch, tending her goats in high mountain pasture, with the jagged outline of the summits in the background' ['une femme drapée dans un pittoresque châle vieux rouge, le corps appuyé sur le tronc lisse d'un bouleau qui garde ses chèvres dans un haut pâturage montagnard, avec en arrière-plan la ligne mouvementée des sommets'],[9] and also 'Rocher St-Michel au Puy' (fig 73 page 69) and 'Portrait de la Mère de l'Artiste,' shown here (fig 1 page 2).

In the mid-1960s, Andrée Valette moved to Beaumont on the island of Jersey, and sold the house in Blacé to a friend of hers, Mademoiselle Denavit. The latter, an admirer of Valette's work, received a number of works from Andrée and she agreed to keep in the attic of the house the works which Andrée could not take to Jersey. Valette's housekeeper, Maria Lafond, who had continued to work in the house for Andrée Valette when Andrée became a widow, also received a number of canvases from Andrée.

In early 1972, Andrée returned to Blacé, in order to choose a large number of canvases to show them at an exhibition of her husband's work in Jersey. This exhibition took place in June 1972 at the A. de Gruchy department store. Already at this point, Andrée was toying with the idea of an 'exhibition on the mainland by collectors who are discovering the unique talents of this artist.'[10] Her wish was made reality when in 1976 the Manchester City Art Gallery organised a major exhibition to commemorate the centenary of Valette's birth, but sadly Andrée was not fortunate enough to be able attend this exhibition as she died in 1973.

4 The Different Facets of Adolphe Valette's Artistic Talent

Sources and Influences: in the Wake of Impressionism

During the two critical decades that cover the early years and artistic training of the young Adolphe Valette, the impressionist movement was at its height. It was transformed from a movement initiated by a few young men rebelling against the prevailing academicism (the official salons initially 'refused' to exhibit their works – hence, their works were displayed in the 'Salon des Refusés'), to the blossoming of this new pictorial approach, despite criticism, and then on to its European flourishing and the unanimous recognition by the art galleries and the State and its vogue with art collectors. The term 'impressionnisme' was coined in 1874 by the critic Louis Leroy in a satirical journal, 'Le Charivari', referring to two canvases exhibited in Paris: that of the 'Champ labouré' by Pissarro and the famous marine scene by Monet 'Impression, soleil levant' [Impression, Sunrise].

Paris was the showcase city, the centre of national and international artistic life. Young painters flocked there from all corners of the earth. It was in the Parisian coteries and through the Salons and dealers such as Durand-Ruel that artists' careers were created, and that painters made a name for themselves. Impressionism was a bombshell for the artistic world; in the provinces, its reverberations were a little delayed and its impact dampened. The provinces always had the effect of tempering Parisian excesses such that Valette's own art followed somewhat this model of holding back and moderation in relation to the great masters of impressionism.

The first painted works of Valette took their inspiration more from pre-impressionism. His first pictures, which were often landscapes, already showed a great interest in nature. One can see in him influences of Daubigny (who also spent time in England) and Corot, and one can already see the impact in terms of composition and colour. The first surviving oils by Valette date from 1906 and 1907. These are still very traditional pictures, such as 'Landscape 1907' (not illustrated) which presents a road bordered by tall cypress trees; it contains a sharp contrast between two horizontals, the one of the sky in which the clouds have been worked in great detail, with perhaps an allusion to Constable's skies, and the horizontal of the sombre mass of the landscape portrayed with a thickening of dark colours in the middle of which four small figures only barely sketched out. These figures contribute to the instantaneity of the picture and are merely suggested by lines of colour, one for the head and the other for the body.

From the same period, there are other canvases with more marked affiliation with impressionism. Thus Valette offered this duality of a painter who, in certain canvases, was holding himself back and did not entirely allow himself his full freedom; but retained a classical and traditional aspect and perhaps never dared to give free rein to the enormous creative and innovative potential he carried within him and which would have placed him in the pantheon of painting, amongst the very greatest.

It was in Manchester that Valette discovered the subjects that he really enjoyed.

In some small paintings of houses made in his Mancunian neighbourhood in 1908 and 1909, Valette opened himself up to modernity. The colours were clear and alive, the brushstrokes relaxed, the movement intense, and the mobility of the individuals walking very well suggested.

The painting 'Plymouth Grove' (not illustrated) dated from 1909, at the time a well-to-do thoroughfare of Manchester where Valette lived when he first arrived there, probably in rented accommodation, has an extraordinary composition; the canvas is filled with a thousand suggestions of colours that bring it to life. The two friends walking accompanied by a little girl in front of the building, which, in contrast, has very clear contours, are remarkable. In the foreground, a mother is with her daughter, walking towards the garden, or towards a barrow pushed by a tradesman with a straw hat. This painting already demonstrates his ability to capture spontaneity of movement and light.

The first known canvas by Valette to have industrial Manchester as its subject is of the Manchester Ship Canal and is dated 18 March 1908 (fig 89 page 86). This is a very refined oil painting, containing all the themes that Valette was to draw upon during the splendid years of his great Mancunian period, up to 1913. In this we can see his desire to encapsulate all the transitory effects of light, the dimension of the sky, and water, and the absence of precisely defined profiles for the buildings. Everything has its mutual basis in each other element, everything is misted into the smog of Manchester pollution. Valette makes full use of the very real symbols of transport and commerce as a pretext for exploring atmospheric effects.

'Forain, Monet, Degas and the French Impressionists were his gods', as one of his students put it.[1]

One of the similarities between Valette and Degas is that of having a special relationship with the Anglo-Saxon environment. Degas spent time in the United States, and also visited London and encouraged Italian painters to visit. Degas contributed to all the impressionist exhibitions but was not really involved in their technical innovations. His preferred subject matter was the study of the human figure, race courses, ballet, café scenes (his canvas 'L'Absinthe' caused a scandal in London in 1893), and brothels. He was also fascinated by the new medium of photography, which he used initially for his studies of how horses gallop and subsequently as a purely creative tool.

Forain is known primarily as a caricaturist and was particularly famous for the satirical drawings that he produced for newspaper publications weekly for almost fifty years. He was close to Degas. Valette admired him perhaps for his talents as a caricaturist, the only artistic domain not explored by Valette. Like Valette, Forain also

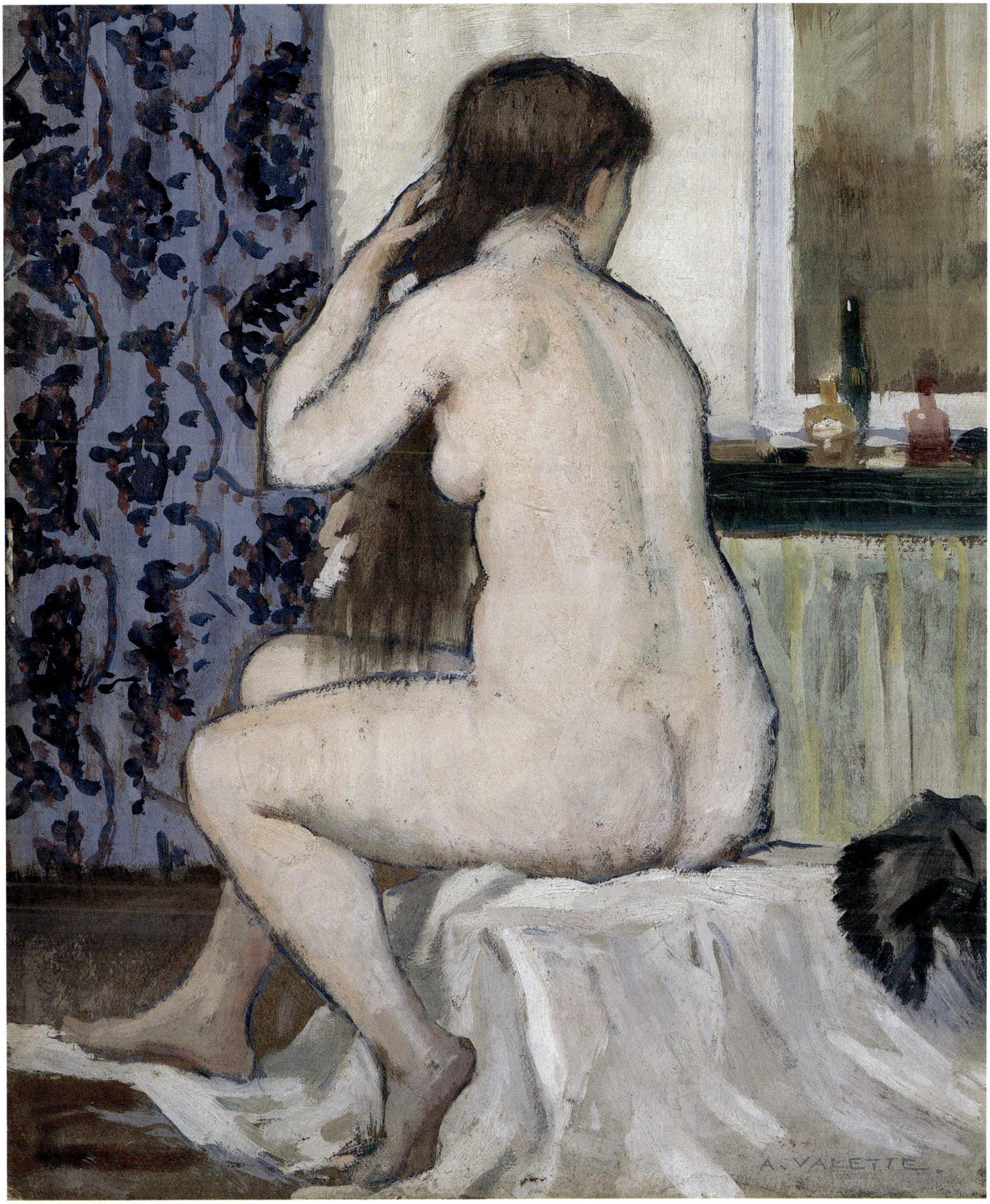

82 *Girl at her Toilet*
Oil on millboard, 40.1 x 32.3
Manchester Art Gallery

worked in engraving and lithography. His drawings are remarkable for their incisive lines and his caricatures for their trenchant style. Forain is less well-known for his landscapes, but did produce scenes in which Valette would have been able to recognise affinities.

In relation to Valette's admiration for Monet, this was very clear in the atmospheric canvases that Valette painted of Manchester, which are reminiscent of Monet's London canvases.

Impressionism is not a formal movement in the sense of a 'school', underpinned by artistic theory. The painters differentiated themselves in their own variations of technique, and each retained his own identity. There is, however, a recurrent element, which is the practice of painting in the open air, founded on the desire to capture an immediate visual impression in relation to a landscape and to render the exact effect of light for a given moment in time.

Another characteristic is the innovative approach to colour which draws its inspiration from the discoveries of Eugène Chevreul (1786-1889) in relation to colouring. Chevreul demonstrated 'that if two brush strokes of the same colour but with a different tone are juxtaposed, the side of the lighter brush stroke tends to appear lighter than the colour really is, as seen next to the darker brush stroke.' ['que si deux bandes de même couleur mais de tonalité différente sont placées côte à côte, le bord de la touche la plus claire apparaît plus clair encore que la bande ne l'est en réalité,

83 *L'Échaudage des Vignes*
Oil on millboard, 12.3 x 17.5
Private collection

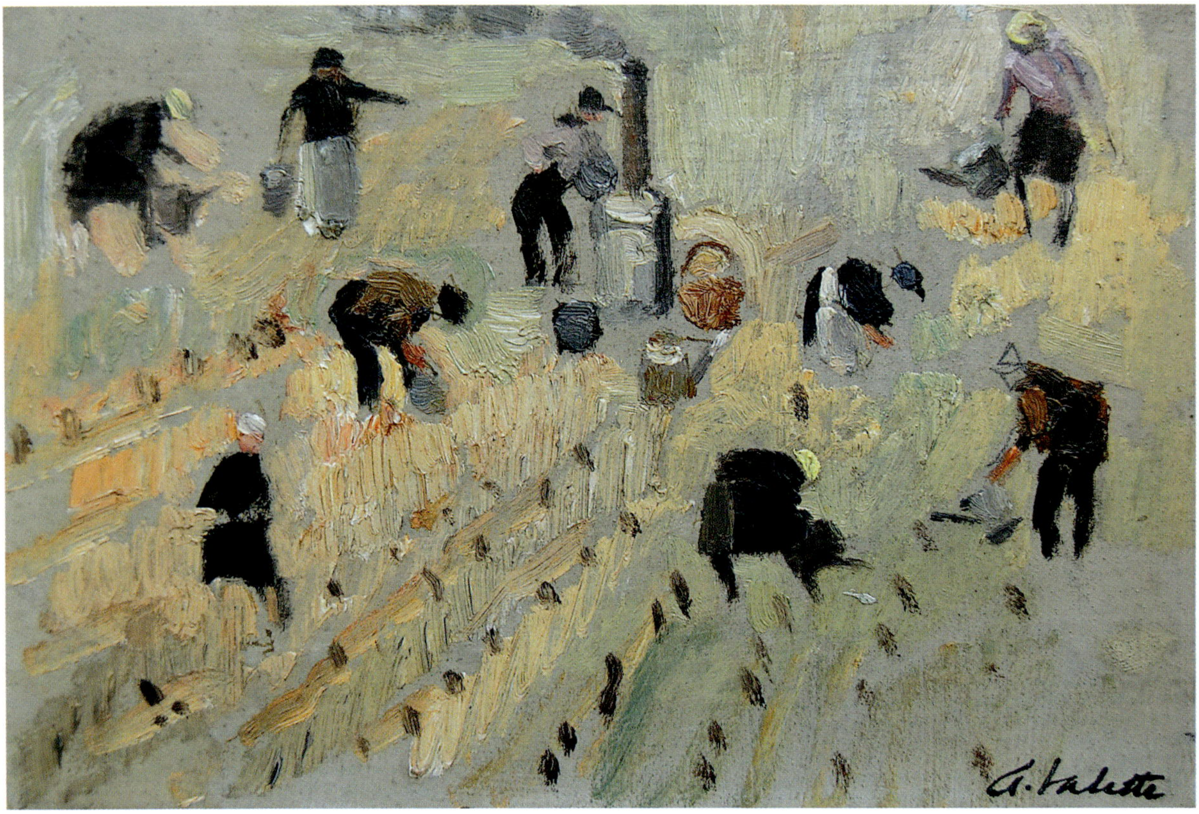

près de la bande foncée.'] He also demonstrated that 'all colours tend to tint its neighbour's colour with the tone of its own complementary colour' ['toute couleur tend à teinter sa voisine du ton de sa complémentaire'].[2] It is sufficient to see how Valette merged colours in some of his large atmospheric canvases of Manchester, for confirmation that he had thoroughly incorporated these concepts.

Valette was a master of open-air painting. It was his greatest happiness to be able to capture nature and light in situ, where his easel had been set up. A painting from 1906 'Open Air Art Class' (fig 37 page 40) shows four of his students painting out of doors, with a small canvas on their knees. The canvas itself is very impressionist in its technique, with its suggestions of poses and attitudes and in the way it juxtaposes and contrasts colours. This liking for open-air painting arrived with the impressionists. Instead of locking themselves away in their studios or closeting themselves in academies to create their pictures, artists went outside and observed the play of light on the surrounding natural contents in situ so that they could achieve an authenticity of atmosphere.

Valette also produced a number of pastels of Manchester such as 'Old Trafford Swing Bridge', and 'Rooftops' (not illustrated). This technique enabled him to capture the instantaneity of the subject. Pastel technique was also something Monet appreciated, for example in his 'Pont de Waterloo à Londres' (1900). He wrote to his wife Alice : 'It is thanks to my pastels, made swiftly, that I realised how to proceed' ['C'est grâce à mes pastels faits promptement qui me font voir comment il faut faire'].[3] Valette's pastels are none the less complete, finished works, with intense detail and movement, and once again show the attraction Valette had to Manchester.

Small Beaujolais and Manchester Views

Valette was known both in Manchester and in the Beaujolais region for his practice of walking around with small pieces of board or card in his hand, and his painting materials slung across his shoulder, and the way in which he used these simple materials to capture fleeting scenes from real life.

In the Beaujolais region, for the greater part, these small paintings consisted of stand-alone subjects: they were above all fragments of landscape or figures seen often in profile

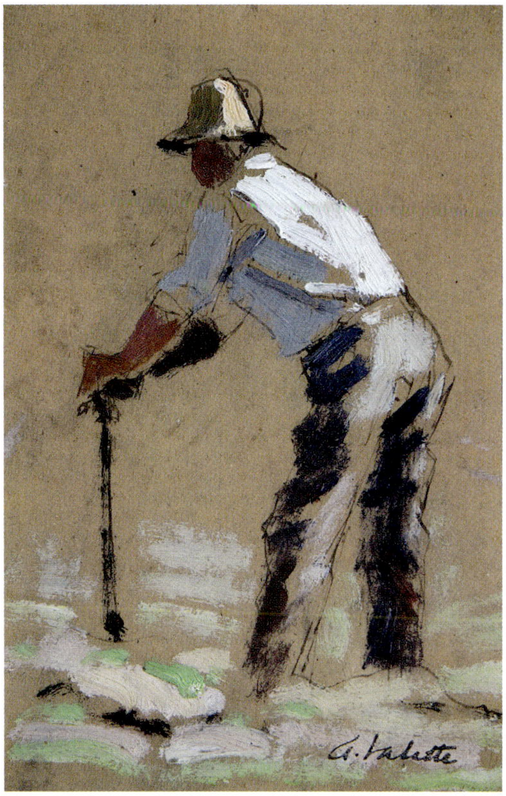

84 Field Worker
Pen and oil on millboard, 16.5 x 10.5
Private collection

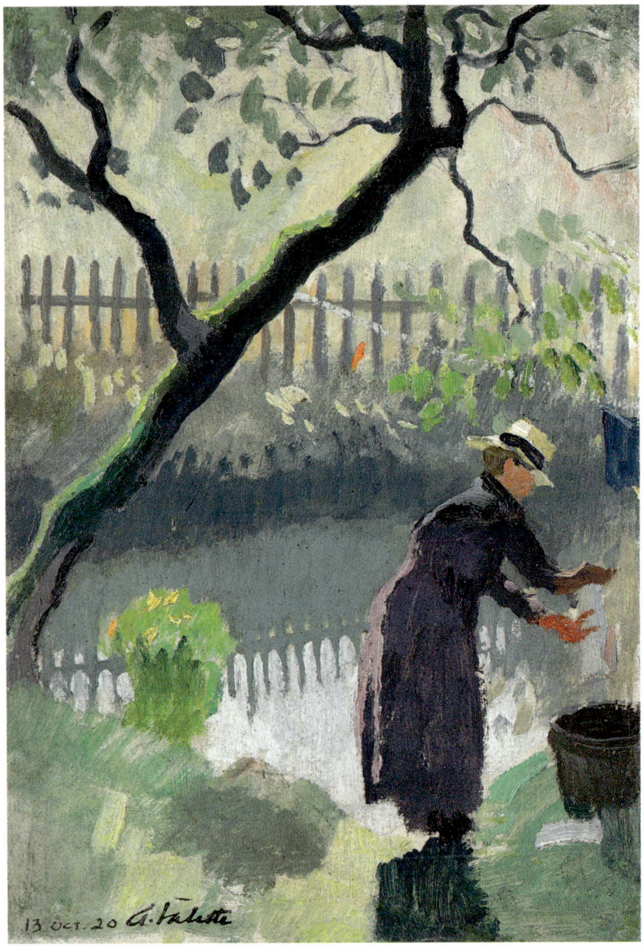

85 *La Laveuse, 13 Oct 1920*
Oil on millboard, 23.5 x 16
Private collection

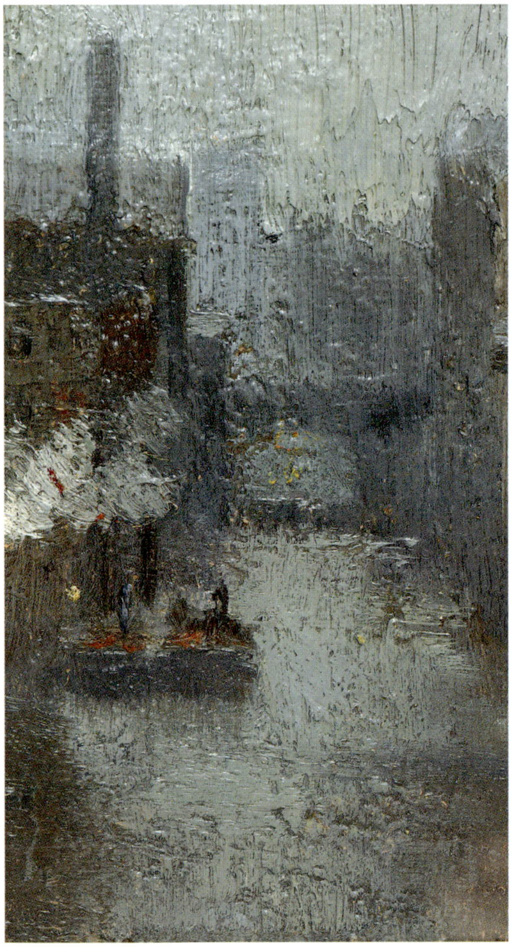

86 *Study for the Irwell*
Oil on board, 15.4 x 8.5
Private collection

or from behind and faceless: harvest workers, gleaners, haymakers, and grape pickers and often cows or goats, which Valette portrayed with considerable modernity. These works can be considered as a distinct category of his oeuvre in themselves, and convey a great freshness of approach.

In Manchester, these little scraps of paintings, often no larger than postcards, fulfilled a dual role. They either served as studies in situ for the composition of much more monumental canvases, which by definition he would have to complete in the studio, or they were small, complete subjects in their own right which he simply enjoyed creating.

In these small Manchester views, one can sense Valette's chosen sphere: the enchantment of light and its effects, the perception of incessant movement; in a word, a love of the transient.

It is in these small postcard format pictures that Valette communicates his energy, a few touches of colour here and there, and with a few brushstrokes his ability to convey an atmosphere. Some of his studies of the Manchester Ship Canal recall Monet's studies of the Thames and others of the 'Central Station' recall the stations painted by Monet. In some of his 'studies' Valette's technique seems more dynamic than in the completed painting it informs.

The 'Manchester-scapes',[4] the Pinnacle of Valette's Art

Atmosphere, … urban architecture and dynamism of the city, waterways and industry, variations of light, smog and haze …

The works described in this section are thorough, carefully thought-out works of art, in which Valette invested all his artistic energies. They are the living manifestos of his art. Major motifs are evinced from these works: buildings, streets, open spaces and squares as well as the waterways. Valette captures them all in their atmospheric variations, such that the stone architecture and urban evocation merge into the tones of the sky and water. All that breaks with the tradition and conventions of the period can be found here: new themes borrowed from contemporary life rather than from mythology and history, a predilection for light, the liberation of touch and a sense of the monumental.

'Manchester Ship Canal, 18 Mars 1908' (fig 89 page 86) and 'Manchester Ship Canal' (fig 90 page 87) bear witness to his debt to Monet and are unconsciously reminiscent of the series painted by Monet of the Thames in London, yet are less evanescent. Valette painted many pictures of the Manchester Ship Canal with his easel set up at the same vantage point. The same contours of buildings are profiled in the background of the paintings. However, the diversity of treatment stems from the variation in colour according to the time of day or the dawn or according to the thickness of the paint used on the canvas. On Valette's canvases of the Manchester Ship Canal illustrated here, two large cargo steamers can be seen, with flat-bottomed river barges and, behind the docks, a tower and grain elevator are shown in profile. The shadows of these elements reverberate on the canal water. Valette thus remodels the industrial, polluted reality of a landscape in order to derive from it an element of poetics. The painter bathes his subject in the

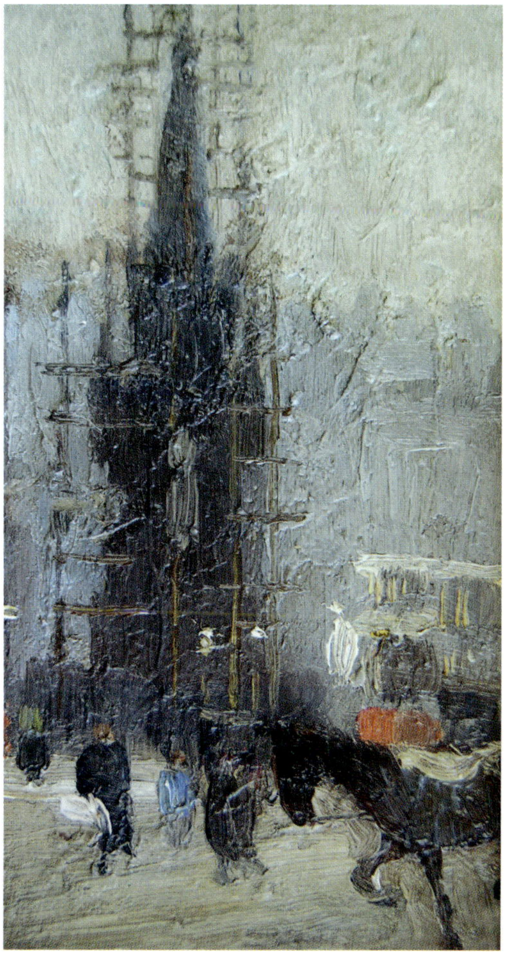

87 *Albert Memorial under Scaffoldings in Albert Square*
Oil on board, 14.8 x 8
Private collection

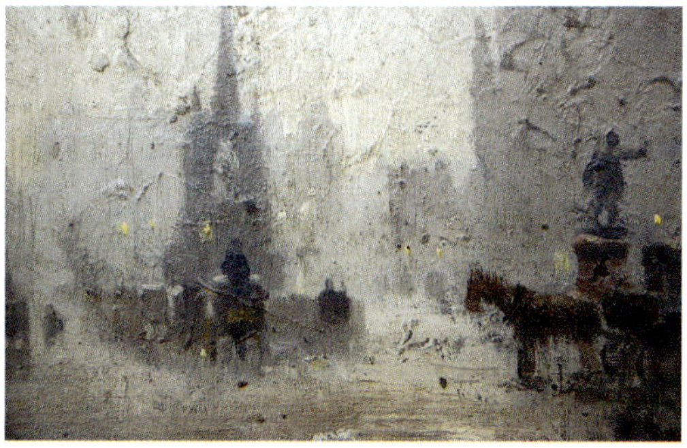

88 *Study for Albert Square*
Oil on board, 15 x 23
Private collection

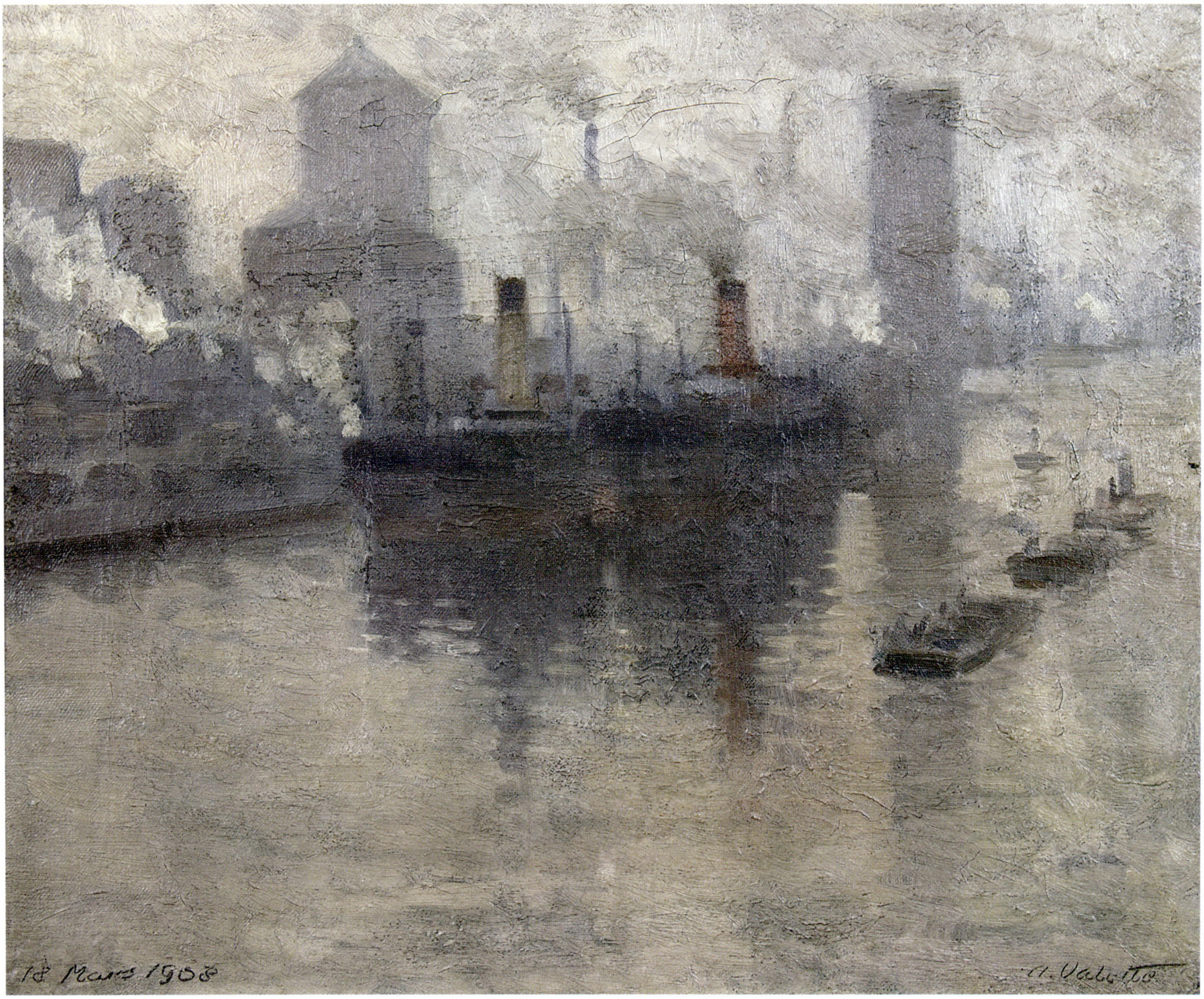

89 *Manchester Ship Canal, 18 Mars 1908*
Oil on canvas, 35.5 x 40
Private collection

blurred atmosphere of the Manchester Ship Canal. The transparency of the colours transfigures the tawdriness of this industrial location by conferring upon it a fascinating dimension. Yet, Valette allows the boats and the industrial buildings of the docks a more structural role than is seen in Monet.

References to Turner and Whistler have often been cited in Monet. One might equally say that Valette was consciously or unconsciously engaged in this exchange of influences, in this artistic dialogue between these three great painters. As we know, Valette explicitly recognised the influence Monet had upon his painting.

Returning to this rationale, one might say that Turner was often seen as a precursor of impressionism. His watery landscapes, his mists, the dissolution of forms, and his work with light have considerably influenced the art of his century and those that

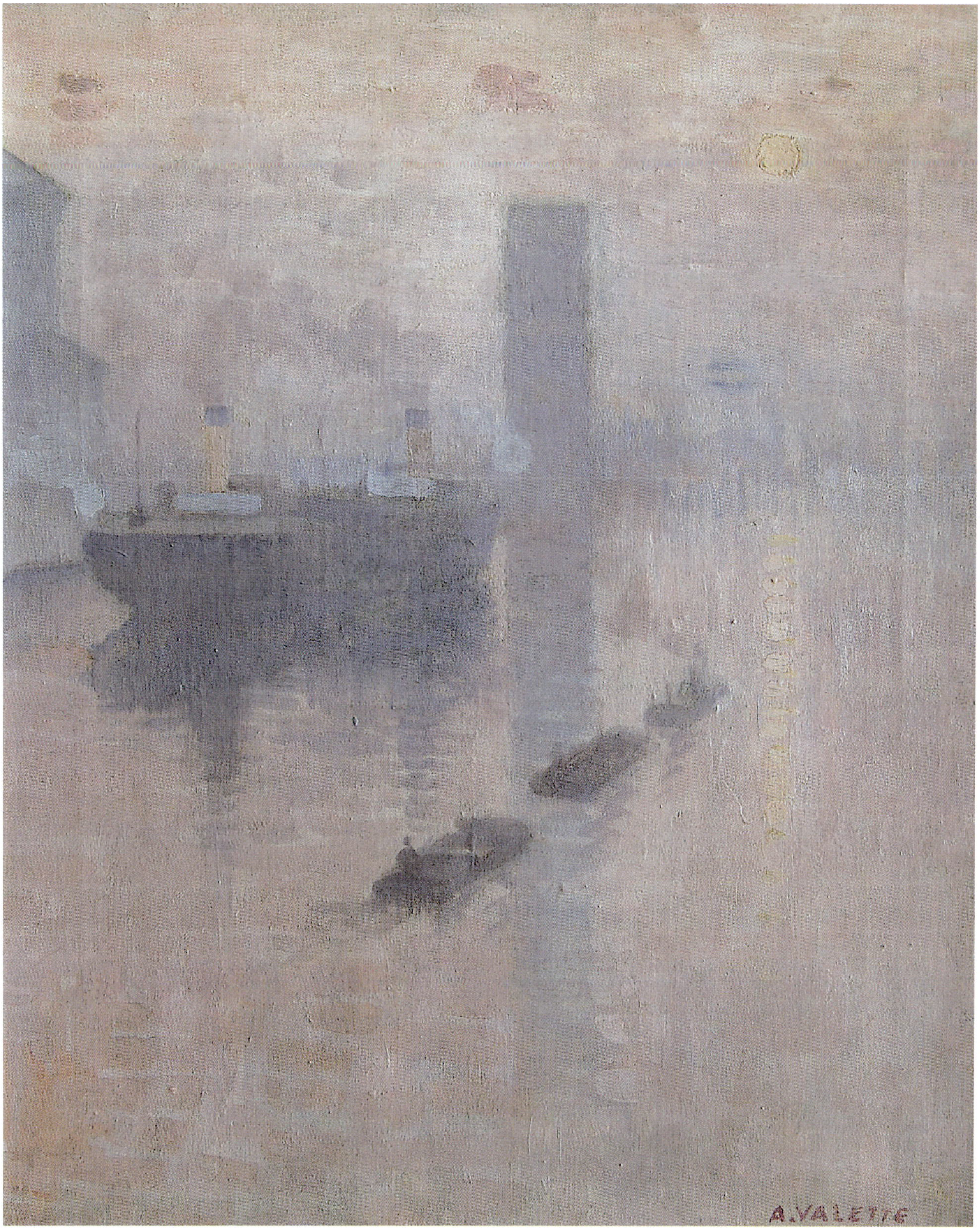

90 Manchester Ship Canal

Oil on canvas, 49.5 x 39.5

Martin Heaps collection

came after. Turner was a travelling painter, which at the time was considered to be an innovative concept. Valette followed in his predilection for travelling, albeit on a far more modest scale. Turner tackled a veritable inventory of European landscapes. He brought back watercolours from his numerous travels to Rome, Venice, the Alps and other regions of France. From the second half of the 19th century after his death and through the legacy of his works to the nation, very many painters were 'nourished' by his works that were exhibited in London. In 1906, the National Gallery loaned to the Manchester Municipal School of Art a collection of Turner's drawings for the School's Autumn exhibition; this was a major event in the art calendar.[5] Adolphe Valette, who was already at the School at this time, would undoubtedly have recognised the significance of the legacy of this great figure in English painting.

Although Valette never referred to it, in some of Whistler's 'Nocturnes' there are elements that must have inspired him, that is, if he ever had the opportunity to see them. All artists draw upon the repertoire of their predecessors and add their own creativity and individual experience. Whistler was an American painter, who was fascinated by European culture. He lived in London, was a Francophile and a friend of Mallarmé who translated into French his famous Ten O'Clock Lecture of 1885. Whistler was fascinated by the effect of mists and pollution: '... and when the evening mist clothes the riverside with poetry, as with a veil – and the poor buildings lose themselves in the dim sky – and the tall chimneys become campanile – and the warehouses are palaces in the night – and the whole city hangs in the heavens, and fairyland is before us – then the wayfarer hastens home – the working man and the cultured one – the wise man and the one of pleasure – cease to understand, as they have ceased to see – and Nature, who for once, has sung in tune, sings her exquisite song to the artist alone, ...'.[6]

'Manchester Ship Canal' (fig 90 page 87) is reminiscent at the same time of Whistler's application of colour in his Nocturnes and also of the manner of the Impressionists. It is a cause for regret that Valette did not produce etchings or lithographic work of Manchester's industrial scenes as Whistler had done for London.

In 'Windsor Bridge on the Irwell', 1909 (fig 15 page 24) one can appreciate the painter's interest in bridges, waterways, boats and barges. The atmospheric variations that impregnate this industrial landscape confer upon it an almost phantasmagorical aspect. The use of the colour mauve which pervades the painting suggests a coldness, or even a sense of mystery which is made even more flagrant by the cloud of strong yellow luminosity projected below the bridge and on the surface of the water. Two minuscule touches of yellow suggest a light in a building in the background and a touch of orange and blue illuminate the barge in a flash. The canal water is punctuated in the foreground with a slight choppiness which somewhat animates the stillness of the canvas; the water is dirty, polluted with industrial waste, but Valette still lights it with minuscule patches of colour which suggest that he none the less saw in it a certain beauty.

A few years later, in 1912, in 'Under Windsor Bridge on the Irwell' (fig 16 page 25) Valette was to position his easel in the same place and reproduce this same atmosphere of effluents coupled with industrial buildings and kept to the same rather

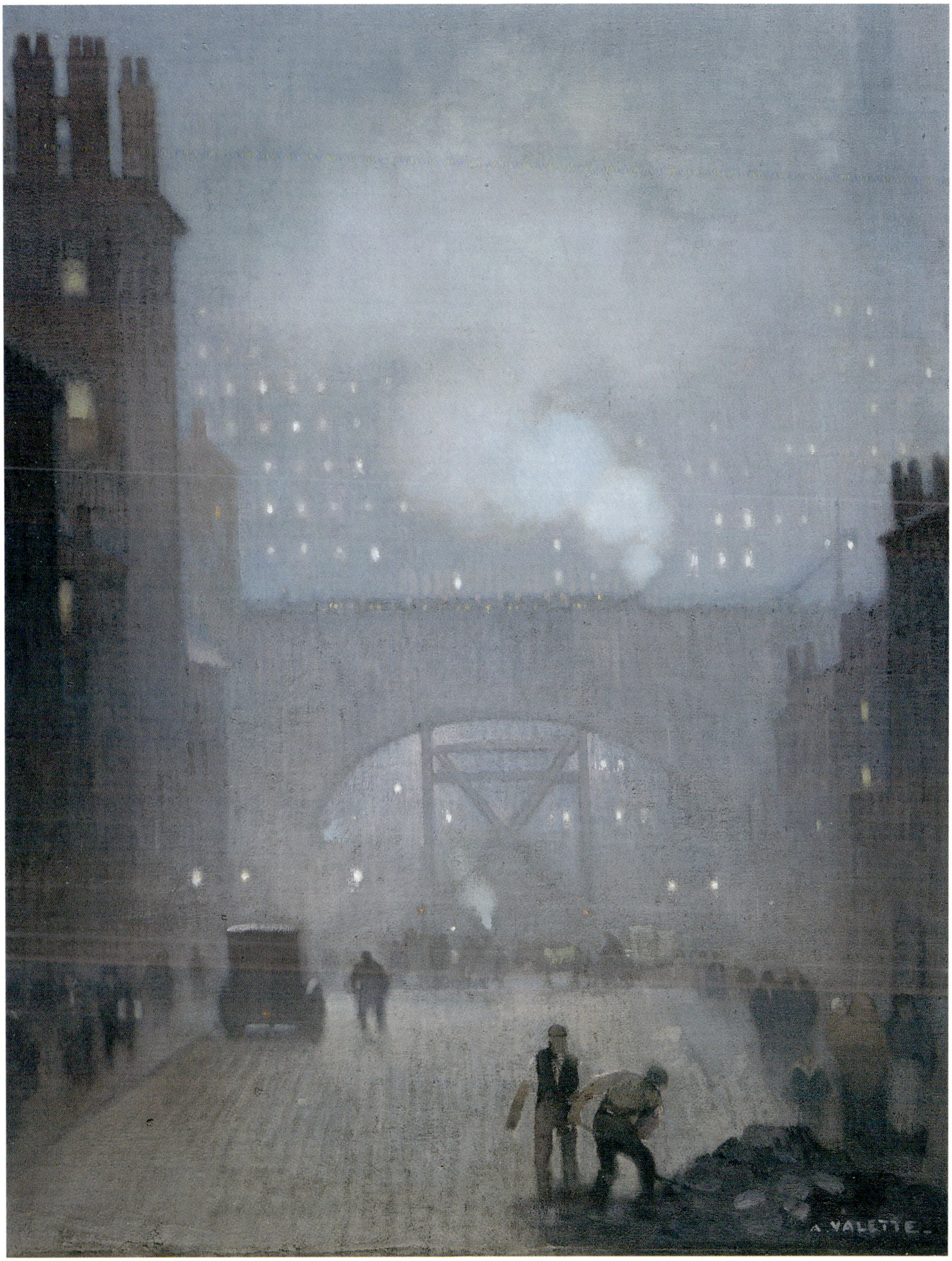

91 *York Street leading to Charles Street, Manchester, 1913*

Oil on linen, 81.3 x 60

Manchester Art Gallery

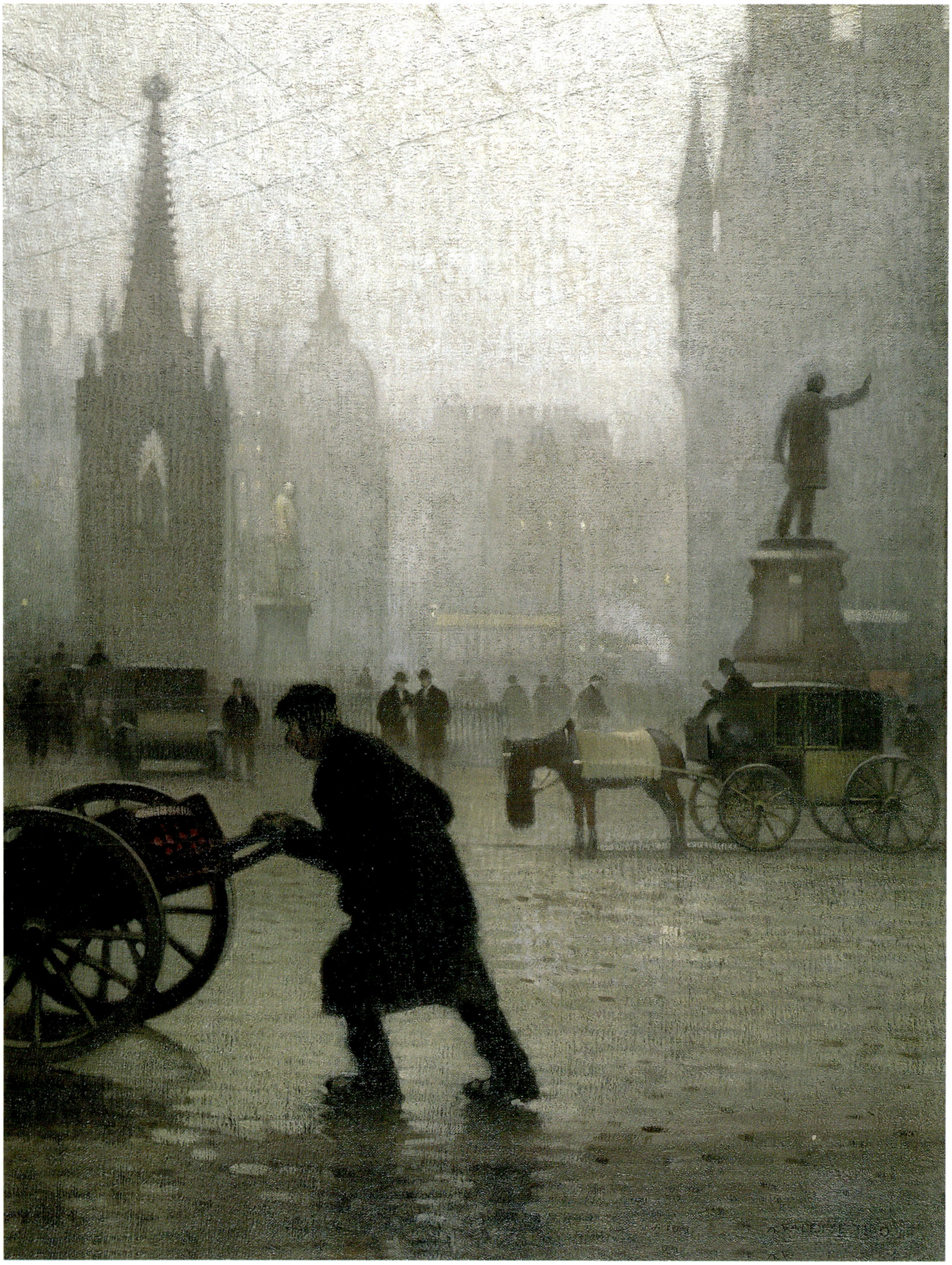

92 *Albert Square, Manchester, 1910*

Oil on jute, 152 x 114

Manchester Art Gallery

dark tones. He also introduced two people into it, on the left a bargee with bent back working on a barge. The other figure in the foreground to the right of the canvas is depicted from behind, merely using rounded lines: he has a round hat, and his shoulders and arms give him a modern, almost extra-terrestrial appearance which suggests the characters that L.S. Lowry, the most famous of Valette's successors, would later include in his paintings. Six small bright points punctuate and light up the painting.

'Bailey Bridge' (1912) (fig 19 page 27), 'India House' (1912) (fig 12 page 21) and 'The Irwell' (1913) (not illustrated) bring us closer to the interior of the city. We are no longer at the docks, but where the canals segment the inner city. We are at the heart of Manchester, within this stark, industrial environment. Valette shows us bridges, cranes, trains, barges, etc ... The compositions of these three paintings are largely the same. The vertical lines of building or warehouses, on both sides of the canvas, are often linked together by bridge arches. The buildings are sometimes rich and solid, but sometimes reinforced by stanchions to keep them from falling down. The train passes through the town centre, like an expression of the imperative of industrial development. In 'The Irwell', the old cathedral dating from the 15th century contributes to this chaotic arrangement of things, relinquishing its solemn and religious character. In these three paintings, Valette handles light with great care and to maximum effect. He creates an aspect of unreality and timeless beauty despite the onslaught of industry. Amidst the degradation of the environment, he is able to suggest the 'ghostly magnificence' of Manchester.[7] The trains are barely discernible, as is their smoke, and that of the chimneys that disperses and mixes with the general smog. Valette renders his pictures iridescent with just a few sparks of light, such as the windows of the building in the background of 'India House' or reflections in the water in 'Bailey Bridge' and 'The Irwell'.

With 'York Street leading to Charles Street' (1913) (fig 91 page 89), 'Albert Square' (1910) (fig 92 page 90), 'Oxford Road' (1910) (fig 10 page 18), we leave the languor conferred by the presence of the water element in Valette's paintings. Valette now takes us to the urban context, to important landmarks of Manchester's business world. In 'York Street leading to Charles Street' (1913), in the background of the painting we have the same façade of the building that features in 'India House', but seen from a different angle. Here the scene is more animated. We are in a very busy street, a crowd of people are about their business, road menders are at work in the foreground – executed in a very modern technique – repairing the road. Here once more Valette uses the theme of the bridge to link the two sides of the composition and the focal point of the steam from the train vanishes in a smog of pollution that covers the city.

In 'Albert Square' (1910) (fig 92 page 90), a huge square adjoining the buildings of Manchester town hall, we have the duality between the working-class world and the business world. In the foreground, we see a bent-over figure, from the world of manual work, pushing a hand cart filled with bottles of wine. This silhouette is again reminiscent of the characters that L.S. Lowry later loved to sketch. This is both the world of manual work and the business world, as the individuals conversing in the

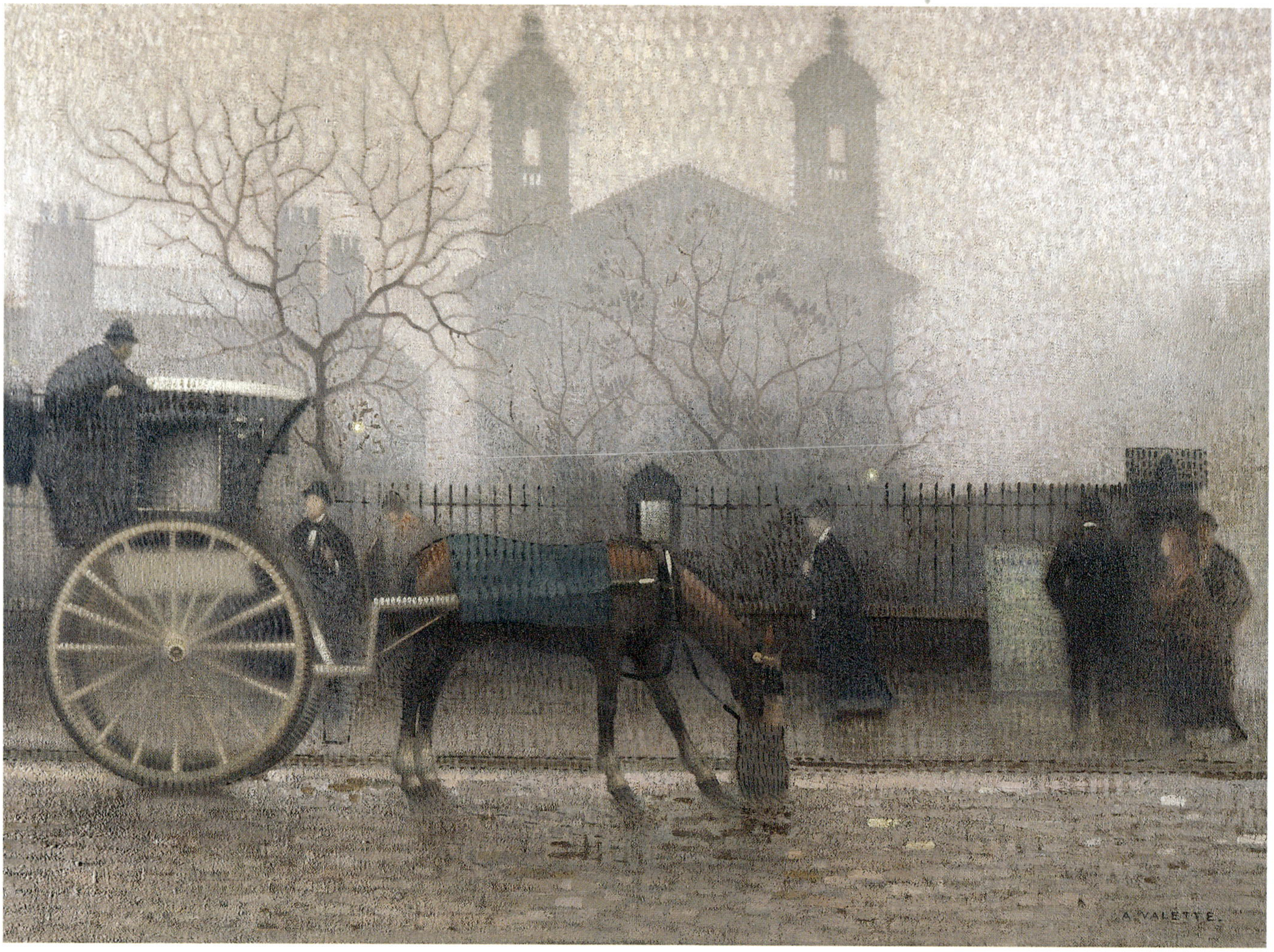

93 *Hansom Cab at All Saints, 1910*
Oil on jute, 115.5 x 155.3
Manchester Art Gallery

square testify. The damp cobbles provide a gilded reflection of the polluted sky. A car with its chauffeur, an emblem of the well-to-do, awaits the owner. The electric cables, symbols of modernity, mark out the opaque sky.

In 'Oxford Road' of 1910 (fig 10 page 18), Valette shows us Manchester's economic dynamism. We are on one of the city's main thoroughfares, there are business people, many horse-drawn hackney cabs, but above all, the car, telegraph wires and tram rails express the town's modernity. The Refuge Assurance Company building under construction, with cranes hanging over it, adds a dramatisation and power to the scene. This amplifies the contrast with the less elevated 19th-century houses, witnesses of a former age, as is the iron of the gas lamps. The misted together mauve and ochre tones render the city light opaque at a time of day when everyone goes, bowler-hatted, about

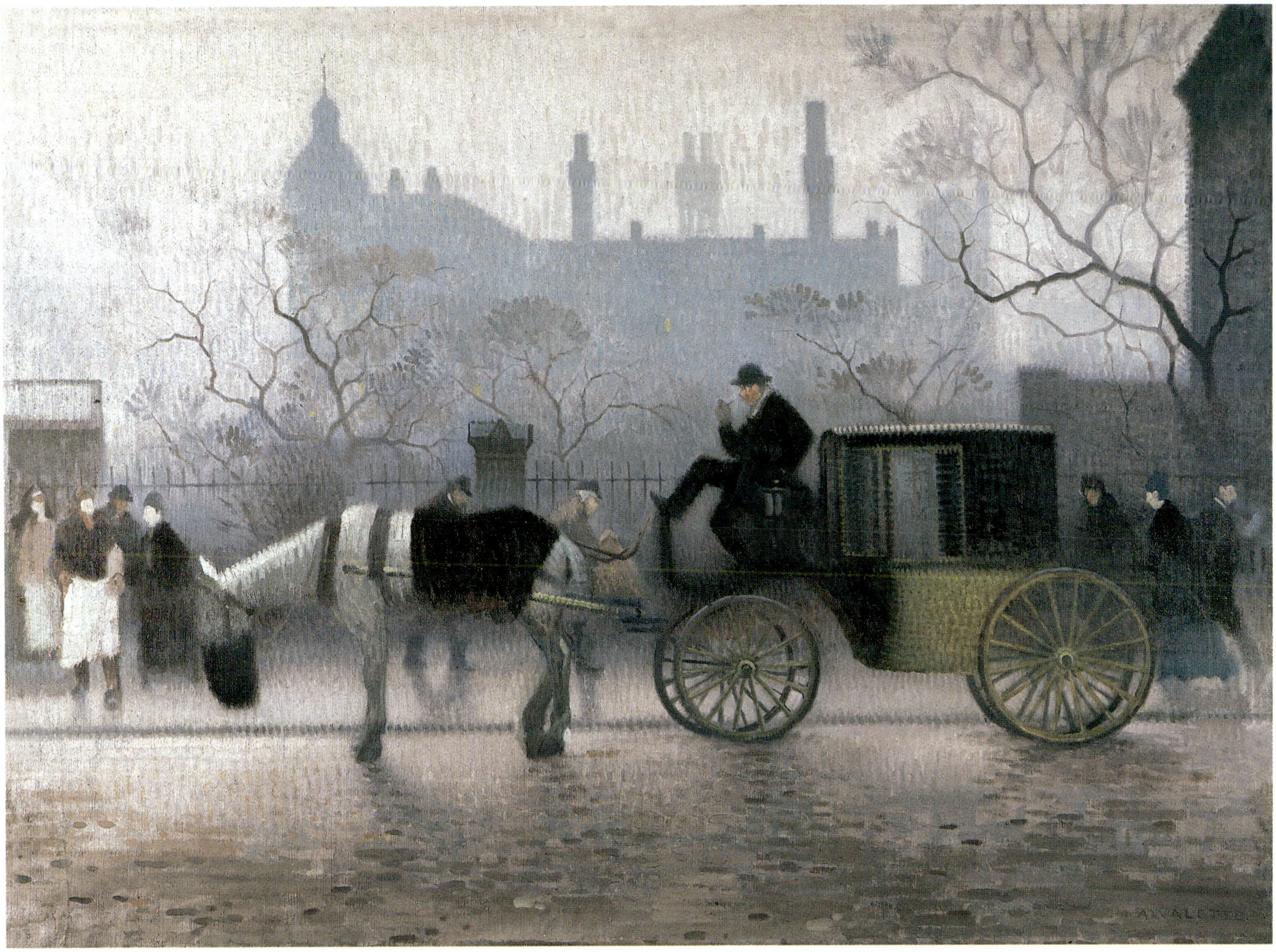

94 Old Cab at All Saints, 1911
Oil on jute, 115.5 x 155.3
Manchester Art Gallery

their business. Valette also conveys to us the street noises of this city under construction: one has the impression of being able to hear the footsteps of this busy multitude, and the crunch of the wheels on the cobbles, the horses neighing, the roar of car engines, the more distant noise of the cranes. For this canvas, Valette, in the guise of a signature, has created his own very finely elaborated monogram of his intertwined initials.

A set of two canvases of the same size representing urban Manchester, 'Hansom Cab at All Saints' (1910) (fig 93 page 92) and 'Old Cab at All Saints' (1911) (fig 94 page 93), demonstrates a slightly different artistic tack moving in the direction of pointillism. The application of the paint is different from that of his other works: it is done with a real juxtaposition of the application of small patches, in an 'optical mix'. The brush strokes are independent, and arranged on the canvas like a small

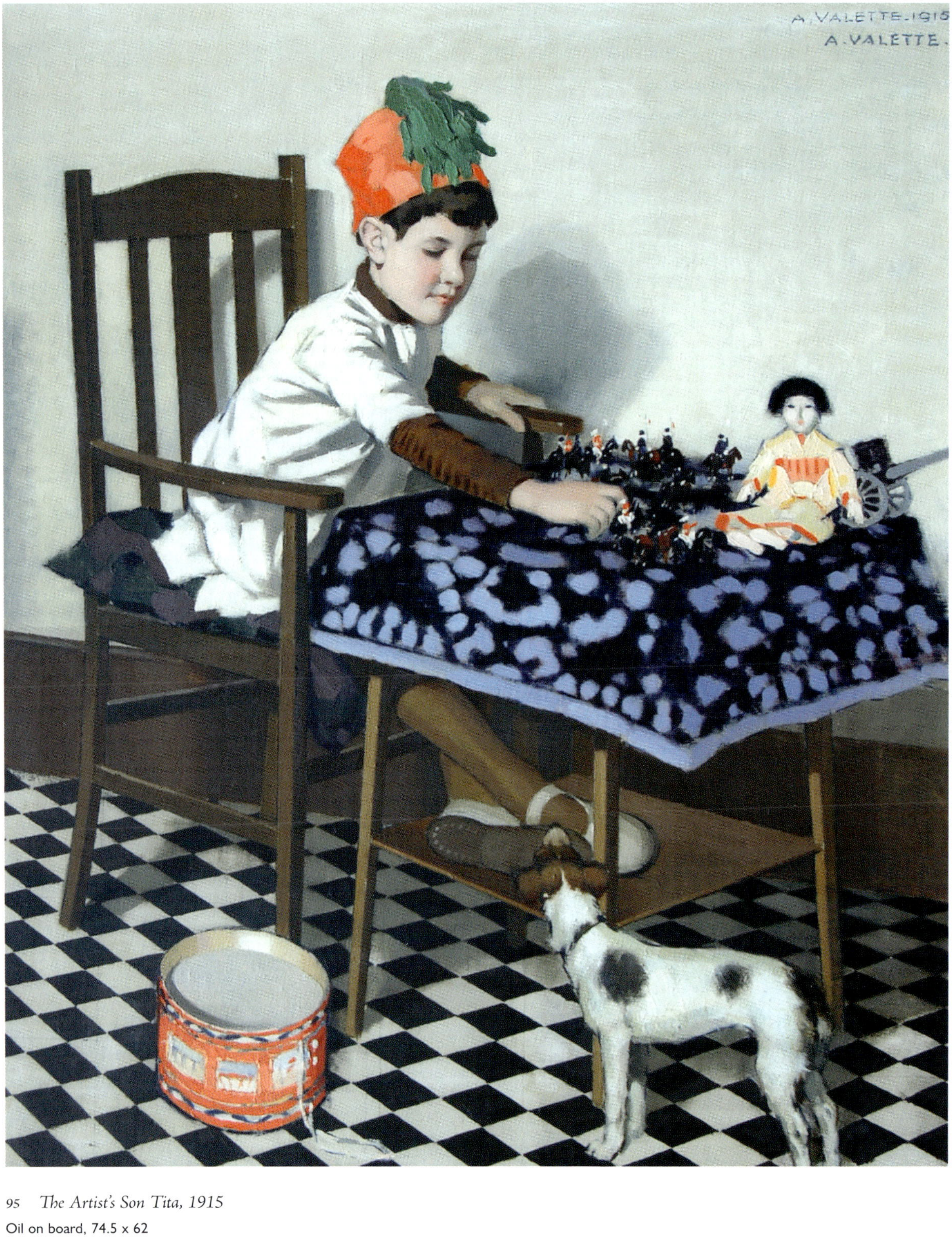

95 *The Artist's Son Tita, 1915*

Oil on board, 74.5 x 62

Private collection

comma of material, coloured in a different shade from those nearby. The sky is made up of three colours: pink, mauve and blue, which are undetectable from a distance, as it gives an impression of uniformity: the retina of the eye reconstitutes the mix that has not been created on the palette. The intensity and chromatic effect are all the more vibrant for it. The same technique is applied to the taxi, the people, the horse, and the 'Registry Office'. The trees, without leaf, give a Japanese impression. In 'Old Cab at All Saints', we find the same technique, but a little less pronounced. These two works are clearly created with a view to their being associated. They are framed by the same design of frame with gilt motif of intertwined leaves that was probably made by Valette's favourite frame-maker, Robert Carruthers, whose portrait he also painted (fig 54 page 55).

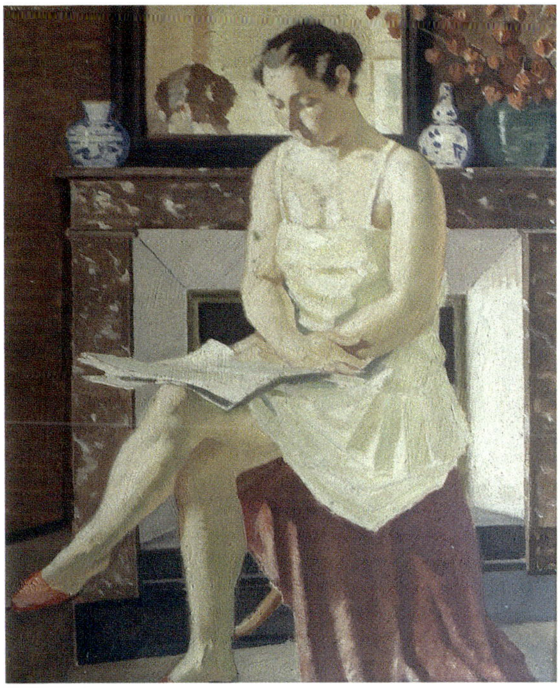

96 *Maria lisant devant la Cheminée*
Oil on board, 61 x 50
Private collection

These works constitute the pinnacle of Valette's art and capabilities. After this magnificent period, which can be said to have lasted until 1913, it must be admitted that the spark that illuminated his work began to fade a little. He no longer pursued the discoveries he had made, he made rather too little call upon his natural talents and allowed himself to subside to some extent into easier options. It would be difficult to imagine him as a cubist or surrealist. Both he and his oeuvre did take a conventional turn, while other revolutionary artistic endeavours followed upon each other at a dizzying pace. Subsequently, after the death of his wife Gabriela in 1917, his inspiration left him and he probably no longer felt equal to drawing out all the modernism he carried within him. He contented himself with returning to a degree of conventionality. On his return to Blacé in France in 1928, he confined himself to a much more traditional style of painting, to which his poor health contributed, at a distance from the new trends. But these were no longer his preoccupation; nature and his circle of friends were sufficient for his happiness. He felt himself to be physically diminished, and simply wished to paint 'to his heart's content'.[8]

Portraits

Adolphe Valette created a large number of portraits. There were many portraits of friends, pupils, and individuals who gravitated to his artistic circle and from the

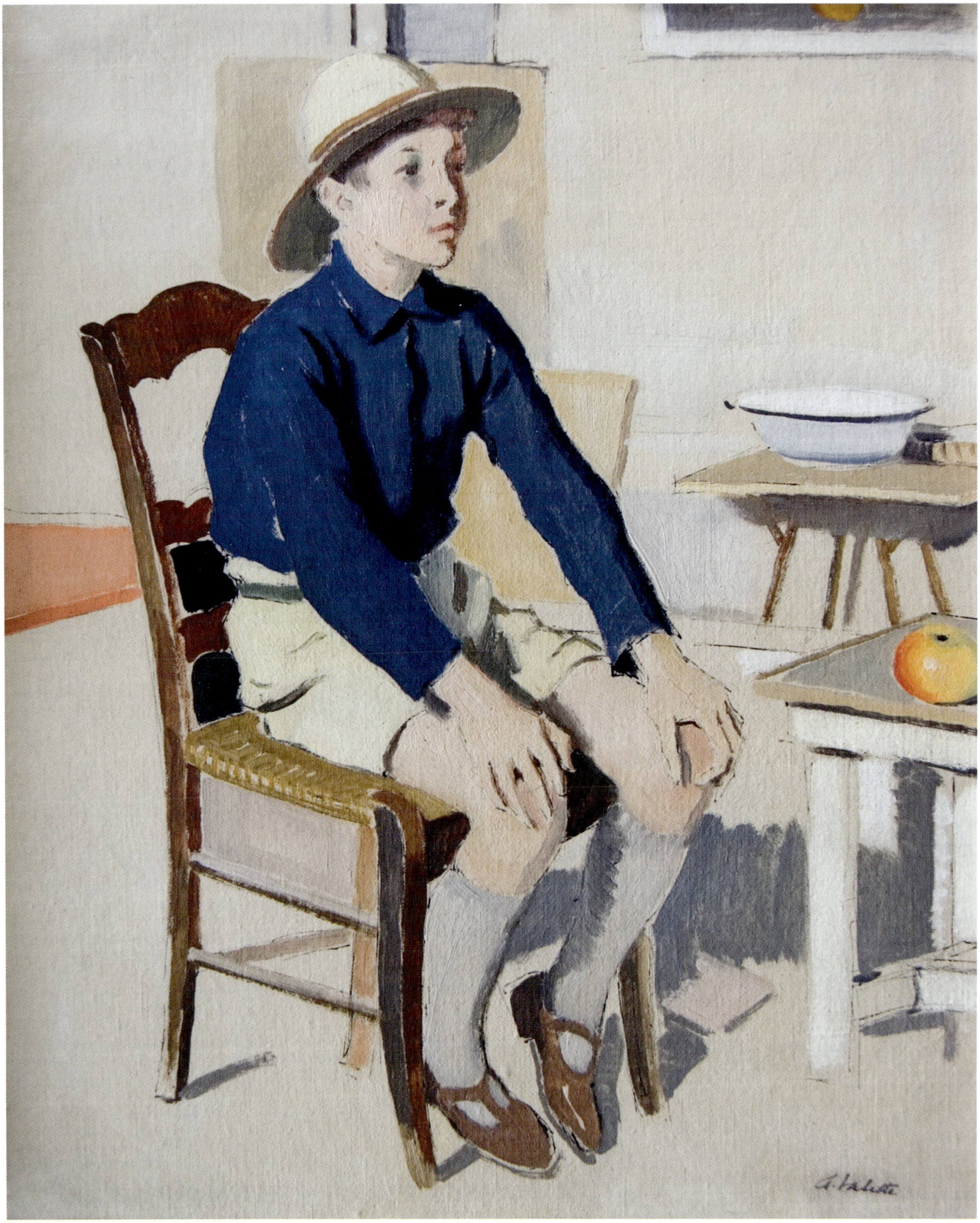

97 *Tita on a Chair*

Oil and ink on canvas, 40.6 x 33.1

Private collection

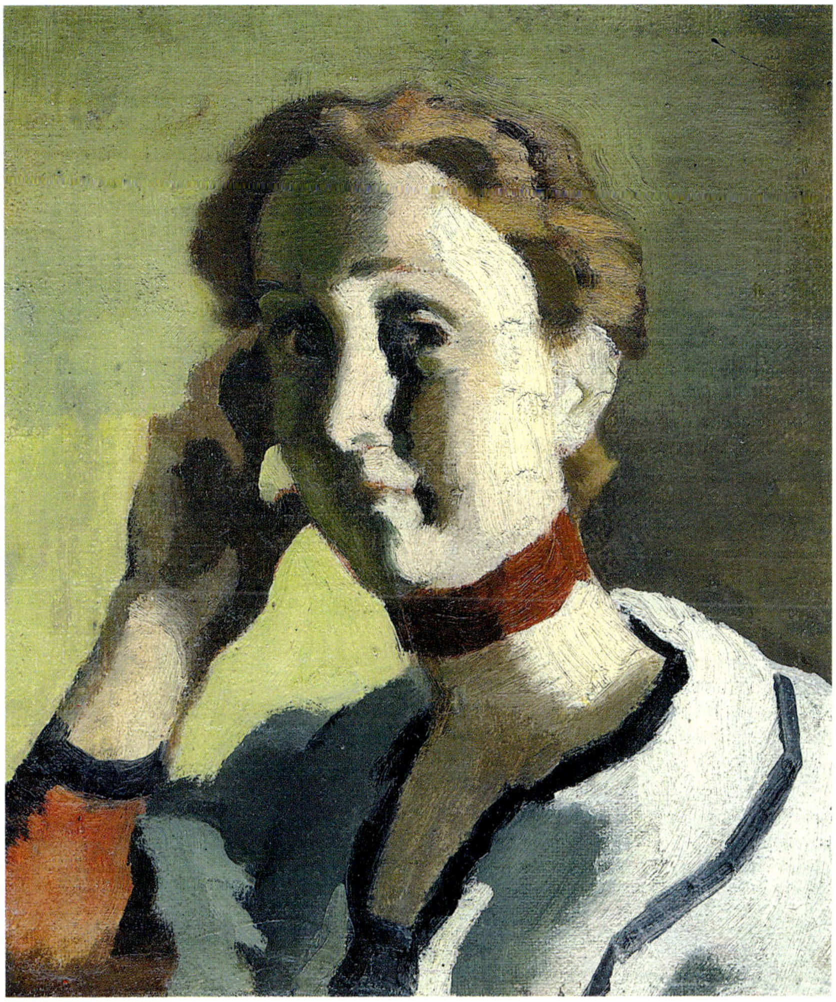

98 *Maria au Collier de Chien*
Oil on canvas on board, 20 x 16.5
Private collection

Manchester Municipal School of Art, such as Bert Wilson, Annie Barnett (fig 121 page 124) (who was a fervent admirer of his work and gave pictures to the Manchester City Art Gallery), Joseph Milner (fig 29 page 35) and Edgar Rowley Smart (fig 25 page 32), one of his favourite pupils, who was a francophile, and who went to paint in Paris. The portrait of Smart received wide critical acclaim: 'His portrait of Mr Smart is a brilliant piece of portraiture wonderfully conceived and executed with an understanding of the qualities of oil-paint seldom seen in this city'[9] and '… to see Mr E. Rowley Smart … passing in front of his own portrait by Monsieur Adolphe Valette is a striking experience, and the likeness is exceedingly faithful.'[10]

His family circle was also a great source of inspiration for Valette's portraits. There are many portraits of his mother, whose strength of character he portrayed very well. We have several magnificently cheerful portraits of his son, who died prematurely, which are of an extraordinary freshness and exemplary degree of refinement that reflect Valette's best period.

99 *Maria à la Robe Rouge*
Oil on canvas on board, 71 x 58
Private collection

100 *Madame Valette reading, 1910*
Oil on canvas, 104 x 130
Private collection

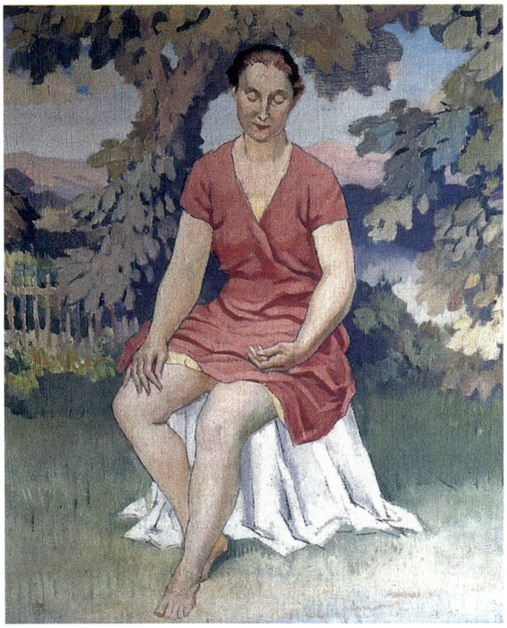

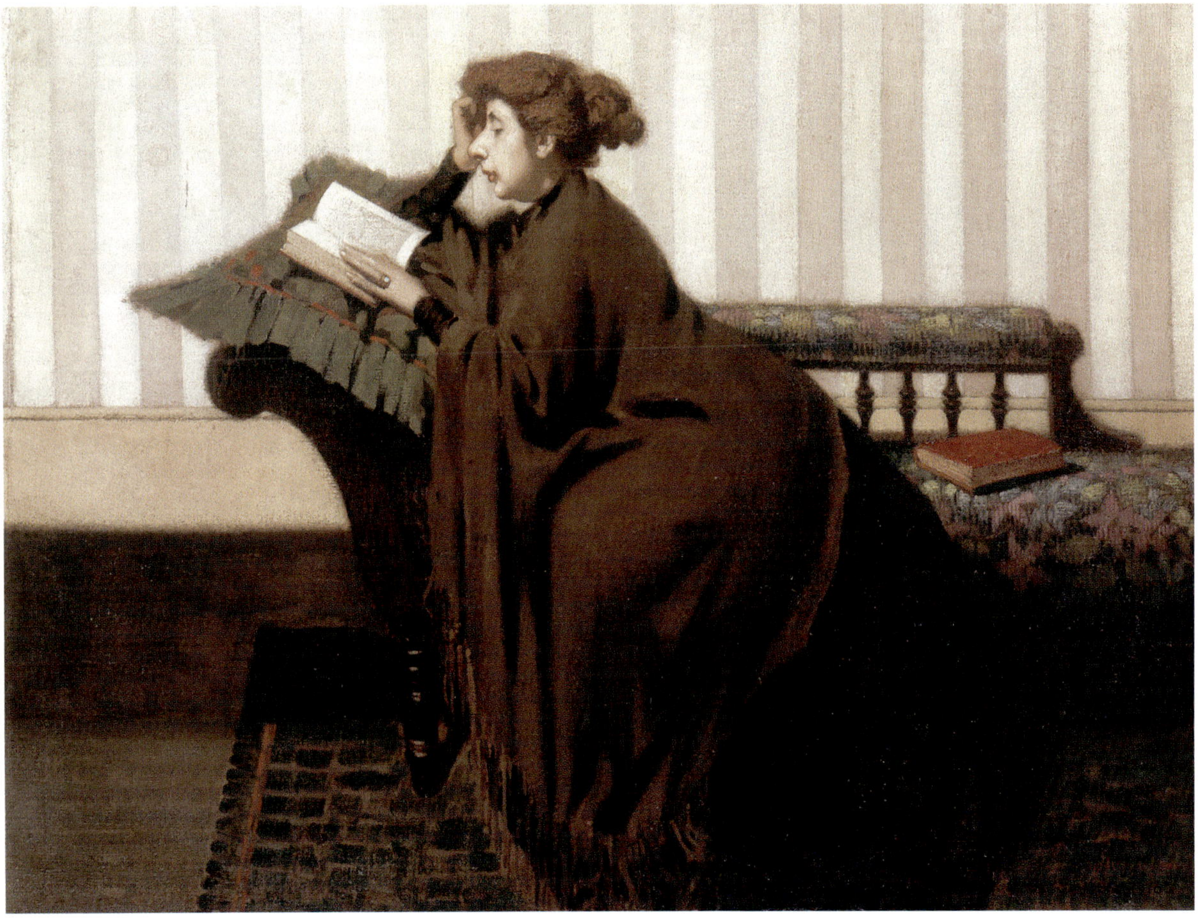

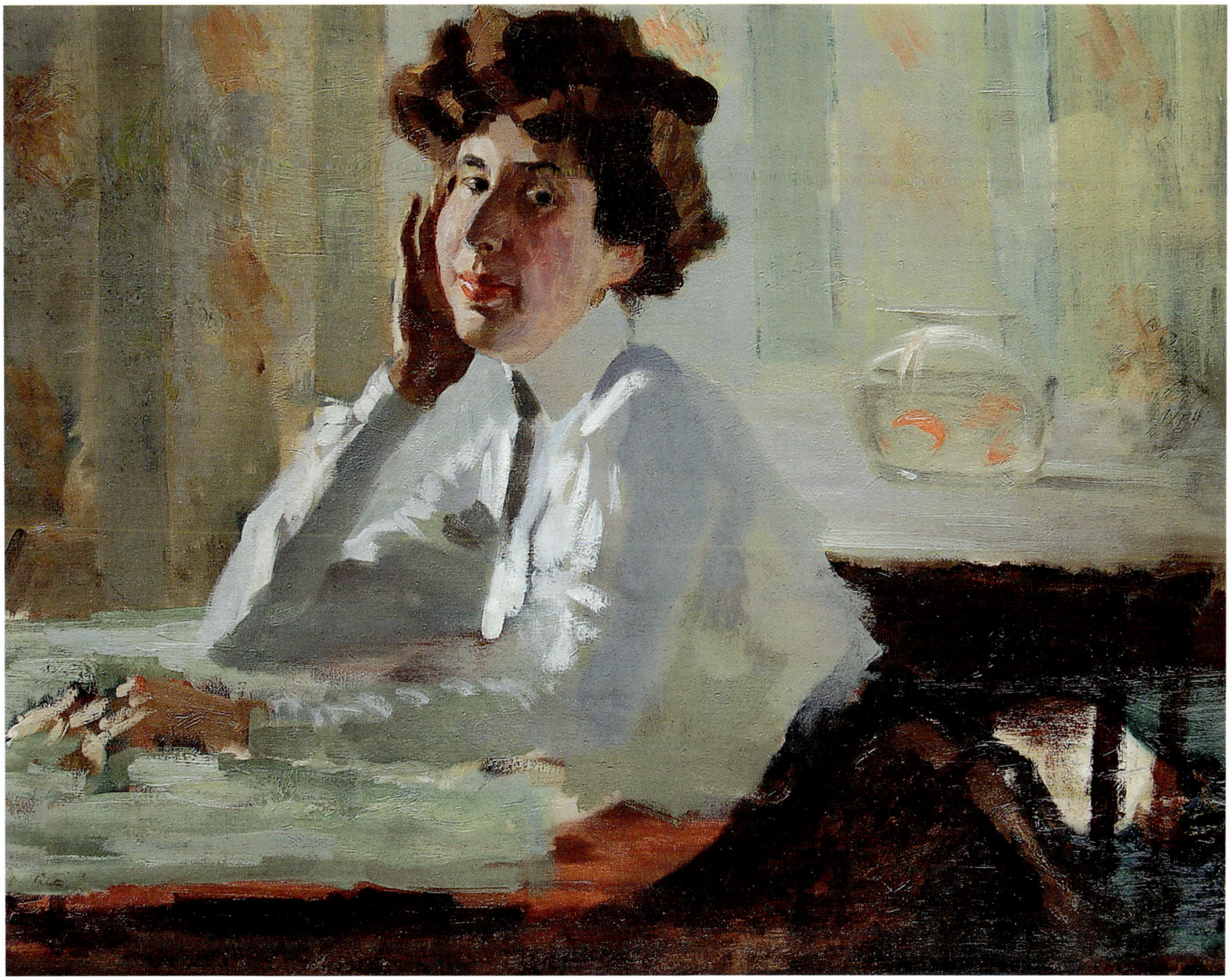

101 Gabriela and Fishbowl
Oil on canvas, 65.5 x 81.5
Martin Heaps collection

Valette's two inspiring muses were undoubtedly his first wife Gabriela and later, to a different extent, his housekeeper in Blaceret, Maria Lafond.

There are numerous portraits of Gabriela, sometimes in very fresh colours, that light up the canvas showing her long neck and fine hair. At other times the colouring is darker and conveys a more well-to-do and bourgeois aspect of the creation. Some of these pictures are in small format, executed simply for the pleasure of sketching his wife; others are very sophisticated works, very complete and very grand. There are some large canvases of Gabriela, in which we see an intimist dimension in the manner of Vuillard, which are reminiscent of the Nabis whose stream of consciousness had a certain influence on Adolphe Valette. In these large paintings of Gabriela, he transfigured his love for his wife by creating truly accomplished pictures in which

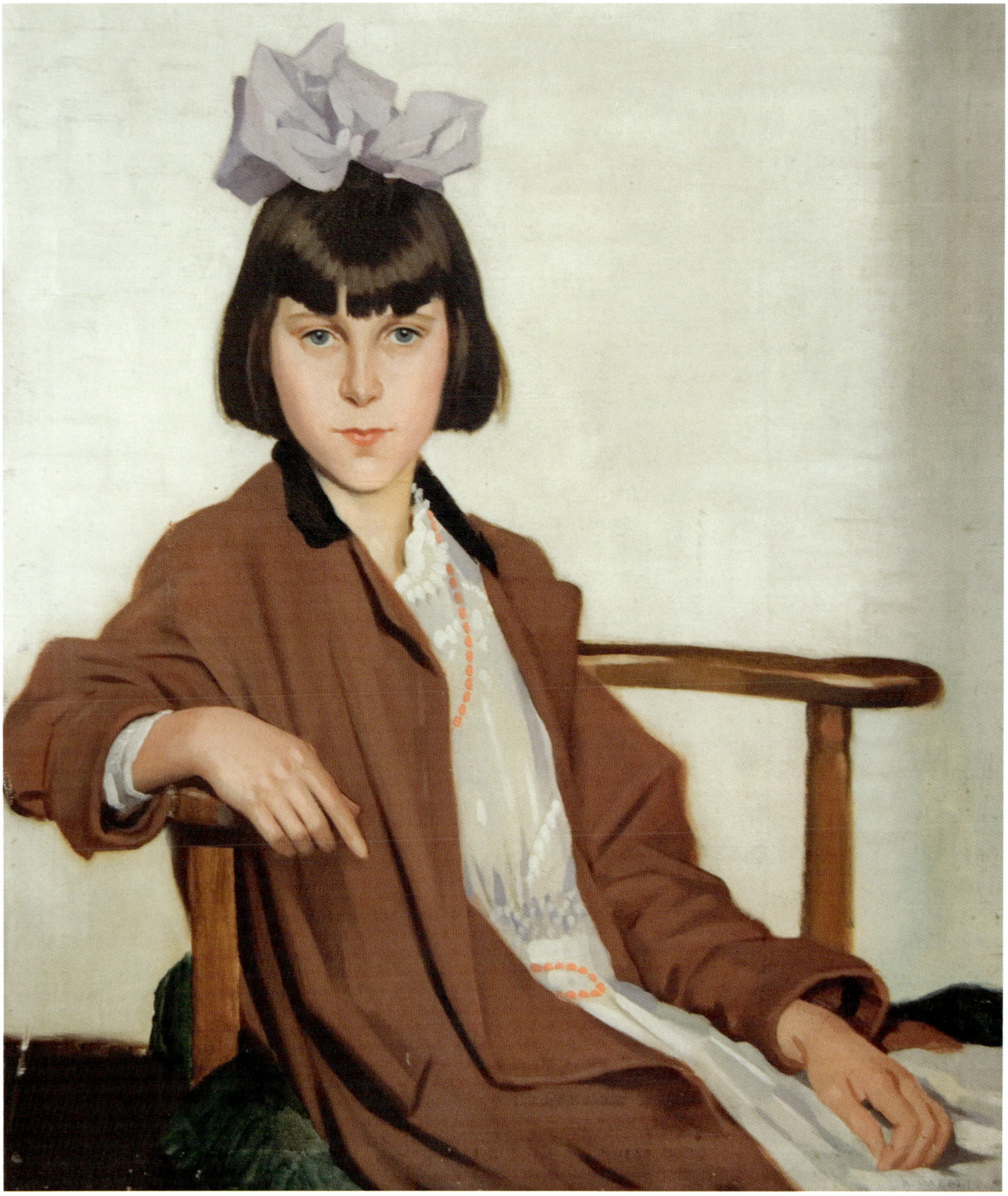

102 Portrait of a sitting Girl with Bow in her Hair
Oil on canvas, 74.5 x 60
Private collection

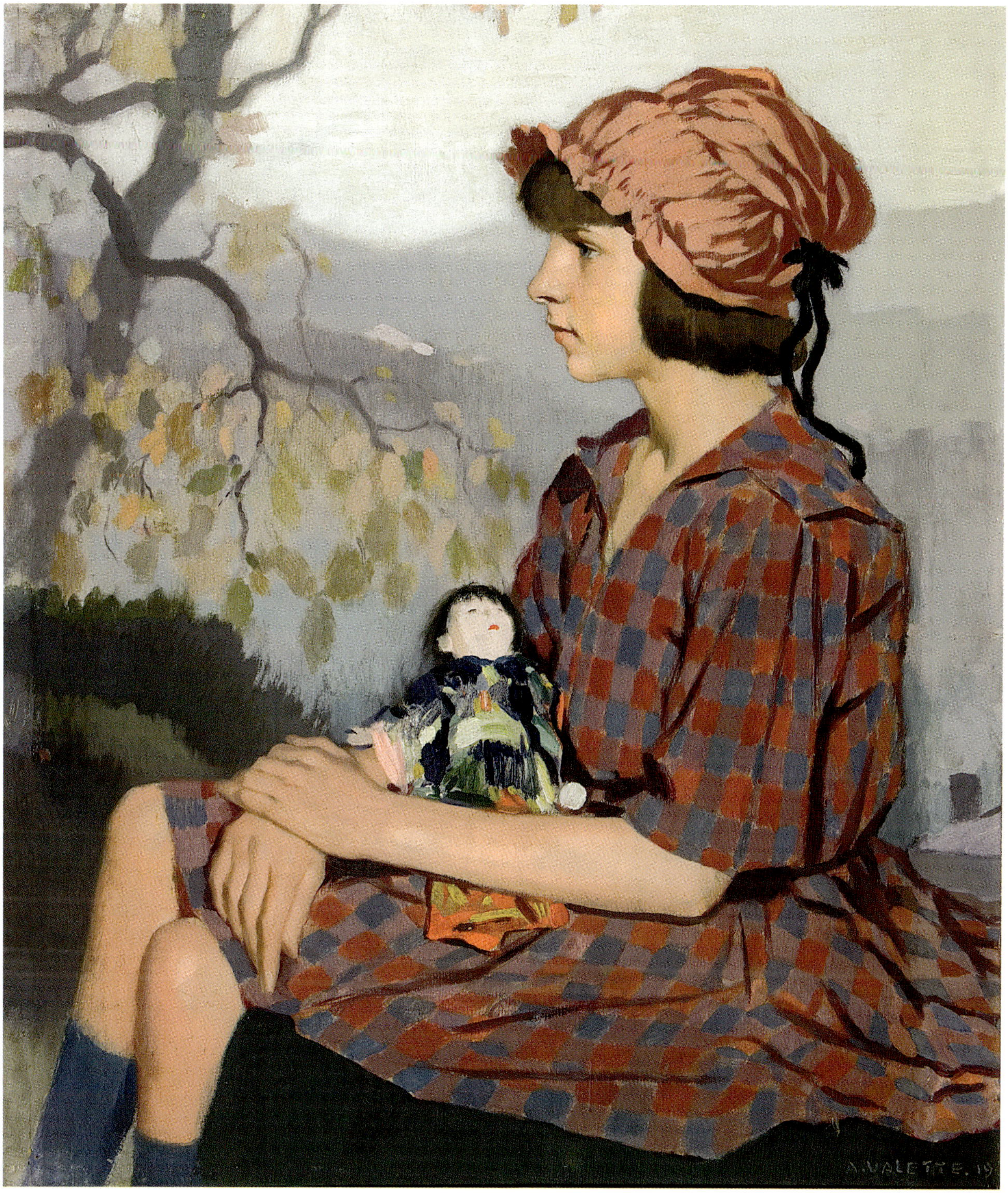

103 Portrait of a Girl with Japanese Doll, 1919

Oil on board, 59.5 x 49.5

Private collection

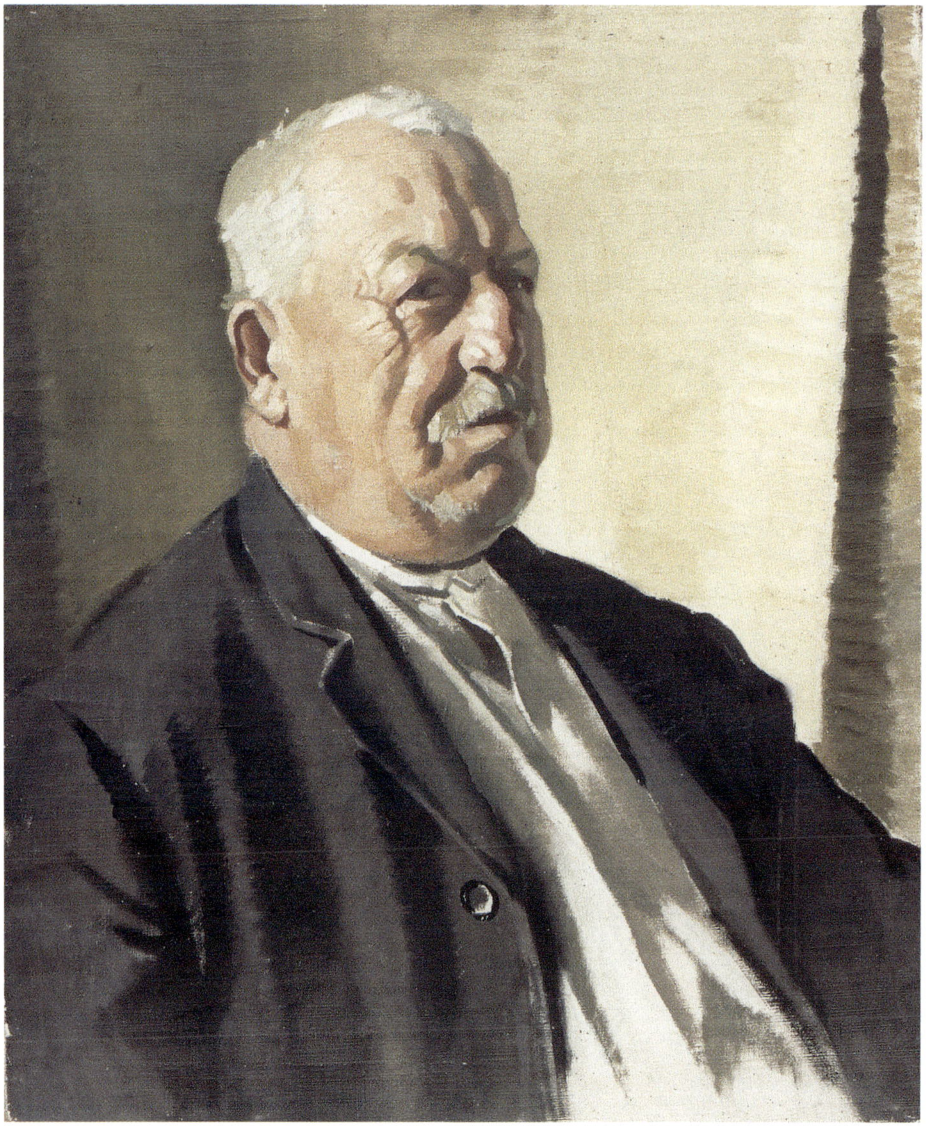

104 Monsieur Chatelet
Oil on canvas, 80 x 66
Private collection

he put a great deal of himself. What strikes us is that loving symbiosis between the painter and the model Gabriela, whose presence transcends the painting and gives it an intimate poetry. Gabriela is the star of the picture, and she is highlighted by the scale of the décor. Valette wants us to share his intimacy, and we enter into his living room. The picture as a whole is a décor. The painter wants us to see how he lives: the wallpaper, the pictures on the wall, the carpets, the furniture, and we enter the Valette couple's private, happy world.

With the impetus of success, from the 1917-18 period, Valette was increasingly approached by the bourgeoisie of Manchester wanting to have portraits of themselves or of their children. Thus, he also left behind a large number of portraits that were

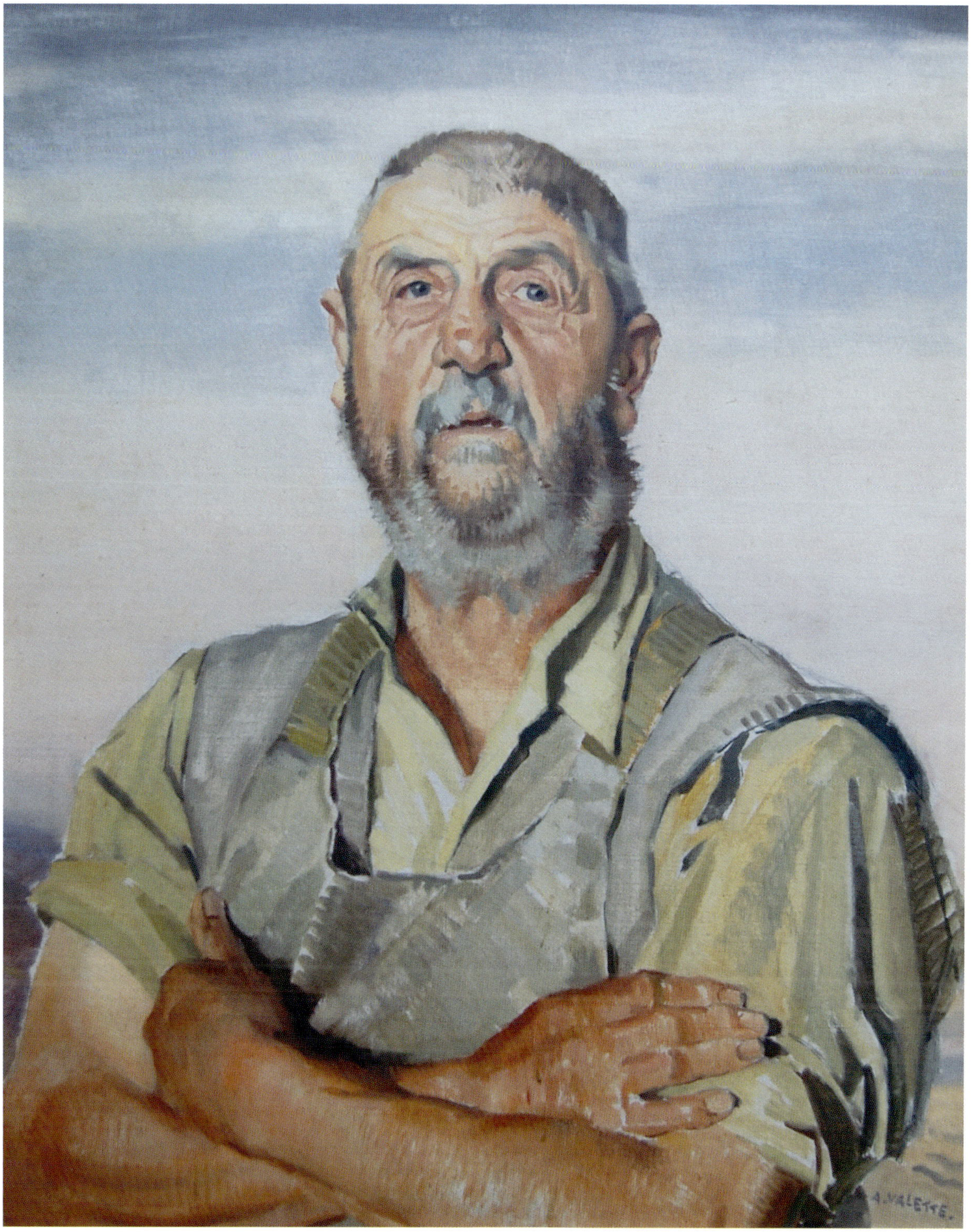

105 French Farmer

Oil on canvas, 79 x 62

Private collection

the result of commissions; the portraits are naturally very conventional in technique, but none the less evidence of a highly disciplined artistic talent. There are also many amongst the drawings he made when he was teaching at the Manchester Municipal School of Art that can be identified as portraits of models.

Towards the end of his life, when he had retired to Blacé, and while his second wife Andrée continued to teach French at Somerville College, Oxford, Valette's day-to-day life was managed by Maria Lafond, a neighbour. She soon became a source of inspiration for Valette. He portrayed her countless times, very often in the garden or going about her household chores or even in more intimist scenes, which are not stylistically unlike certain portraits he produced of Gabriela. Valette left us some very

106 *Sheep grazing under a Tree, 1919*
Oil on canvas, 38 x 48
Private collection

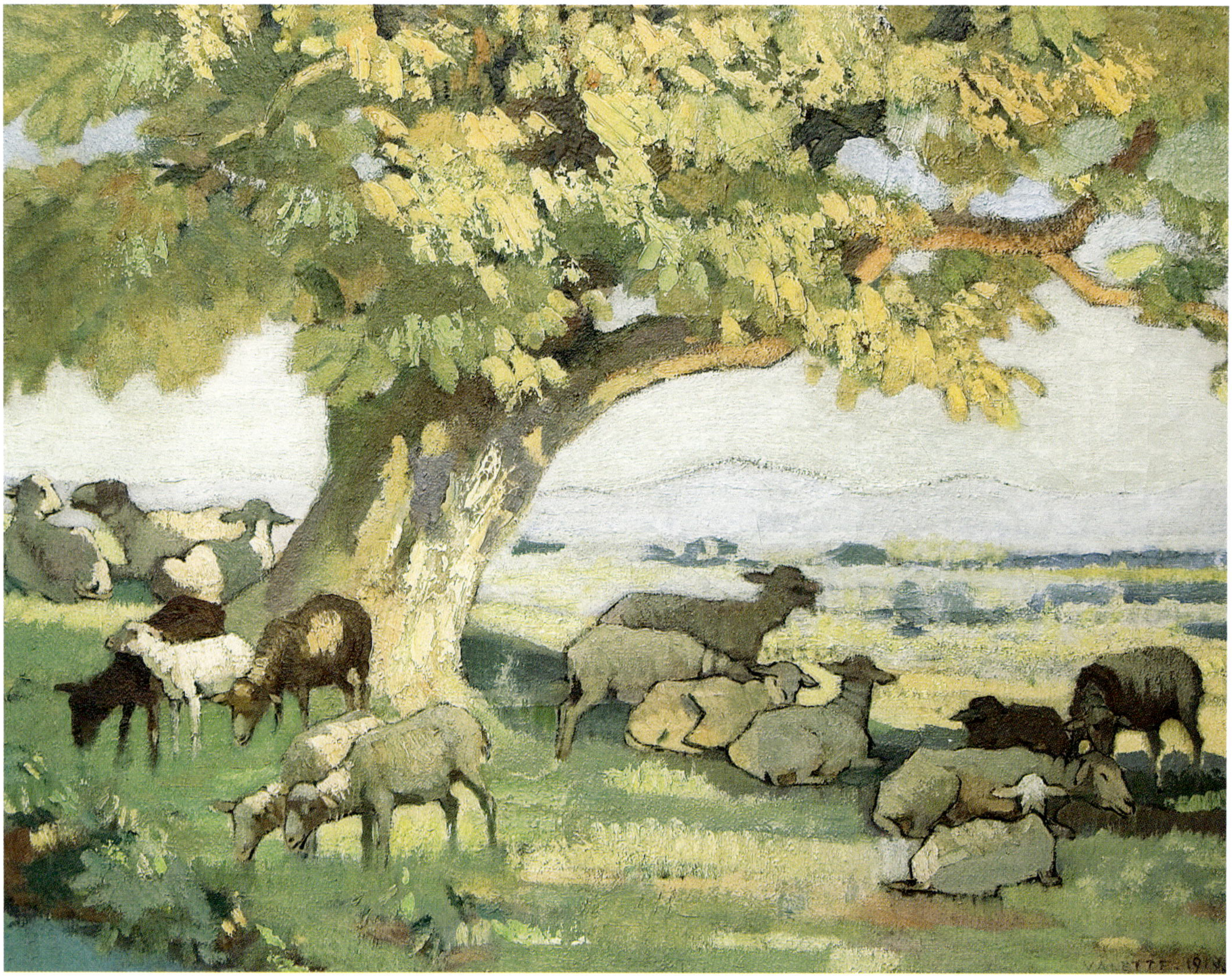

lively portraits of local individuals with very expressive features. Thus, for example, we know the genesis of the portrait of Monsieur Chatelet (fig 104 page 102): while out walking in the village, Valette chanced upon Monsieur Chatelet, a retired railway worker, sitting on a wall. He went up to him, struck up a conversation and told him that he had a 'tête de Gaulois'; he asked him if he would like to pose for him to which Mr Chatelet agreed. When Valette had completed the portrait, he presented it to Mr Chatelet![11]

Landscapes and Animals

Valette had a liking for open-air painting. He would literally set up his easel anywhere he went. This approach to working gave him a great feeling of freedom.

107 Grimaud

Pencil and watercolour on paper, 27.5 x 38

Private collection

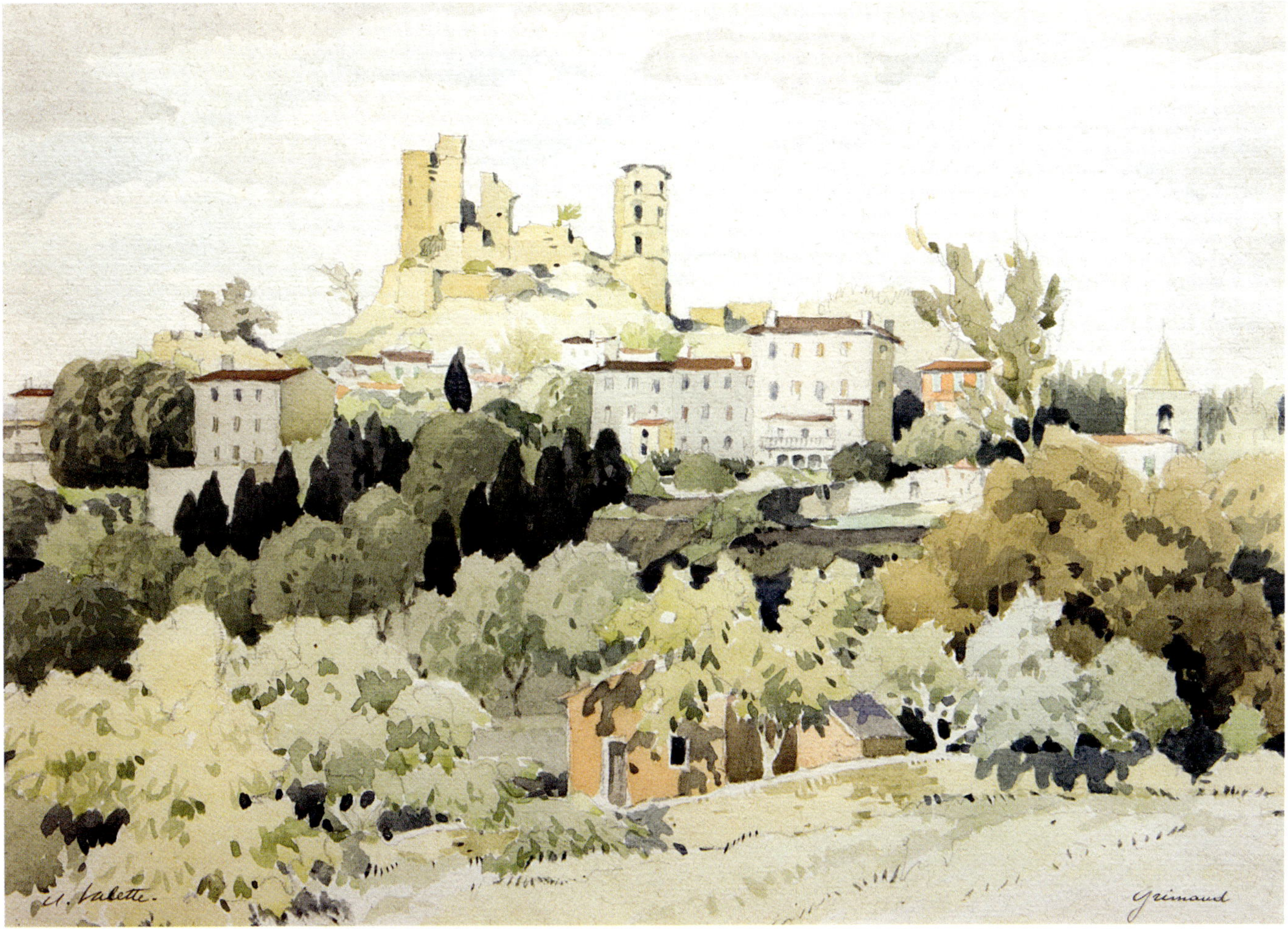

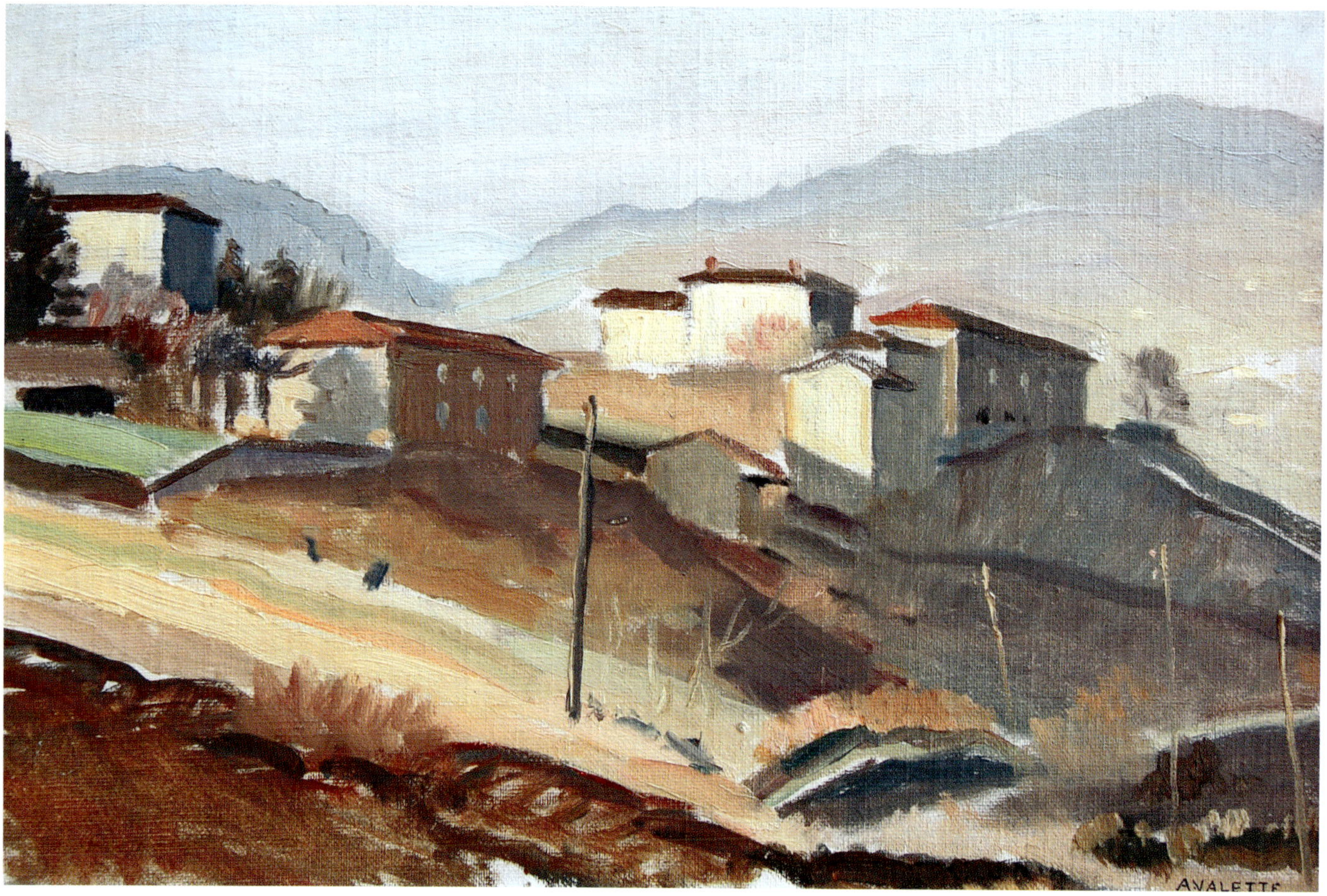

108 Chatenay St-Julien
Oil on canvas on board, 33 x 41
Private collection

Valette was very fond of farm animals. A portfolio of more than two hundred sketches of animals has recently been discovered. This portfolio confirms to us that, in Blacé, Valette lived with a pencil in his hand. His day-to-day life was punctuated by little pieces of paper, sheets on which he jotted down sketches of animals. His sketchpad was never far away and he was quick to capture the movement of the animal, and would draw the animal a great number of times, make small annotations and would repeat the process at will, often in preparation for future subjects. In his sketchpads there are cocks, cows, goats, sheep, horses, dogs, pigs, drawn in pencil or charcoal or lightly watercoloured. These are only studies, but they also have an important historical value and, as one realises, even on these small pieces of paper, a record of the innate talent of the draughtsman. Valette used any paper that was to hand: headed paper from the Municipal School of Art, wallpaper or the backs of letters. As well as farm animals, Adolphe Valette loved dogs; he and his wife Andrée had many dogs, often terriers, which are often represented in his pictures, such as that of his dog Cora.

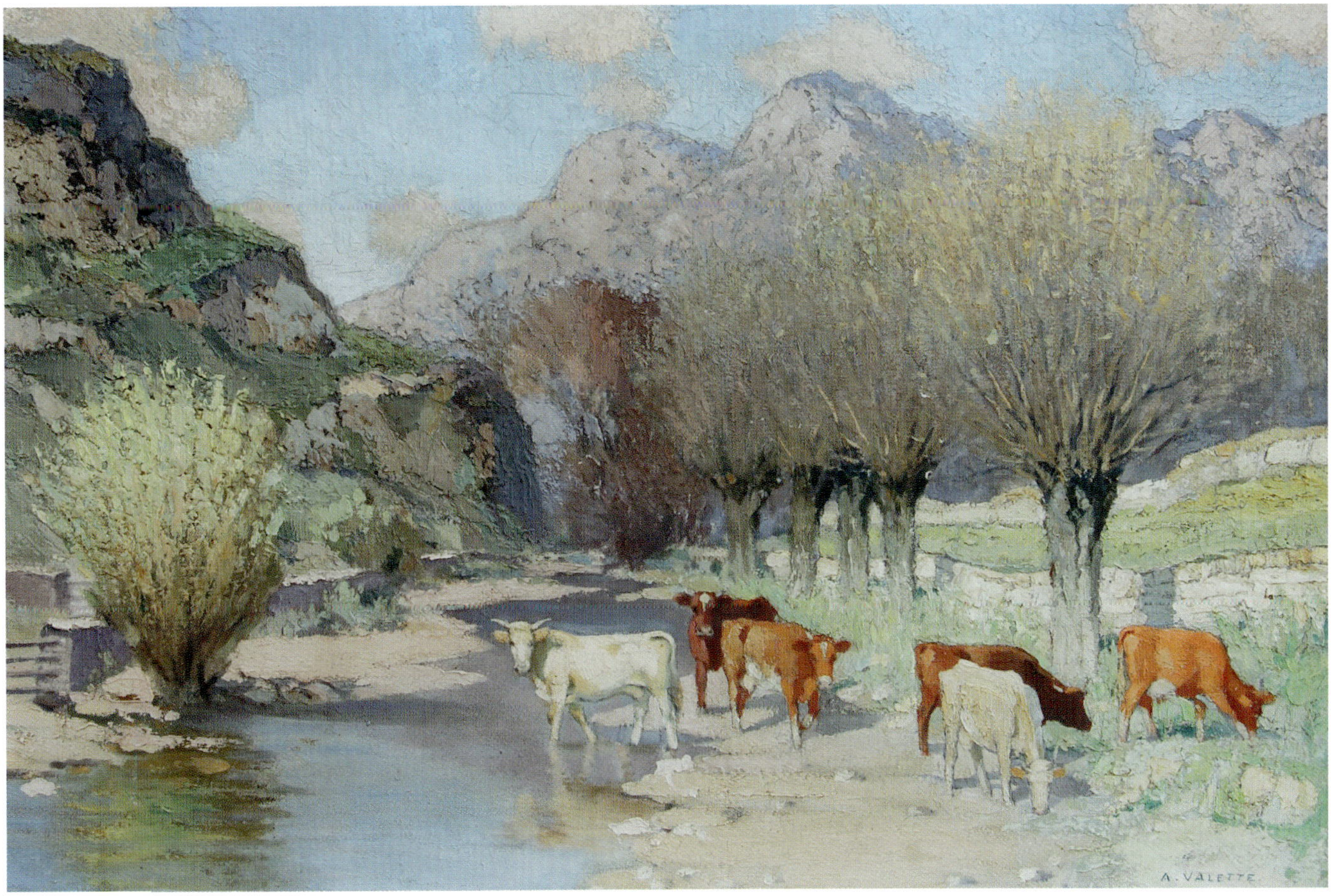

109 Vaches, Rivière et Saules
Oil on canvas, 61 x 81
Private collection

Thanks to this portfolio of sketches, we can see how Valette prepared some of his landscape paintings: he would mark out a sheet of paper, he would then outline the landscape and would reproduce the contents of each square in large format in his oil painting.

Valette also produced a very large number of watercolours of landscapes. These watercolours enable us to retrace the Valettes' steps on their travels and their favourite places. A large number of his watercolours were executed in situ, others perhaps pre-sketched in situ in pencil with colour being added subsequently. Valette applied the paint in a very fluid way, with an economy of colours, and their luminosity was derived from the contrasts between the juxtaposed colours. These watercolours were certainly intended to be used to provide a constant income for the painter who had little difficulty in selling them, due to the classicism of the subjects chosen. Many of these watercolours retrace the travels in the Midi and Balearic regions by Adolphe and Andrée Valette. Unlike many artists who were stunned by the violence of the Mediterranean light, the sun in this region did not cause an outburst of bright colours from his palette. On the

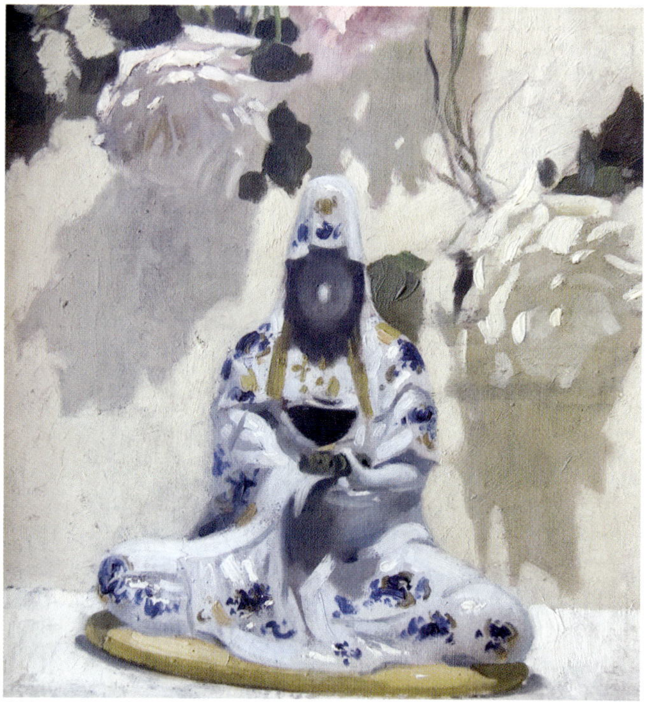

110 Still Life Porcelain Figure on sunlit Ledge with Roses above
Oil on canvas, 43.8 x 40.5
Private collection

contrary, when one looks at the watercolours of Saint-Tropez (fig 76 page 72), Grimaud (fig 107 page 105) and others scenes, the tones are faded and muted. They reflect more the stones and the soil than the direct brightness of the sun.

These are charming watercolours, but nonetheless lacking the pictorial substance we see in some of his other works. However, the watercolour method does enable misted and fading effects. Sometimes Valette was known to have painted watercolours on both sides of the paper. Alongside the refined and completed watercolours ready for sale, there are also a large number which are studies of detail or preparations for larger scale compositions.

Adolphe Valette often also used oil paints for landscapes; throughout his life as a painter, Valette executed landscapes in many different ways: 'minimal' small views of beach scenes (fig 24 page 30) (fig 118 page 118) executed with long horizontal strokes of the brush, and landscapes of his native region executed with a vivid and colourful palette. In yet another genre is a very poetic landscape with sheep and a shepherd boy (perhaps reminiscent of his own son) playing the flute, which is a decorative synthesis of the symbolism of Puvis de Chavannes with a neo-impressionist application of the brushstrokes (fig 7 page 11). Towards the end of his life he executed quite a number of traditional landscapes at Blacé and in the Beaujolais region; there are views of Salles, Chatenay, villages and fine residences in the surrounding region. The earth, the sky, a particular building, a few trees, or some vines enable him to allude to his emotion in the place where he is painting.

Still Life

Valette's still life paintings demonstrate a sparseness in their composition, which can in itself be powerful. Some objects, which include household implements, a vase, flowers or fruits are arranged on the canvas, often kept at a distance from each other. There are sometimes bulrushes, a jar, a teapot, cups with Far Eastern motifs, that were very fashionable at the time. Japan invited itself into the day-to-day life of the French via the major universal exhibitions. In middle-class interiors it was seen as a sign of culture to decorate one's interior with Japanese fabrics, and to own Japanese ceramics and bibelots. It has been reported that Valette himself had a large trunk in his house containing a variety of Far Eastern objects and clothing.

For his still life pictures, Adolphe Valette was at a crossroads with post-impressionism. He distances himself from atmospheric effects, but shows an interest

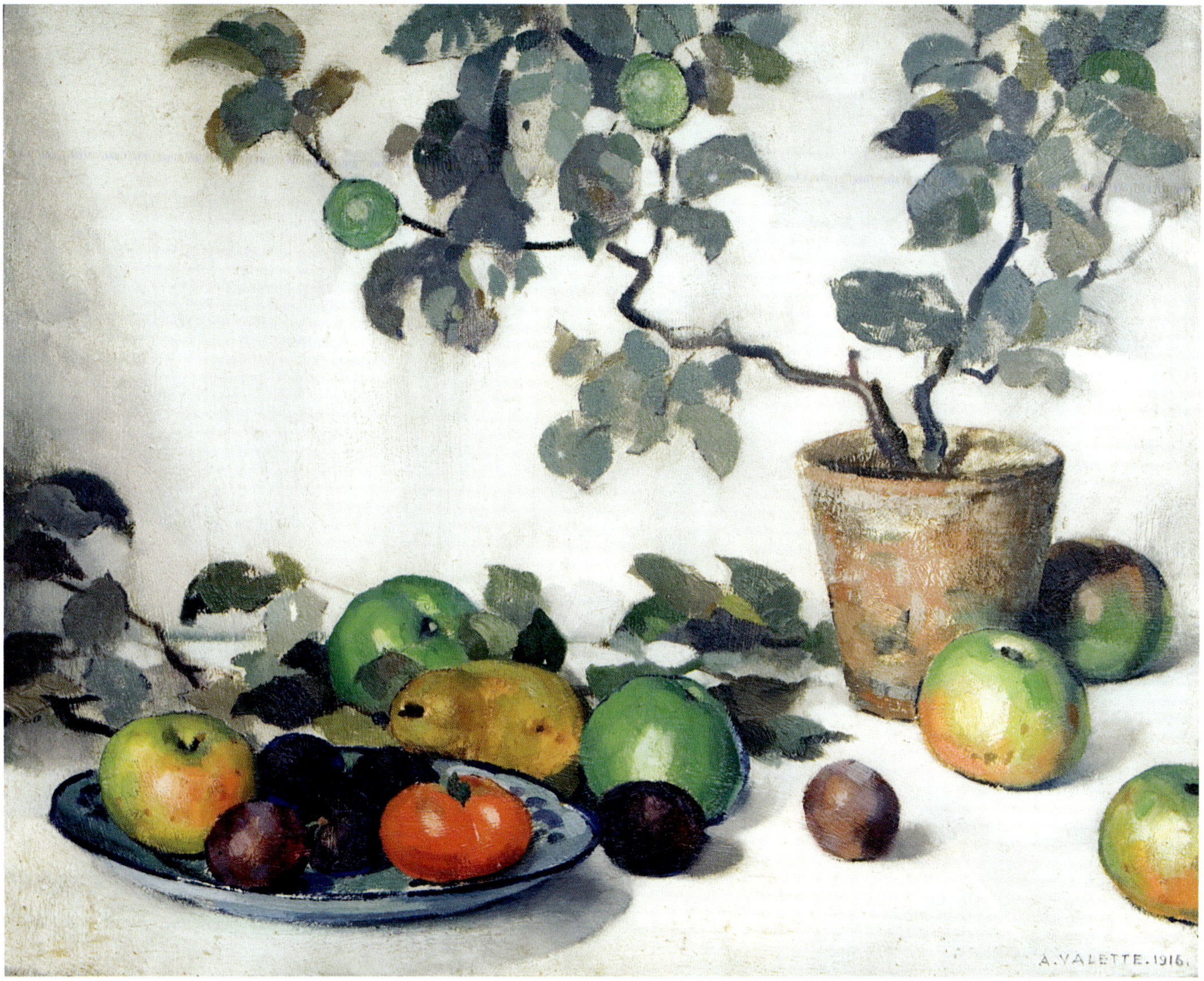

111 Still Life with Potted Plant, 1916
Oil on canvas, 50.8 x 61
Bill Clark collection

in the arrangement of objects on the canvas. He chose bright colours, and represented his objects in contrast on white or very pale background. The tones were delicate, without dramatic effects, and the still life is peaceful but at the same time ordered in the sense of the balanced arrangement of the objects.

The technique used by Valette for his still life pictures is striking in its refinement. Each object on the canvas is highlighted individually, and is often presented, at a distance from the others, on a cloth or tablecloth. Each element exists in itself alone, but functions in harmony with the whole composition. His palette is sometimes lively,

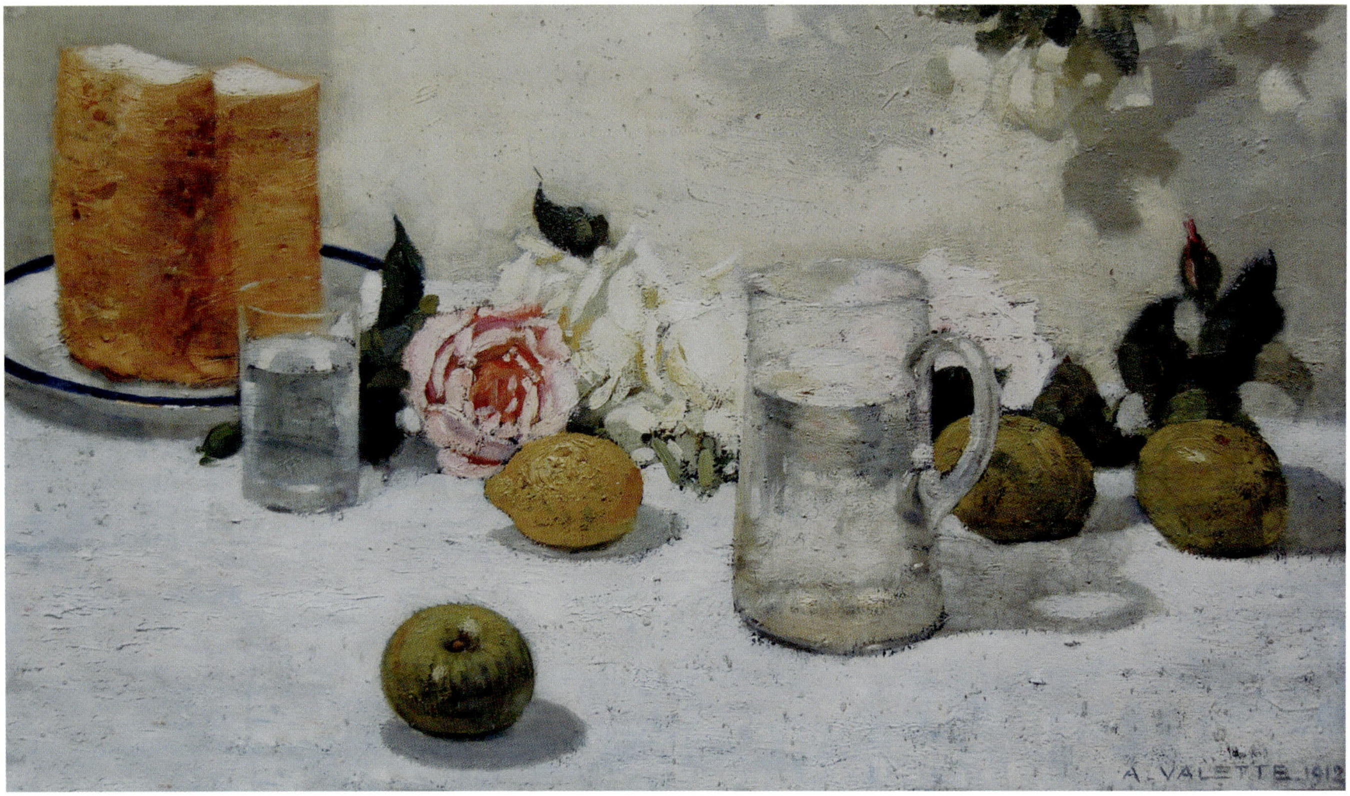

112 Still Life (Fruit), 1912
Oil on canvas, 44 x 75
Stockport Art Gallery

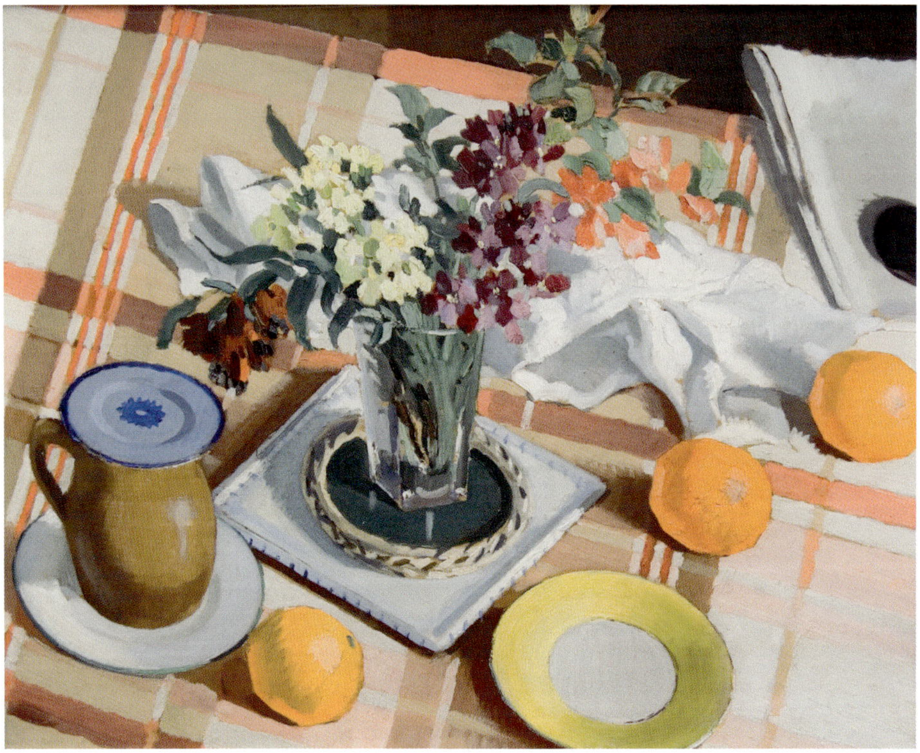

113 Still Life with Chequered Cloth
Oil on board, 48 x 59
Martin Heaps collection

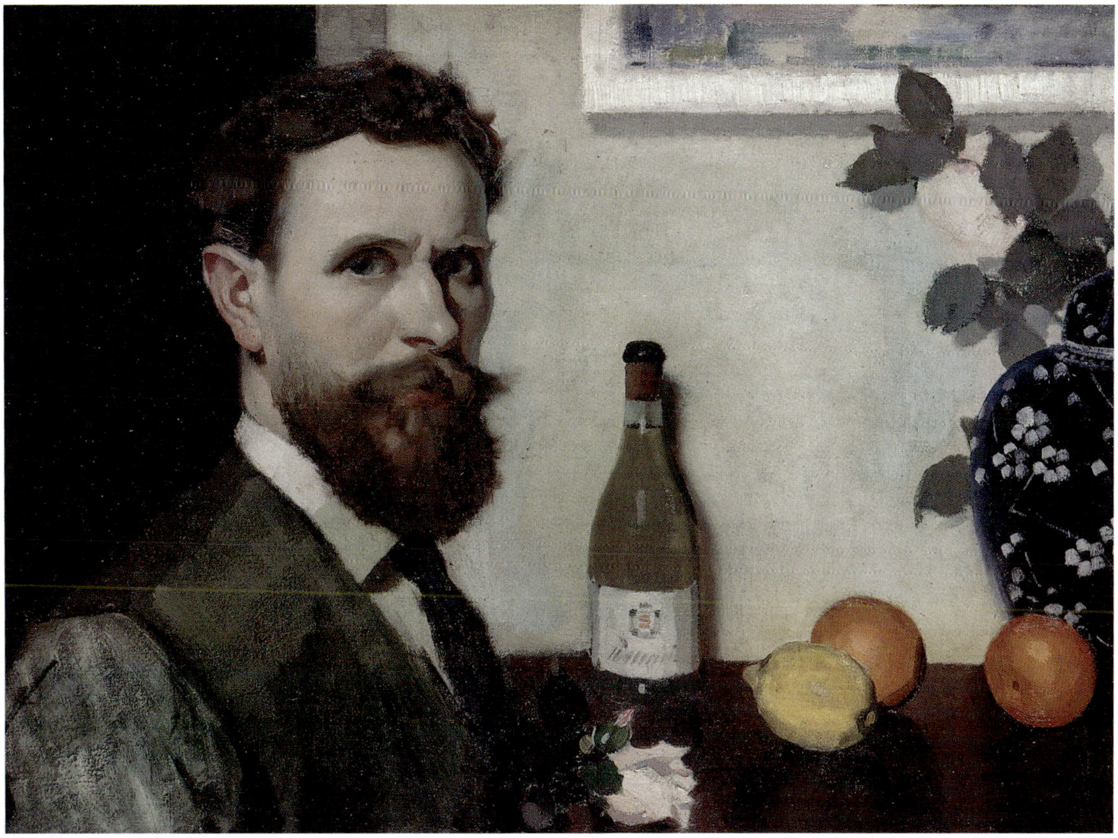

114 Self-Portrait
Oil on linen, 45 x 60.4
Manchester Art Gallery

but very often remains in the softer tones, with pale ochres, whites, pearl whites as in 'Still Life (Fruit)' from 1912 (fig 112 page 110) or greys as in 'Still Life with Potted Plant' from 1916 (fig 111 page 109).

Interestingly, a still life finds itself implanted onto his own 'Self-portrait' (fig 114 page 111), executed around 1917, when he was fifty. He is seen, standing out on a black background, to the left of the picture, both serious and shy, with a moustache and thick beard. Certain objects, including a wine bottle in the Burgundy shape, a lemon, two oranges and a Chinese vase, occupy the space to the right of the canvas, and stand out on a white background.

Sometimes even, on one or two rare canvases, there may be a suggestion of a rapprochement, albeit a very timid one, with fauvism. We should not forget that in France he knew Paul Signac and Jean Puy. Similarly, in the 'Society of Modern Painters' that he co-founded in Manchester, we know that latest trends in art were welcomed, as were fauvism and cubism. Thus, in 'Still Life with Chequered Cloth' (fig 113 page 110),

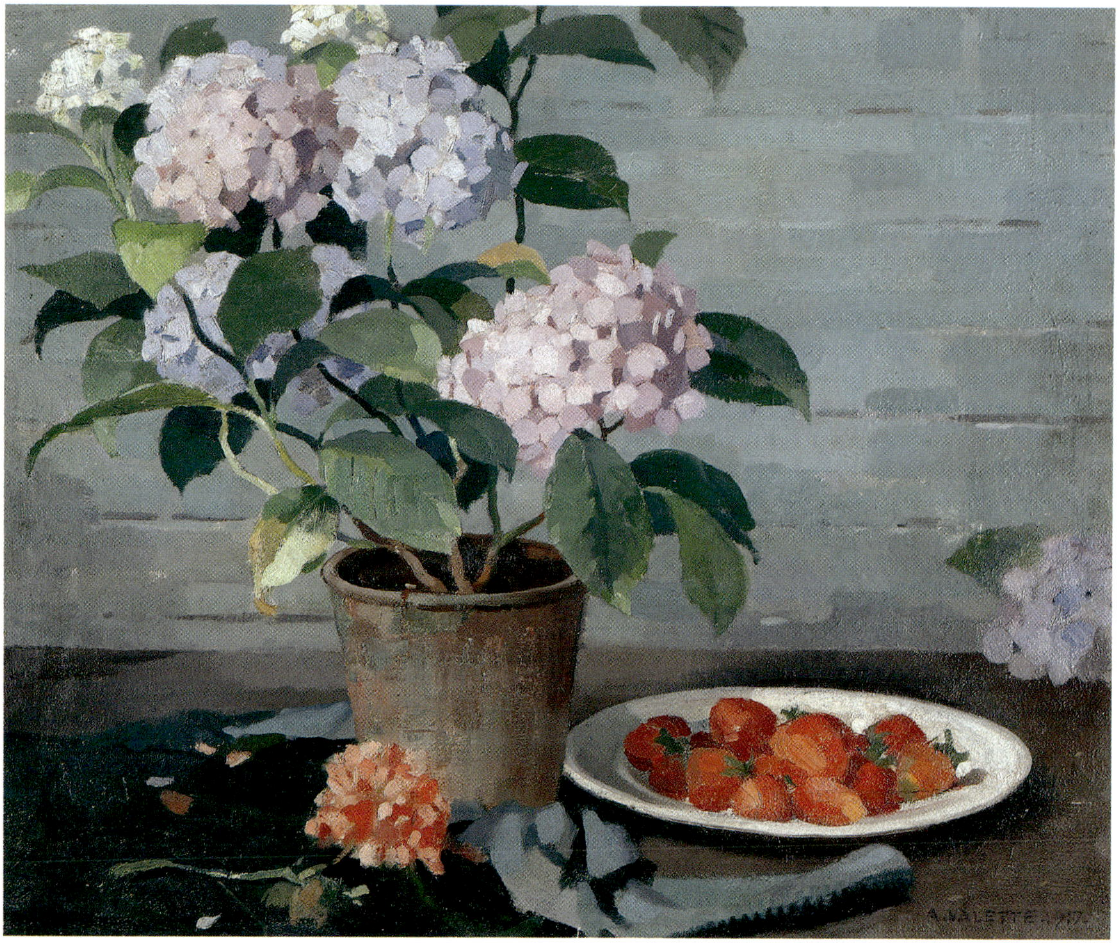

115 Flowers and Fruit, 1917
Oil on canvas, 49.8 x 58.8
Manchester Art Gallery

the colours come straight off the palette and Valette plays with the gaps in the picture to create space, and brings down the objects onto the surface of the painting, somewhat as though it had been painted as seen from above, but this remains an exception.

The critics liked the still life works, such as William Weatherby, of the *Manchester City News*, on the occasion of the exhibition of the 'Society of Modern Painters' of 1913: 'In another category are some highly original still life combinations, daring in conception and colouring and entirely pleasing.'[12]

Valette also left floral still life paintings, which, without showing signs of any particular audacity, certainly must have delighted collectors of more conventional tastes.

5 The Heirs and Advocates of the Work of Valette

Students at the Manchester Municipal School of Art

Some art critics state that Adolphe Valette had initiated a school of artists in Northern England. Thus, in 1926, on the occasion of the exhibition for the 25th anniversary of the 'Society of Modern Painters', of which Valette was one of the founder members, a critic noted that 'Monsieur Adolphe Valette is ultimately responsible for the style of most of our younger painters ...'[1] Valette had generated an enthusiasm amongst this rather doleful Northern England school and many of his own pupils were amongst his most fervent admirers.

We look with interest at the photograph of Adolphe Valette, with the beard, surrounded by his Life class in 1910 at the Manchester Municipal School of Art (fig 116 page 113). To the right of Valette in the photograph, by the easels, is William E. Daly who was later to study in Paris and subsequently returned to England

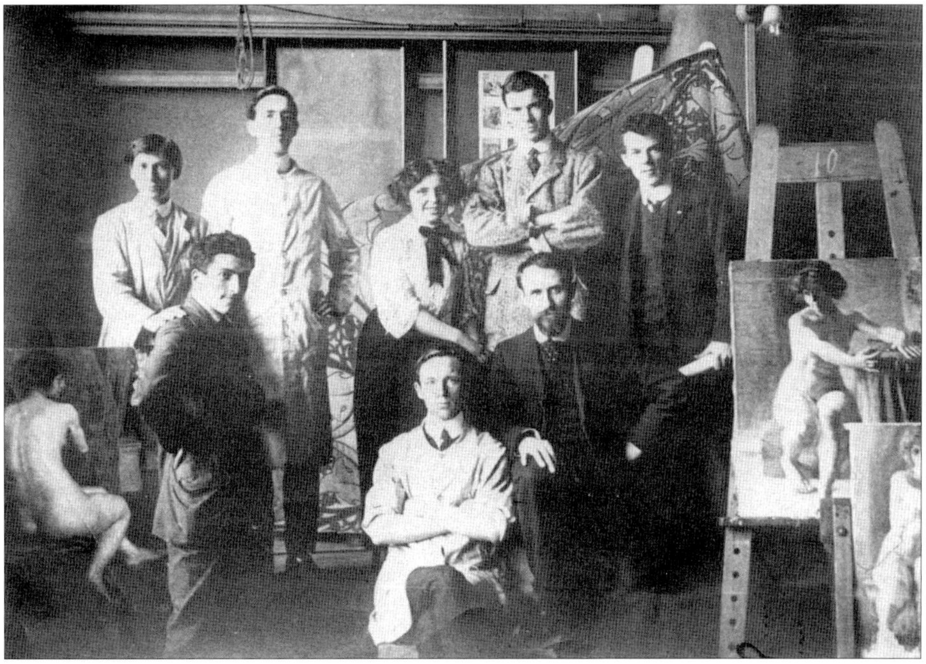

116 *Valette's Life class at the Manchester Municipal School of Art, in 1910*
Manchester Metropolitan University Special Collections

where he became principal of an art school in Kidderminster, in the Midlands. Like Adolphe Valette, he spent some time creating decorations for churches and schools in Manchester. Behind Valette is Harry Coller who later specialised in magazine and advertising illustrations. Also next to Valette, is Charles Whitham, one of his most prize-winning pupils, and behind him we see the model Louise Gunnery. (See also fig 50 page 49.) Next to her is Joseph Milner, to whom Valette was to dedicate a portrait with the caption 'à mon ami Milner' [to my friend Milner]. Milner was one of Valette's intimate circle of friends, dating from his arrival in England. (See fig 29 page 35.) Next to Milner is W.H. Myers, who in 1908 won the bronze medal for his drawing after the antique style, and in front of him is David Ghilchick who made a career for himself as an illustrator for *Punch* magazine. Ghilchick, with his future wife Josephine Duddle, also one of Valette's pupils, illustrated a journal written by Josephine, which was a humorous account of day-to-day student life at the Manchester Municipal School of Art. In the Special Collections of the Manchester Metropolitan University (into which the School of Art has been incorporated), there are two nude studies by Ghilchik of two models (one of them most certainly being Louise Gunnery) which are familiar to us for having seen them in Valette's own life drawings. It should be remembered, as has already been highlighted, that Valette liked to work alongside his students.

To the students in this photo should be added, amongst Valette's disciples, Karl Hagedorn, Emmanuel Levy, Edward Harrison Richardson, Edgar Rowley Smart, Charles B. Wilson, Henry Vitofski and L.S. Lowry. Karl Hagedorn, who was of German origin, had an early career quite similar to that of Valette: he worked for a textile firm and designed fabrics. He had a particular interest in etching and lithography techniques at the Manchester Municipal School of Art and spent some time in Paris. Like Valette, he was also involved with the 'Society of Modern Painters', where he caused a sensation, in 1913, by exhibiting a work in the cubist tradition.[2] Emmanuel Levy was also one of Valette's students, and was also recommended by Valette as successor to his position of Master of Drawing when he left Manchester in 1928. Sam Rabinovitch, who changed his name to Sam Rabin, had an astonishing career. He was noticed as a talented draughtsman at the Manchester Municipal School of Art; he later became a sculptor and fairground wrestler. He produced pictures associated with the boxing. Edward Harrison Richardson also absorbed a strong influence from Valette as was very visible from his choice of subjects (Manchester, mists, the waterways and urban life) and their post-impressionist mode of representation. He was mid-way between Valette and Lowry, about whom we shall hear more later. Edgar Rowley Smart of whom Valette produced a stunning portrait (fig 25 page 32), was a friend from the very earliest days, and, like Valette, a founder member of the 'Society of Modern Painters'. He spent some time living in Paris, where he led a fairly dissolute life and also produced some pictures; he then went to Sweden. Charles Wilson worked, like Valette, at the Norbury Natzio and Co Ltd printing works, and then studied under Valette; he then went to Paris, and eventually returned to Manchester where he founded his own printing company. Henry Vitofski, another of Valette's friends who exhibited with the 'Society of Modern Painters', left us an interesting portrait of his master.

What is striking here, in drawing up the list of students he taught, is the kinship Adolphe Valette was able to engender with them. The dissemination of his expertise did not stop at the doors of the Manchester Municipal School of Art. Valette often spent time with students, not merely in the context of a teacher–student relationship but in a relationship of one artist to another, and between friends. Valette had made his educational duties his raison d'être and his students responded in kind in a way that was testimony to their affection for him.

In all that precedes, it is clear that none of his students achieved true fame, with the major exception of L.S. Lowry.

During a brief stay in Manchester in 1933, Valette regretted this fact, as was reported by a journalist in the *Evening News*: 'We walked today in the studio of one of his old pupils. That bright smile which has won him a hundred friendships disappeared when we came to talk of art in Manchester. 'The Manchester I remember had a large number of picture galleries. Where are they now? I have searched in vain for them. And the artists – my old pupils at the Art School – where are they? Yes I know where many of them are. They are hiding in poverty. Brilliant men I had hoped to meet on this visit have not been heard of for years. They are starving. For the men who scorned commercial art there is no work.' [3]

L.S. Lowry (1887-1976)

The industrious student whose fame was to outstrip that of his teacher.

One of Valette's students attained the highest echelons of the artistic world in an extraordinary fashion; he attended various classes given by Valette throughout the years he was at the Manchester Municipal School of Art and Valette's influence upon him extended to more than a mere imprint. The student in question was L.S. Lowry.

The destinies of Valette and Laurence Stephen Lowry were sealed with their respective enrolments as students at the Manchester Municipal School of Art in 1905. Valette was 29 at the time and Lowry seventeen.

As we know, Valette's talent very quickly won over his teachers and he was himself offered a teaching post. Thus within a few months Lowry found himself in Valette's class as a student, in a new student/teacher relationship.

Lowry was only able to attend evening classes at the Manchester Municipal School of Art, as he worked during the day in an insurance company in Manchester and subsequently as a rent collector for the Pall Mall Property company in Salford, another industrial city adjacent to Manchester. Lowry was never encouraged by his family circle in the pursuit of a career as a painter and had a very austere Victorian upbringing constrained within the yoke of respectability.

Lowry reports that he enjoyed these evening classes: 'I saw people there. I liked the life. It was good to meet people there. My temperament made me very unsociable, although that was not my wish.'[4] In the eyes of his fellow students at the Manchester Municipal School of Art, Lowry was an unusual and strange individual. While his colleagues rejoiced in the more relaxed social values offered by the new Edwardian society, with its emerging new visions for the century, and the laissez-faire ambience of the artistic circles, Lowry retained the Victorian values of his childhood.

Valette was, like everyone else, slightly taken aback by this unusual student; initially, it seems, Valette paused before Lowry's work, as he did with all his students, as he passed among the easels, making a small annotation or sketch, applying a small correction to demonstrate the balance of a face or drawing of the hand; however, after a while he stopped doing this in Lowry's case. Subsequently, he paused by him occasionally, and gave Lowry a friendly tap on the shoulder, uttered some unintelligible words in English and frowned. Another student, Cyril Greenberg, remembers Valette complaining about Lowry's representation in caricatures.[5] At the Manchester Municipal School of Art, Lowry confessed that the Antique Drawing class presented him with a problem: he confided that drawing a plaster statue was much harder than drawing a living model in the Life class: 'If you draw from life, whatever you do, you can say it was like that when I drew it, but it moved. You can't say that about the antique.'[6]

Even so, although Valette had not yet fathomed Lowry's future talent, he always surrounded him with an aura of understanding and warmth, as well as an influence of both sympathy and authority. In early 1907, Lowry asked Valette to give him private lessons. Valette declined but recommended another artist to him, William Fitz, 'who did him a lot of good.'[7] It may even be the case that there was a kind of understanding between Lowry and Valette, albeit one that went unexpressed, in that they were both so different from the others: Valette, a French artist somewhat out on a limb in Manchester, with an imperfect grasp of the language, Lowry locked into his own private environment by his upbringing and individual way of drawing and painting.

Lowry did in fact later express his gratitude for Valette's contribution. 'I cannot over-estimate the effect on me at that time of the coming into this drab city of Adolphe Valette, full of the French Impressionists, aware of everything that was going on in Paris. He had freshness and a breadth of experience that was a very wonderful thing, as I saw it done by himself and his friends. I had not seen drawings like these before – for artistry. They were French life-class drawings, and he painted and drew in the same way. I was fascinated by it, and whilst I never drew in that way – I couldn't have done, it wasn't my way of drawing – I greatly admired him and they helped me very much. They were great stimulants.' [8] What Lowry took with him from Valette was more than just technique, it was the enthusiasm he conveyed as well as a confidence in his talent. Much later, without Lowry knowing it, Valette visited Lowry's father to plead his case and allow him to continue with the classes 'because he thought I had something in me.'[9]

At the Manchester Municipal School of Art, Valette and Lowry necessarily shared the same models for the Life class. It is interesting to see side by side the drawings that Valette and Lowry made of these models. Among the male models was one Julian Aeronson, who posed both for the teacher and the student (fig 117 page 117) (fig 119 page 119). Lowry later came across Julian, at the Salford Art School, where he enrolled in 1915, having left the Manchester Municipal School of Art. Lowry very willingly acknowledged his appreciation of the varied company of students and models. The

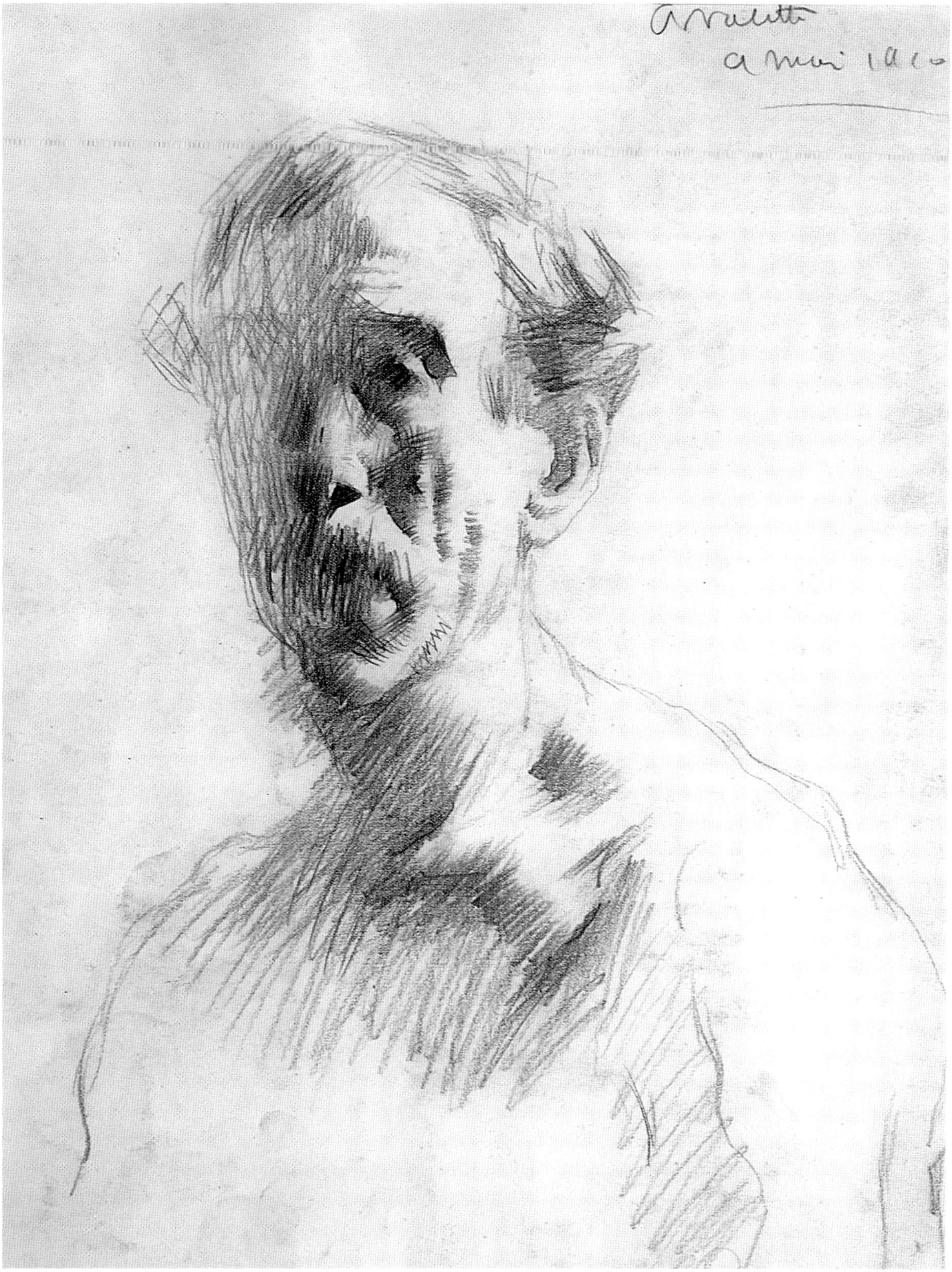

117 Julian, 9 Mai 1910

Pencil on paper, 33 x 27.7

Private collection

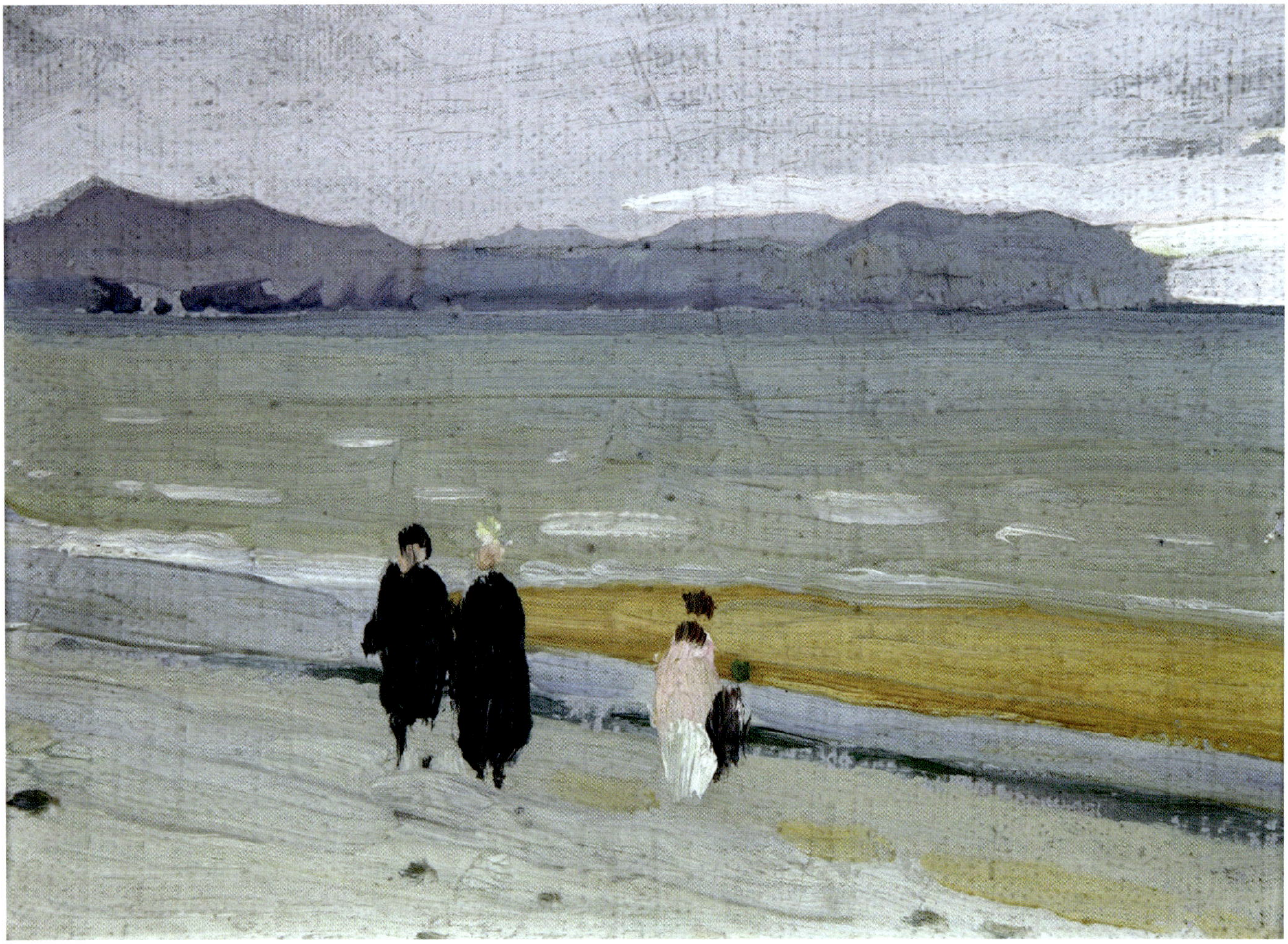

118 Beach Scene, North Wales
Oil on board, 11 x 17
Sefton Samuels collection

models and students were not the type of people he could ever meet in his family milieu: the Pachito sisters, the Italian Valenti who also posed for Lord Leighton, Hetty the Magnificent and also a model discovered in an Altrincham chemist's shop, a young 16-year-old beauty with Titianesque hair 'who posed for the master, at a wage of four shillings an hour, with tea and biscuits.'[10]

In two of Lowry's oils, 'Landscape' of 1912 and 'Country Lane' of 1914, one can see an influence from Valette in the composition and the application of colour. Lowry admits this himself: 'I was going through my impressionist period.'[11] In an interview[12] in which he made reference to his tutor Adolphe Valette, Lowry himself stated that he had been influenced subconsciously by impressionism. In his own words: 'People say that I was influenced by what was happening in France, but I was not aware of it. I could have been subconsciously influenced by Valette.' A little further on in the interview, Lowry is more specific and willingly admits to having been influenced by Valette for his 'seascapes of the Fylde coast', but, he adds, not by Valette's still life work,

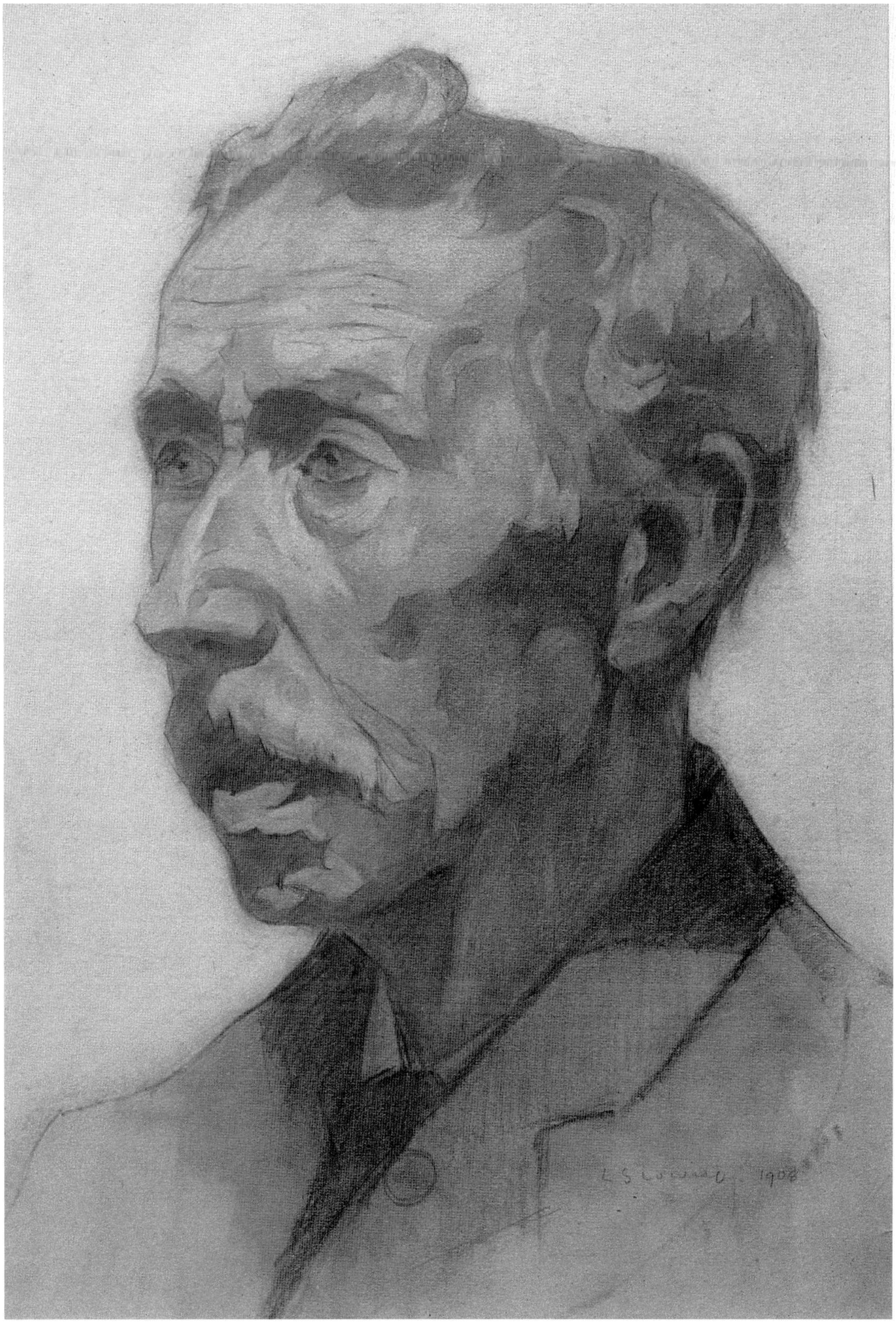

119 L.S. Lowry. Portrait of a Man, 1908

Pencil on paper, 40.2 x 22.7

The Lowry Collection, Salford

as he had never seen them. Later, in adopting his own style, Lowry detached himself from the technique of impressionism that conveyed the changes in colour determined by light. Lowry only used the colours he had originally chosen (ochre, blue, black, white and red), separating them on the canvas.

The theme that made both Valette and Lowry famous is the portrayal of the urban and industrial landscapes of the North of England, in shades of the greyness of the smoke from the factories trapped by mist and fog.

Our view is that Lowry was most certainly influenced, either consciously or unconsciously, by Valette, in his choice of subjects. He had seen the greater majority of Valette's canvases, having spent a decade in close proximity with him at the Manchester Municipal School of Art, and even though the influence of his master became less pronounced ('We didn't see eye to eye at all about my painting; I didn't show them to him again,' as he put it),[13] Valette was nonetheless present as part of his artistic baggage. They both transcended the industrial, urban environment. They were the first artists to place Manchester 'centre stage'; for them, Manchester was raised to the level where the city itself was in the spotlight in their paintings. It was, furthermore, for this specific reason that Mancunians so revere these two artists. Valette had told Lowry, as he told all his students, to look at everything around him 'with the eye of the artist'.[14] Lowry himself accepted that 'When I was young, I did not see the beauty of the Manchester streets. I used to go into the country painting landscapes and the like. Then, one day I saw it . . . I suddenly saw the beauty of the streets and crowds.'[15] Valette also commented in a Studio interview in November 1923, that 'there is a beauty in Manchester'.[16]

The handling of industrial landscapes by Lowry was clearly not the same as that of Valette, who was more focused on colours misting over and mixing in a Turneresque, impressionist atmosphere. While Lowry's early industrial landscapes are reminiscent of those of Valette, he very soon acquired his own style in a more down-to-earth handling of the scene with the characters themselves having been reduced to stark silhouettes.

It is entirely possible that it was Valette who encouraged his pupil to send canvases to the Salon de Paris and to the Salon d'Automne in the 1920s when Valette himself spent some time in Paris; in 1928 a number of Lowry canvases were exhibited in the Galerie Goupil where Théo van Gogh had previously hung works by his brother Vincent.

In 1925, canvases by Valette and Lowry hung side by side in the exhibition of the Society of Modern Painters, in Manchester.

From when in 1928 Valette left Manchester, his reputation began to decline. On the other hand, in 1939 Lowry experienced his first great successes in London with his first personal exhibition, which established his reputation on an upward path. In 1965, television broadcast further enhanced his reputation and in 1966 and 1967 another major retrospective exhibition focused entirely on him; despite this, Lowry continued to lead a spartan existence, although he had been able to retire from his job as a rent collector and had become by then a full-time professional artist. Lowry declined the offer of a several honours, including a knighthood; he did, however, agree to become a member of the Royal Academy and he received honorary doctorates from two universities.

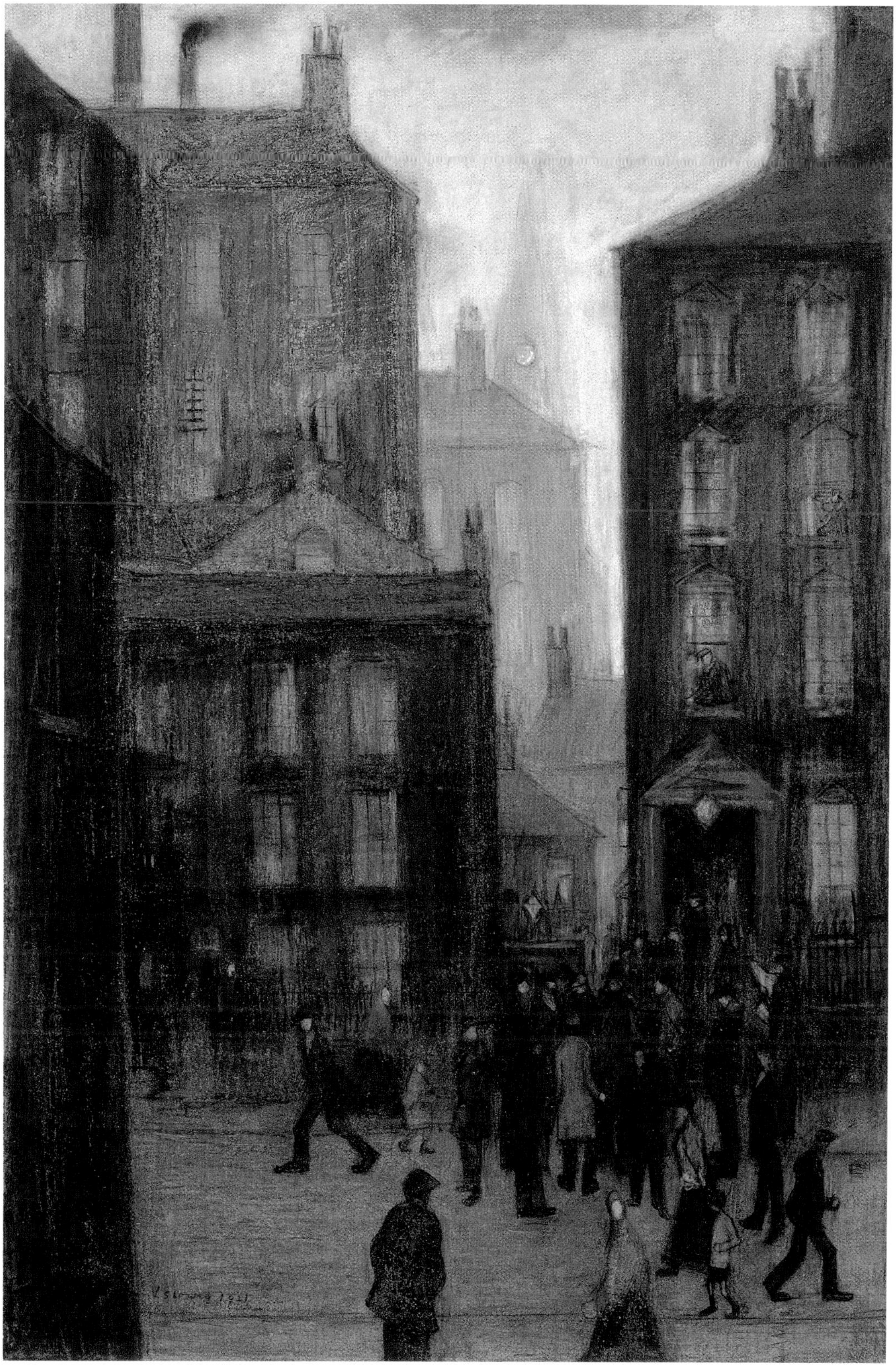

120 L.S. Lowry, *The Lodging House, 1921*
Chalk on paper, 50.1 x 32.6
The Lowry Collection, Salford

Like Valette had done at the Manchester School of Art, Lowry enjoyed being able to provide the simplest form of support to the students of the Salford School of Art that he himself had previously attended from 1915. 'Lowry used to pass by the Salford Art Gallery in Peel Park to see how his works where being exhibited. Then, he would look in on the art classes and enjoyed talking to the students and offering advice. Mr Lowry was a very modest man', we were told by one of the students of the time who feels privileged to have met him at the Salford School of Art.[17]

In 1976, a few months after the death of Lowry, a retrospective exhibition of his works at the Royal Academy in London broke all attendance records and provoked a considerable range of opinions amongst the critics. Some saw Lowry as a great artist with an original vision while others considered him a minor talent, while acknowledging his status as a social commentator.

With the increasing fame of Lowry's work in 1976, which coincided with the retrospective exhibition in the Manchester City Art Gallery marking the celebration of the centenary of the birth of Adolphe Valette, there was a heightening of the public consciousness of the tutor/student relationship between Valette and Lowry spanning many years. This heightened awareness directly impacted the revival of interest in Valette.

In 2000, the city of Salford, where Lowry had spent most of his life rendered him a perpetual homage, 24 years after his death, creating a major public art gallery in his honour, eponymously named 'The Lowry' housing more than 350 of his works of the L.S. Lowry Collection that the Salford Museum and Art Gallery had collected since the 1930s. In comparison the 17 canvases by Valette exhibited in the new extension of the Manchester Art Gallery are the image of the barometer of popularity of these two artists.

At the point where the student overtakes his tutor, it is an appropriate time to ask whether Lowry harboured a certain resentment against Valette, who, it should be remembered, had Lowry as his student for a decade in his Life class; in point of fact in one of Lowry's 'course records' at the Manchester School of Art there is the verdict 'failed' for the Life class and for Drawing from the Antique.[18] On no occasion did Lowry achieve any commendation for his work at the Manchester Municipal School of Art. Our view is that Lowry did not bear a grudge against his tutor for the poor marks he had given him. He acknowledges the influence Valette had upon him and had fond memories of the motivative ambience in the classes and the unique individuals one met there.

In the 1970s, thirty years after the death of Adolphe Valette, his widow, Andrée, wrote to Geoffrey Green, who was selling the works of Valette through the Tib Lane Gallery in Manchester. Andrée asked him to explain the reason for the enthusiasm for Lowry's painting and why it sold so well, while that of Valette had virtually fallen into oblivion. Geoffrey Green, mustering all the tact he could, responded: 'The line in Lowry's drawing is exquisite. Though the image may not always be correct in terms of perspective, the personality of the artist overcomes that, through the beauty and the quality of his line.'[19]

The objective of this book, following the example of Madame Valette's initiatives, is to seek to prove that Valette is far more than just 'the man who taught Lowry'.[20]

The Advocates of Valette's Work

As most of his disciples had not managed to establish their reputation as painters, they turned into ardent champions of Valette's work. Thus, for example, Charles Holmes, in 1928, persuaded Manchester City Art Gallery to acquire works by Valette. Holmes felt that these works had historical significance for the city of Manchester. The Art Gallery acquired nine large canvases by Valette representing Manchester, for £200, which in the money of the time represented a very good deal for the Manchester City Art Gallery. Even so, Valette was very happy to see his pictures of Manchester finding a permanent home in the city in which they had been created.

Already in 1927, the Art Gallery had accepted the portrait of John Henry Reynolds, the Principal of the College of Technology (see fig 26 page 33); this was a donation on the part of the daughter of the former director of one of the colleges of the institution at which Valette taught.

About ten years later, in 1938, Annie Barnett (fig 121 page 124), of Macclesfield, persuaded the Manchester City Art Gallery to accept her gift of four more of his works. Annie Barnett was a former student of Valette; and since his early days at the School of Art she became a good friend of the couple Gabriela and Adolphe Valette. Gabriela died in 1917, without having made a will, and, on the Letters of Administration of Gabriela's estate, we can read that Annie Barnett acted as surety (guarantor) which indicates how close she was to the Valettes. After Gabriela's death, Annie gave Adolphe Valette practical and moral support, preparing meals for him at the School of Art.

From 1928, when Valette left Manchester, until the 1970s, it would be fair to say that Valette's works were neglected and had become forgotten. The years of the depression, followed by the war years, put paid to all the initiatives to revive the artist's memory. Valette's canvases remained in reserve storage for many years, until in 1970 they returned to the foreground of the Manchester art scene when the Manchester City Art Gallery decided to set up 'a small exhibition of works by Valette and his followers' to be held from 8-30 November, which was extended to 31 December 1970.[21]

At about the same time, on the scene of the private art galleries in Manchester, it was brought to the notice of Geoffrey Green of the Tib Lane Gallery that he should contact Valette's widow Andrée, who was by then over 80 years old and living in Jersey and had preserved her late husband's artistic heritage. Geoffrey Green had been familiar with Valette's name since 1961, as, in a book published in that year and written by Mervyn Levy, he had read L.S. Lowry's acknowledgement of a debt of gratitude to his tutor from the Manchester School of Art, Adolphe Valette. However, Geoffrey Green had never seen the works of Valette. He then travelled to Jersey, met Andrée Valette, and was immediately won over by what he saw of the collection of the works of the painter. He proposed an exhibition that was arranged in haste and held from 16-28 November 1970 at the Tib Lane Gallery in Manchester with paintings priced at £35 and £45. The show generated an enthusiastic response from the public and practising artists.[22]

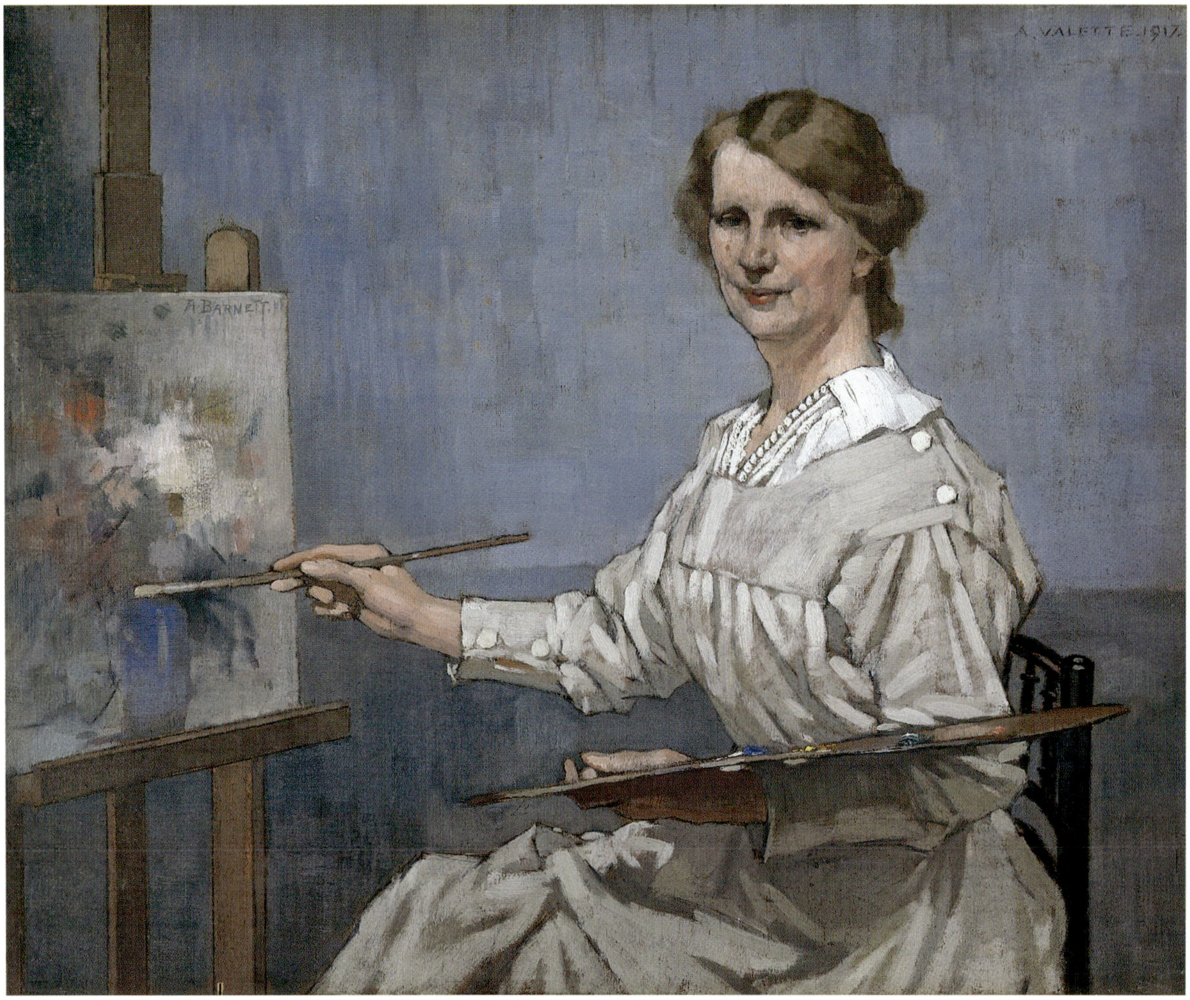

121 *Annie Barnett, 1917*
Oil on board, 39.5 x 46.9
Manchester Art Gallery

With the conjunction of the exhibition at the Manchester City Art Gallery and the private show held at the Tib Lane Gallery, interest in the painter revived in quite a phenomenal way. Andrée Valette finally had the satisfaction of seeing her husband's paintings valued once more in the city in which they had been created more than fifty years earlier.

Also during the 1970s, Valette's first major private collectors, Mr and Mrs Perera, assembled a large collection of works. The collection was started coincidentally in 1967 when Mr Mario Perera from Portsmouth was on a routine business trip to Jersey during which he planned to buy a birthday gift for his wife Rosemary. It happened to be a small landscape by Valette which Andrée Valette had put on display in a local department store. This purchase was the impetus that would lead the Pereras to acquisitions that amounted to a total of 70 works in 1983 (which were exhibited in Portsmouth City Museums in February-March 1983) and 150 works in 1984 (which were exhibited in Salford, in the City of Salford Art Gallery in September-October 1984, under the title 'The Perera Collection of paintings, drawings and etchings by Adolphe Valette'). In 1987 and 1991, a large part of the Perera Collection was dispersed at auctions held in Christies, London from where they have found their way into many private collections.

Still in the 1970s, the exhibition organised in 1976 by the Manchester City Art Gallery to mark the centenary of Valette's birth was another significant event in the development of Valette's artistic ascendancy in Manchester as it had a real impact upon a new generation of artists who were confronted with these canvases for the first time. One only has to look at certain canvases by Bob Richardson, William Turner, and many others, to realise that these artists have been able to draw upon the melting pot cast by Valette. In 1994, the Manchester City Art gallery mounted another exhibition of Valette's work: 'Adolphe Valette, a French Influence in Manchester'. More recently, other younger artists have continued to draw inspiration from him. Liam Spencer, a contemporary artist who depicts the city of Manchester with instinct, colour and rhythm, has acknowledged the significance of the small direct studies painted from life by Valette.[23] These are the 'second generation heirs', who did not know Valette during his lifetime, but who are living proof of the ever-present influence of Adolphe Valette on art in the North West of England.

Epilogue

Having traversed the life of Adolphe Valette, the overwhelming feeling we are left with along the way is one of having learned an important lesson about life. This talented man, with such a lively and creative spirit, who left his homeland for the North of England which he proceeded to glorify, compels our admiration.

His oeuvre is a work of love and truth. He represented the beauty, tumult and vigour of Manchester in his misted lights and atmospheric effects. Subsequently, he depicted the gentleness of the Beaujolais region, its brown, green, pink or gilded land, its farms and its hillsides. And, throughout his work as a portraitist, he transcended the love and affection he held for those individuals he cherished.

Adolphe Valette was an indefatigable worker in the pursuit of excellence, a man with an open spirit. His bounty could be read in the calm smile that we see in his self-portraits or in the rare photos that we have of him.

His passion was for his work: his work as a painter.

It is because of his joy in painting that he was able to set aside the dramas and difficulties of his life, all the bitternesses, sadnesses and pain.

Thus, we imagine him, at the twilight of his years, in the midst of wartime, in his house in Blaceret, cleaning his palette and brushes, sharpening his pencils, to prepare himself, despite his poor health, for the next day's session; as it was painting that gave him his life spirit, and which was his passion.

In the course of our research, we were able to locate his tomb at the cemetery of Villefranche-sur-Saône.

Go there and pay him tribute, and, after the Manchester haze, allow yourself to be touched by the gentleness of the region where he spent his last years and that he loved so much.

Brief Chronology

13 October 1876
Born in Saint-Etienne, to a middle-class family.

Circa 1891
Enrolled at the Ecole Régionale des Arts Industriels in Saint-Etienne; in 1893, he came first in the engraving class. Amongst his tutors was Jean Dablin, who was later to be the founder of the 'Société des Arts du Forez' of which Valette was to become a member.

1895
Enrolled at the Ecole Municipale de Dessin de la Guillotière in Lyon, where he won a large number of distinctions. Amongst his teachers was Tony Tollet, a painter very much in vogue in Lyon at that time.

1900
Enrolled at the Ecole Municipale de Beaux-Arts et des Arts Décoratifs in Bordeaux. He won numerous academic distinctions and worked during the day as a 'professional draughtsman'.

1903 and 1904
First exhibitions in Bordeaux, at the Société des Arts Girondins.

1904 or 1905
Arrived in England, for unknown reasons. Studied for a while in London at Birkbeck College and then went to Manchester. Worked during the day at the printing company Norbury Natzio and Co Ltd and in the evening as a student at the Municipal School of Art.

1905/6
He was appointed 'Master of Painting and Drawing' at the Manchester Municipal School of Art. He was much liked by his students, who valued the contribution of his French experience and his understanding of impressionism. L.S. Lowry was one of his pupils in the 'Life Drawing' classes and remained so for many years.

1906-7
First known oil paintings by Valette that have survived.

1908
First known 'Manchester-scape' by Valette: this is dated 18 March and has as its subject the Manchester Ship Canal.

1909
Married one of his students, Gabriela de Bolivar, of Venezuelan nationality; Gabriela was to be the artistic muse for his portraits.

Creation of 'Windsor Bridge on the Irwell'.

First exhibition of his canvases in the UK at the Autumn Exhibition at the Walker Art Gallery in Liverpool. He contributed further to this annual exhibition up to 1912.

1910
Birth of his only child, Pierre, who was soon nicknamed Peter or Tita.

Creation of 'Albert Square', 'Oxford Road', and 'Hansom Cab at All Saints'.

1911
Creation of 'Old Cab at All Saints'.

1912
Co-founder of the 'Society of Modern Artists'. Seven of his own works were shown at the first exhibition of this society.

Creation of 'India House', 'Bailey Bridge', and 'Under Windsor Bridge on the Irwell'.

1913
Change of name of the 'Society of Modern Artists' to the 'Society of Modern Painters'. At the exhibition of 1913 the avant-garde tendencies of certain members of the Society generated criticisms from some art critics.

New teaching roles at the Manchester School of Art, including the 'Etching Class' which had begun on an unofficial basis in *c*.1909.

Creations of 'York Street leading to Charles Street', and 'The Irwell'.

1917
Death of his wife Gabriela.

1918
Valette's timetable at the Manchester School of Art is extended by the addition of numerous additional courses.

First solo exhibition at the Finnigans Showrooms, in Manchester, which was a resounding success and confirmed his reputation.

1919
Married a fellow French national, Andrée Pallez, who was a teacher of French at the University of Manchester.

1920
Second solo exhibition at the Finnigans Showrooms in Manchester which was equally as successful as the first.

Promoted to the position of 'Principal Master of Drawing' at the School of Art.

Health worries, amongst others arising from the poor working conditions at the School. He resigns his position.

Given that his reputation was at this point well-established, he began to receive an increasing number of commissions from public and private establishments.

1921
Took a part-time teaching position at the Bolton Municipal School of Art.

1922
In parallel with his role at the Bolton Art School, took up a further part-time teaching role at the University of Manchester.

1924, 1925, 1926 and 1928
Further exhibitions with the 'Society of Modern Painters'.

1928
The purchase of nine of Valette's major canvases by the Manchester City Art Gallery.

Leaves Manchester and moves permanently to Blacé to the house he had inherited following the death of his mother.

His wife Andrée remained in England to continue teaching and Valette retained the services of a housekeeper, a young neighbour, Maria Lafond, who became his second artistic muse, for his portraits.

Revived the links he had always maintained with the 'Société des Arts du Forez', in Saint-Etienne.

From 1928 to 1940, he made many trips in the Midi, Alps, Pyrenees and other parts of France, and to the Balearics, and each time returned with a large number of water colours and oil paintings that he continued to sell in Manchester.

1929
Death of his son Peter, who had remained in England, from tubercular meningitis.

Purchase by the Musée de Saint-Etienne, of the canvas 'Rocher Saint-Michel au Puy'.

Exhibition at the Société Lyonnaise des Beaux-Arts, to which he continued to send works until 1939.

1930
Co-founded, with, amongst others, Jean Puy, the 'Association des Artistes Foréziens' in Saint-Etienne. Paul Signac was an honorary member.

Exhibition at the Salon des Artistes Foréziens, to which he continued to provide works until 1935.

1931
Personal exhibition of his works at the Galerie Livet in Saint-Etienne.

1936
Exposition at the Salon d'Automne, in Lyon, to which he continued to provide works until 1940.

1940 and thereafter:
Deteriorating health.

1942
Died on 18 April in a hospital in Lyon. He was buried in Lyon in the public graveyard in the Guillotière Nouveau cemetery.

1943
His widow Andrée arranged for his remains to be exhumed from the grave in Lyon and laid to rest next to those of his mother in a perpetual concession of his family in the cemetery of Villefranche-sur-Saône, where he still lies.

Summary of Documented Exhibitions by Valette during his Lifetime

1903
Société des Artistes Girondins, Salon d'Automne, Bordeaux.
Two charcoal drawings, one of an Autumn landscape.

1904
Société des Artistes Girondins, Salon d'Automne, Bordeaux.
Two drypoints.

1909
Autumn Exhibition, Walker Art Gallery, Liverpool:
324. Windsor Bridge, Manchester £30
885. Matinée d'Eté £60
1276. Portrait of a Child (drypoint) 3gns
1293. Portrait of an Old Man (print) 3gns

1910
Autumn Exhibition, Walker Art Gallery, Liverpool
93. Oxford Road, Manchester £80
172. Intimité £30
1424. Soleil Couchant (print) 1gn
1705. Affamés (coloured etching) 3gns
1724. Le Vieux Berger (ditto) 3gns
1851. Rêverie (drypoint)

1911
Autumn Exhibition, Walker Art Gallery, Liverpool:
1285. Albert Square £100

1912
Autumn Exhibition, Walker Art Gallery, Liverpool
9. Pastorale £120
165. Dover Street, Manchester £100

Society of Modern Artists, Orme's Buildings, Manchester (September)[1]
42. The Hill
43. Still Life
44. Oxford Road. £85
45. The Bridge, Salford
46. Portrait
81. Portrait d'Enfant
82. Coloured etching

1913
Society of Modern Painters, Orme's Buildings, Manchester (October)[1]
52. The Irwell £21
53. Dover Street £31
56. Swinton Bridge 15gns
57. Point de Salles (pastel) 10gns
58. Idol £21
59. Aiguille de Varens 10gns
60. Whitworth Institute 15gns
61. Vallée de l'Arve 10gns
160. Trafford Bridge 12gns

1915
Manchester War Fund Art Union Exhibition[1]
193. A Welsh Farm

1918
Finnigans Showrooms, Deansgate, Manchester (4-21 October)[2]

Oils and Pastels
1. Albert Square £105
2. Le Sol Natal £60
3. At the Seaside £35
4. The Old Cab £105
5. Group of Cattle £60
6. Landscape, Anglesey £35
7. Landscape, Derbyshire £35
8. Landscape, Anglesey £35
9. India House £80
10. Landscape, Wales. £65
11. Cattle in Wales. £60
12. All Saints, Manchester £105
13. Langdales Pikes £40
14. Landscape, near Soissons £35
15. Landscape, near Matlock £35
16. Scène Champêtre. £60
17. The Bridge, Salford £105
18. Landscape, Anglesey £40
19. Le Retour des Champs £50
20. Flowers and Fruits £21
21. La Paix £25
22. La Moisson, Hartennes £30
23. Landscape, Haute Savoie 15gns
24. Benllech Bay £21
25. Plymouth Grove (Pastel)
26. The Grain Elevator, Manchester £25
27. Landscape, near Ambleside £30
28. York Street, Manchester. £40
29. Trafford Bridge £35
30. Beaujolais, France. £80
31. Flowers £30
32. Under the Bridge, Salford £40
33. Cueillette de Pommes. £25
34. Plymouth Grove, July £50
35. La fuite en Egypte £30
36. L'Orage £30
37. Scène Antique 15gns
38. Leda 15gns
39. La Toilette 15gns

40. Portrait of an Artist
41. An Artist in her Studio
42. Portrait of my Son
43. A Discovery ... £21
44. Landscape of the Alps ... 12gns
45. Portrait
46. In the Garden
47. Portrait
48. Breeze of the Sea
49. Still Life ... £25
50. Point de Salles, France (Pastel) ... £25
51. Aiguille de Varens, France (Pastel) ... £25
52. Le Mont Blanc, France (Pastel) ... £25
53. Suzette ... £50
54. Baigneuses (Décoration) ... £80
55. Scène des Champs ... £65
56. Alpes Françaises ... £30
57. The Model ... £40
58. The Ghost, Hamlet (Pastel) ... £25
59. Vallée de l'Arve (Pastel) ... £25
60. Study of a Head ... -
61. Still Life ... £21
62. A French Girl ... 10gns
63. Girl with Flowers ... 12gns
64. Still Life ... £35
65. Sous le Feuillage ... £60
66. Portrait ... -
68. Portrait ... -
69. Portrait (Pastel) ... -
70. Portrait ... -
71. Cluses, France ... 15gns
72. Vieux Berger ... £25
73. Faucheurs ... 15gns
74. In Summer ... 15gns
75. The Turning of The Road ... £21
76. Paysan et ses Chèvres ... 15gns
77. Peasant Resting ... £21
78. Landscape, Cumberland ... 15gns
79. Paysan Français ... 15gns
80. Scene in Wales ... £21
81. Landscape in Wales ... £21

Watercolours

82. A View of Matlock ... 8gns
83. Benlech Bay ... 10gns
84. Chapel Stile ... 8gns
85. Farm in Cumberland ... 8gns
86. Farm at Cronford ... 8gns
87. A Road, Matlock ... 8gns
88. Landscape, near Ambleside ... 8gns
89. Farm at Burnage ... 8gns
90. Landscape at Burbage ... 8gns
91. The Road to Matlock ... 8gns
92. The Road to Ambleside ... 10gns
93. The Langdale Valley ... 10gns
94. Buxton ... 8gns
95. Bakewell ... 8gns
96. Farm at Langdale ... 8gns
97. Landscape, near Windermere ... 8gns
98. Matlock, Bath ... 10gns
99. The Road to Chapel Stile ... 10gns
100. Elterwater, Lake District ... 8gns
101. Benlech Bay, Anglesey ... 10gns
102. Landscape, near Matlock ... 10gns
103. Romeo and Juliet ... 10gns

Oils and Pastels

104. Autumn, Winter ... 15gns
105. Spring, Summer ... 15gns
106. Ceiling for a Ballroom ... 15gns
108. Orpheus ... 15gns
109. Sweet Peas ... £21
110. The Goats ... £25
111. Le Soir (Décoration) ... £25
112. Roses ... £21
113. Sketch for Decoration ... 15gns
114. A Canal, Manchester ... 12gns
115. Still Life ... 15gns
116. Au Bord de la Mer (Décoration) ... £30
117. Les Bûcherons (Décoration) ... £30
118. Still Life ... £30
119. Scène Pastorale (Sketch) ... £21
120. Sketch for Decoration ... 15gns
(No 121 in Catalogue)
122. Baigneuses ... £25
123. Landscape with Goats (Pastel) ... 15gns
124. Still Life ... £25

Etchings

125. Coloured Etchings ... 4gns
126. L'Agonie ... 3gns
127. Femme nue ... 3gns
128. Sunset ... 2gns
129. The Cliff ... 3gns
130. Coloured Etching ... 4gns
131. Evening ... 3gns
132. A Shepherd and his Dog ... 3gns
133. Landscape ... 2gns
134. André ... 3gns
135. Les Moutons ... 3gns
136. Job ... 4gns
137. Les Alpes, France ... 3gns
138. Landscape ... 2gns
139. Portrait d'Enfant ... 3gns

1920

(December) Finnigans Showrooms, Deansgate, Manchester[2]

Watercolours

1. View from Church Stretton ... 12gns
2. Cattle resting ... 12gns
3. At Church Stretton ... 12gns
4. Cattle in Wales ... 12gns
5. La Tallebarde, Beaujolais ... 12gns
6. Blacé, France ... 12gns
7. Ludlow Castle ... 12gns
8. Old Bridge, Ludlow ... 12gns
9. A Walk at Ludlow ... 12gns
10. Near Grasmere ... 10gns
11. Round the Castle, Ludlow ... 12gns
12. Cheadle ... 12gns
13. Sunset in Cumberland ... 12gns
14. La Fenaison ... 12gns
15. Shropshire Castle ... 12gns
16. View of Church Stretton ... 12gns
17. The *Hotel Capel Curig* ... 12gns
18. A Cottage, Rudyard Lake

Etchings

19. Paysan Français ... 3gns
20. St-Séverin, Paris ... 3gns
21. Landscape with Cows ... 4gns

22. A Picnic..2gns
23. Cows Resting..4gns
24. Cow and Calf..4gns
25. Baigneuses..2gns

Watercolours
26. A group of Cattle..10gns
27. Cattle in the Shade..10gns
28. Le Vacher..10gns
29. Vaches au Pâturage..10gns
30. Vache en montagne..10gns
31. Cattle drinking..12gns
32. Cattle in Westmorland..12gns
33. Bishop's Castle..12gns

Oils
34. Farm Yard..£60
35. Moutons à l'Ombre..£30
36. Sheep in Wales..£25
37. Morning Effect..£35
38. Still Life..£35
39. The Poultry Yard..£80
40. Vieux Jardin..£16
41. Paysan et ses Chèvres..£21
42. Sketch for a War Memorial..£50
43. Castle on the Hill Top..£75
44. Still Life..£35
45. Leda..£63
46. Still Life..£35
47. Still Life..£25
48. Still Life..£25
49. Henry Vitofski, Esq..-
50. Rolda..£21
51. Portrait (lent by Mrs Hurst)..-
52. Sketch of a Boy..£15
53. Sketch of a Girl..£15
54. Ship Canal..£21
55. Portrait of Miss Hayes..-
56. Laveuse..£12
57. Portrait in Open Air
58. Portrait of a Little Girl
59. In the Shade..£60
60. Sketch for a Portrait
61. Portrait of an Old Lady
62. Portrait of an Old Man
63. Le Peintre H. Vitofski
64. Portrait of my Mother
65. Profile (lent by Mrs Dowling)
66. Portrait (lent by L.V. Gladwell)
67. Portrait (lent by Mrs Gladwell)
68. Portrait (lent by Mrs Forbes)
69. Portrait of R. Carruthers
70. Portrait (lent by H. Doyle, Esq)
71. Portrait (lent by Mrs Rowland)
72. Portrait (lent by H.B. Nicolas, Esq)
73. Portrait (lent by Mme L.L. Pallez)
74. Portrait (lent by H. Doyle, Esq)
75. Portraits d'Enfants (lent by Mme E. May)
76. Group (lent by Mrs Gonne)
77. Portrait (lent by J. Milner)
78. Portrait (lent by Dr Dowling)
79. Portrait
80. Portrait (lent by J.H. Reynolds, Esq)
81. Tita

Watercolours
82. Church Stretton..12gns
83. Old Château, Blacé..12gns
84. Place Carnot, Lyon..12gns
85. Whitcliff, Ludlow..12gns
86. Near Church Stretton..12gns
87. View at Cromford..12gns
88. Castle Walk, Ludlow..12gns
89. On the Hills, Capel Curig..12gns
90. Near the Lake..12gns
91. Stokesay Castle..12gns
92. Place Bellecour, Lyon..12gns
93. Verrex, Italy..12gns
94. View of Bishop's Castle..12gns
95. Rudyard Lake..10gns
96. Street, Church Stretton..12gns
97. Landscape, Cattle in Wales..12gns
98. Montaud, St-Etienne..12gns
99. View from Church Stretton..10gns
100. Cow and Calf..10gns

1924

(December) Society of Modern Painters 33 Blackfriars St., Manchester[1] (complete list not known, but exhibits include picture of horsemen and clouds)

1925

(20-31 January) Society of Modern Painters, 33 Blackfriars St., Manchester[1]

Watercolours
50. The Bridge on the Loire..6gns
51. Landscape, St-Bonnet..8gns
52. Mill at La Voute..8gns
53. Polignac..8gns
54. St-Julien..8gns
55. Montinelas..8gns

1926 (April) Society of Modern Painters, 2 Mount Street, Manchester[1] (full list not known, but several portraits including ones of Ahmed Loutfi, an Egyptian poet; a girl reading the *Daily Mail*; H. Vitofski, no 49 and Rowley Smart, no 126)

1928 (March) Society of Modern Painters, City Art Gallery, Manchester[1]
213. Studland..12gns
214. Flowers..£21
215. Flowers..£21
223. Le Pont Neuf..15gns

1929

Société Lyonnaise des Beaux-Arts, Salon 1929, Palais Municipal, Quai de Bondy, Lyon
485 Portrait
486 Fleurs

1930

Les Artistes Foréziens, Ier Salon de Printemps, 3-25 May 1930, Hôtel de Ville de Saint-Etienne
Le Turban Rose
Fleurs
Les Nouvelles
L'Eglise (Rochetaillée)
Les Ruines

Société Lyonnaise des Beaux-Arts, Salon 1930, Palais Municipal, Quai de Bondy, Lyon
486. Paysanne et ses Chèvres
487. Portrait

1931
Les Artistes Foréziens, IIème Salon de Printemps, 18 April-10 May 1931, Hôtel de Ville de Saint-Etienne
Complete list of exhibits not known, except
160. Devant la Maison

Société Lyonnaise des Beaux-Arts, Salon 1931, Palais Municipal, Quai de Bondy, Lyon
495. Esthera
496. Paysage
497. Fleurs

1932
Les Artistes Foréziens, IIIème Salon de Printemps, 9 April-8 May 1932
101. Paysanne et ses chèvres... ... ... 1.800 francs
102. Rochetaillée... ... ... 1.500 francs
103. Saint-Julien ... ... 1.500 francs
104. Vieille Maison .. .. 1.500 francs

Société Lyonnaise des Beaux-Arts, Salon 1932, Palais Municipal, Quai de Bondy, Lyon
502. Le Turban Rose

1933
Les Artistes Foréziens, IVème Salon de Printemps, 7 April-7 May 1933, Palais des Arts de Saint-Etienne
234. L'Échaudage des Vignes
235. Paysans
236. Le Chevrier
237. Paysage
238. Jeune Polonaise

Société Lyonnaise des Beaux-Arts, Salon 1933, Palais Municipal, Quai de Bondy, Lyon
495. Caladoise
496. Fillette et ses Chèvres

1934
Les Artistes Foréziens, Vème Salon de Printemps, Hotel de Ville de Saint-Etienne
Le Chien Malade

Société Lyonnaise des Beaux-Arts, Salon 1934, Palais Municipal, Quai de Bondy, Lyon
433. Femme lavant
434. Le Chevrier

1935
Les Artistes Foréziens, VIème Salon de Printemps, 24 February-24 March 1935, Hôtel de Ville de Saint-Etienne
388. Un Notable
385. Maison Beaujolaise.. ... ... 1.200 francs
386. Fleurs.. ... ... 1.200 francs
387. Au Pays de Galles ... ... 2.400 francs

Société Lyonnaise des Beaux-Arts, Salon 1935, Palais Municipal, Quai de Bondy, Lyon
437. Paysage
438. Après-midi

1936
Société Lyonnaise des Beaux-Arts, Salon 1936, Palais Municipal, Quai de Bondy, Lyon
449. Portrait
450. Fleurs

Société du Salon d'Automne, 4 October-15 November 1936, Palais Municipal des Expositions, Quai de Bondy, Lyon
126-1. Basse-cour
126-2. Tête de Femme

1937
Société Lyonnaise des Beaux-Arts, Salon 1937, Palais Municipal, Quai de Bondy, Lyon
395. Nus
396. Portrait

Société du Salon d'Automne, 9 October-14 November 1937 Palais Municipal des Expositions, Quai de Bondy, Lyon
118-1. Nu
118-2. Portrait
118-3. Fleurs

1938
Société Lyonnaise des Beaux-Arts, Salon 1938, Palais Municipal, Quai de Bondy, Lyon
395. Jeune Fille
396. Paysans

Société du Salon d'Automne, 1938, Lyon
115-1. La Ménagère
115-2. Scène Champêtre
115-3. Arundel's Farm
115-4. Ferme Beaujolaise

1939
Société Lyonnaise des Beaux-Arts, Salon 1939, Palais Municipal, Quai de Bondy, Lyon
417. Portrait d'Enfant
418. Burrington Hall, Herefordshire

1940
Salon d'Automne de Lyon, 1940, Lyon
107-1. Ombre et Lumière
107-2. Le Retour
107-3. Vaches au Pâturage
107-4. Paysan

Union des Sociétés Artistiques de Lyon, Salon Unique 1940, Palais Municipal, Quai de Bondy, Lyon
193. Polignac (watercolour)

Works by Valette in Public Collections

MANCHESTER ART GALLERY
Life Drawing of a Male Nude with a Cane
Chalk on paper, *c.*1910-12,
62.3cm x 47.5cm

Drawing from the Antique: Cast of a Faun
Charcoal on paper, 1901 or 1904
61cm x 45.5cm

Life Drawing of a Male Nude
Pencil and black chalk on paper, April 1911
61cm x 46.5cm

Les Graces de Pilon
Black crayon and pencil on paper
60.8cm x 45.6cm

Life Drawing of a Bearded Man
Black chalk, red chalk and white heightening on paper
63.5cm x 46.5cm

Self-Portrait
Oil on linen, *c.*1917
45cm x 60.4cm

Old Cab at All Saints
Oil on jute, 1911
115.5cm x 155.3cm

Hansom Cab at All Saints
Oil on jute, 1910
115.5cm x 155.3cm

India House, Manchester
Oil on jute, 1912
142.4cm x 86.1cm

Portrait of Rowley Smart
Oil on panel, 1925
66.3cm x 55cm

Windsor Bridge on the Irwell
Oil on jute, 1909
50.4cm x 61.1cm

Flowers and Fruit
Oil on canvas, 1917
49.8cm x 58.8cm

Annie Barnett
Oil on board, 1917
39.5cm x 46.9cm

Study for the Irwell
Oil on cardboard, *c.*1913
16.3cm x 8.8cm

Castlegate, Salford
Oil on canvas, 1912
Size not stated

Interior of a Cathedral
Etching and aquatint on paper, 1907
20.1cm x 13.5cm

Girl at her Toilet
Oil on millboard
40.1cm x 32.3cm

Bailey Bridge
Oil on jute, 1912
155cm x 115cm

Portrait of John Henry Reynolds
Oil on canvas, 1919
81.7cm x 56.2cm

Oxford Road, Manchester
Oil on canvas, 1910
127.4cm x 101.5cm

Under Windsor Bridge on the Irwell, Manchester
Oil on linen on jute, 1912
48.2cm x 61cm

Albert Square, Manchester
Oil on jute, 1910
152cm x 114cm

Study for Albert Square
Oil on cardboard, *c.*1910
12cm x 15.5cm

Study for Albert Square
Oil on board, *c.*1910
Size not stated

Study for Base of Statues, Albert Square
Oil on board, *c.*1910
8cm x 15cm

Study for Albert Square
Oil on board, *c.*1910
14.5cm x 23cm

Le Puy
Oil on canvas, *c.*1920s-1942
14.6cm x 23cm

Self-Portrait Study
Oil on canvas mounted on board, *c.*1912
60.8cm x 48cm

Portrait of May Aimee Smith
Oil on panel, 1918
55.5cm by 38.1cm

York Street, leading to Charles Street, Manchester
Oil on linen, 1913
81.3cm x 60cm

PRESTON, HARRIS MUSEUM AND GALLERY
Near Ambleside
Watercolour, 1916
23.4cm x 30cm

SAINT-ETIENNE METROPOLE, MUSEE D'ART MODERNE
Rocher St-Michel au Puy
Oil on canvas
57cm x 98cm

Portrait de la Mère de l'Artiste
Oil on canvas
42cm x 32cm

SALFORD, CITY ART GALLERY AND MUSEUM
Still Life
Oil on canvas, 1916
49cm x 64cm

SALFORD, THE LOWRY
Drawing from the Antique
Charcoal on paper
60.7cm x 45.5cm

THE STOCKPORT WAR MEMORIAL AND ART GALLERY
Still Life (Fruit)
Oil on canvas, 1912
44cm x 75cm

THE UNIVERSITY OF MANCHESTER, THE WHITWORTH ART GALLERY
Etching on paper
Size not stated

Saint-Tropez
Watercolour and pencil on paper, 1934
28cm x 37.9cm

References

***Introduction*, pp.xiii-xv**

1. Article signed J.C. in an unnamed Saint-Etienne newspaper, published in 1942, with the title 'Adolphe Valette, peintre et graveur'. [Adolphe Valette, painter and engraver.]

1. *The Formative Years in France*, pp.1-15

1. Marriage certificate of Adolphe Valette and Gabriela de Bolivar in the District of Chorlton in 1909, and marriage certificate of Pierre Adolphe Valette and Hélène Andrée Pallez in the District of Chorlton in 1919.
2. Sandra Martin, *Adolphe Valette, A French Influence in Manchester*, Manchester City Art Galleries, 1994, p.11.
3. *Op. cit.*, p.12.
4. E. Hardouin, 'La peinture stéphanoise', in *Grande Encyclopédie du Forez et des Communes de la Loire*, sous la direction de Gilbert Gardes, Horvath.
5. *Ibid.*
6. Article signed J.C. in an unnamed Saint-Etienne newspaper, published in 1942, with the title 'Adolphe Valette, peintre et graveur' [Adolphe Valette, painter and engraver].
7. Procès-verbaux de la Distribution des Prix aux Elèves de l'Ecole Nationale des Beaux-Arts et des Ecoles Municipales de la Ville de Lyon, 1896, 1897, 1898 and 1899.
8. Ecole Municipale des Beaux-Arts et des Arts Décoratifs, Ville de Bordeaux, 'Concours de 1901' and 'Concours de 1902', Bordeaux, printed in Bordeaux, Delmas.
9. Ecole Municipale des Beaux-Arts et des Arts Décoratifs, Ville de Bordeaux, Concours de 1903, Distribution des Prix, Prix accordés aux Elèves de l'Ecole, Bordeaux, printed in Bordeaux, Delmas, 1903, p.18.
10. Archives Municipales Bordeaux, 'Ecole Municipale des Beaux-Arts et des Arts Décoratifs, Concours 1903, Rapport du Jury, printed in Bordeaux, Delmas, 1903, p.18.

2. *The Manchester Years: The Flourishing of an Artistic Personality*, pp.16-62

1. Elisabeth Lee, 'Pierre Adolphe Valette (1876-1942)', Final Year thesis for BA (Hons) course, Department of History of Art, University of Manchester, 1976, p.5.
2. *Ibid.*
3. *Blue Guide*, France, Ian Robertson, A. & C. Black, London and W.W. Norton, New York, 1988.
4. Cecil Stewart, *A Short History of the Regional College of Art*, Manchester, 1954, pp.3 and 9.
5. Alexis de Tocqueville, *Oeuvres complètes: Voyages en Angleterre, Irlande, Suisse et Algérie*, Ed. J.P. Mayer, t. V fasc. 2, Gallimard, Paris, 1958, pp.78-82.
6. *Liverpool Courrier*, 17 September 1910.
7. *Daily News*, 1910, 'Art in Liverpool – Autumn Exhibition at the Walker Art Gallery – British and Continental Pictures compared'.
8. Elisabeth Lee, 'Pierre Adolphe Valette (1876-1942)', Final Year thesis for BA (Hons) course, Department of History of Art, University of Manchester, 1976, p.18.
9. Letters to Alice Monet, 26 Jan., 3 Feb., 10 March 1901 (Wildenstein 1974-91, IV, letters 1588, 1593, 1616) in Sylvie Patin, Catalogue of the exhibition *Turner, Whistler, Monet*, Tate Publishing in association with the Art Gallery of Ontario, p.180.
10. Alan Kidd, *Manchester*, Ryburn Publishing, Keele University Press, 1993.
11. Stuart Hylton, *A History of Manchester*, Phillimore, 2003, p.103.
12. *Op. cit.*, p.191.
13. *Op. cit.*, p.189.
14. Alan Kidd, *Manchester*, Ryburn Publishing, Keele University Press, 1993, p.167.
15. Alexis de Tocqueville, *Oeuvres complètes: Voyages en Angleterre, Irlande, Suisse et Algérie*, Ed. J.P. Mayer, t. V fasc.2, Gallimard, Paris, 1958, pp.78-82.
16. Alan Kidd, *Manchester*, Ryburn Publishing, Keele University Press, 1993.
17. *Ibid.*
18. Stuart Hylton, *A History of Manchester*, Phillimore, 2003, p.165.
19. *Op. cit.*, pp.160, 188.
20. Elisabeth Lee, 'Pierre Adolphe Valette (1876-1942)', Final Year thesis for BA (Hons) course, Department of History of Art, University of Manchester, 1976, page 5.
21. *Ibid.*

22. Manchester Geographical Society, addressed in the Geographic Hall, on Tuesday 16 February 1909.
23. Manchester Academy of Fine Arts, Exhibition Catalogues 1908 and 1909.
24. Municipal School of Art, Calendar for the Session 1907-8.
25. Sandra Martin, *Adolphe Valette, A French Influence in Manchester*, Manchester City Art Galleries, 1994, p.19.
26. Minutes of the Board of the School of Art, 1906.
27. Elisabeth Lee, 'Pierre Adolphe Valette (1876-1942)', Final Year thesis for BA (Hons) course, Department of History of Art, University of Manchester, 1976, p.9.
28. *Manchester Guardian*, 19 August 1942, obituary notice of Adolphe Valette, by Laurence Haward.
29. Cecil Stewart, *A Short History of the Regional College of Art, Manchester*, 1954, Royal Manchester Institution.
30. D. Jeremiah, *A Hundred Years and More*, Manchester Polytechnic, 1980, p.28.
31. *Op. cit.*, p.34.
32. Shelley Rohde, *L.S. Lowry, A Biography*, The Lowry Press, 3rd edition, 1999, p.75.
33. *Manchester Evening News*, 'City honours the French Collection, and artist Bert, 95, explains why', 1994.
34. Shelley Rohde, *L.S. Lowry, A Biography*, The Lowry Press, 3rd edition, 1999, p.69.
35. *Manchester Evening News*, 'City honours the French Collection, and artist Bert, 95, explains why', 1994.
36. D. Jeremiah, *A Hundred Years and More*, Manchester Polytechnic, 1980, p.17.
37. School Calendar of the Municipal School of Art, 1907-8, 1909-20.
38. D. Jeremiah, *A Hundred Years and More*, Manchester Polytechnic, 1980, p.34.
39. Minutes of the Board of Studies, Municipal School of Art, 1907-8.
40. From a letter written by A.H. Knighton-Hammond to the Editor of the *Manchester Guardian*, 24 August 1942, in Elisabeth Lee, 'Pierre Adolphe Valette (1876-1942)', Final Year thesis for BA (Hons) course, Department of History of Art, University of Manchester, 1976.
41. *Manchester Guardian*, 19 August 1942. 'Obituary notice of Adolphe Valette', by Laurence Haward.
42. Mervyn Levy, *Laurence Stephen Lowry, A Short Monograph*, Painters of Today Series, 1961, Studio Books, London.
43. School Calendar of the Municipal School of Art, 1911-12.
44. Minutes of the Board of Teachers, Municipal School of Art, 17 May 1909.
45. Cecil Stewart, *A Short History of the Regional College of Art*, Manchester, 1954, Royal Manchester Institution.
46. Minutes of the Board of Teachers, Municipal School of Art, 7 July 1915.
47. Josephine Duddle, 'Journal', Sept 1911-July 1914.
48. Sandra Martin, *Adolphe Valette, A French Influence in Manchester*, Manchester City Art Galleries, 1994, p.29.
49. Interview of L.S. Lowry, North West Sound Archive, 1967.
50. *Manchester Guardian*, 17 September 1910, 'Liverpool Exhibition'.
51. Elisabeth Lee, 'Pierre Adolphe Valette (1876-1942)', Final Year thesis for BA (Hons) course, Department of History of Art, University of Manchester, 1976.
52. *Manchester Guardian*, 6 May 1937, Article entitled 'A Manchester Movement'.
53. *Manchester Guardian*, 19 September 1912.
54. *Ibid.*
55. *Manchester Guardian*, 23 October 1913.
56. *Ibid.*
57. *Ibid.*
58. *Manchester Guardian*, 6 May 1937.
59. *Manchester City News*, 25 October 1913.
60. *Manchester City News*, 24 April 1926.
61. Sandra Martin, *Adolphe Valette, A French Influence in Manchester*, Manchester City Art Galleries, 1994, quoting the *Manchester Guardian*, p.73.
62. *Manchester Evening News*, 4 October 1918.
63. *Manchester City News*, 5 October 1918.
64. *Manchester Guardian*, 9 December 1920, 'Pictures by Mr A. Valette', signed B.D.T.
65. Minutes of the Board of Studies, 7 July 1919.
66. Cecil Stewart, *A Short History of the Regional College of Art*, Manchester, 1954, p.23.
67. Minutes of Senate, University of Manchester: 11 October 1917, 6 June 1918, 5 June 1919 and Annual Report of the Department of French for academic session, 1917/18.
68. Preface by Geoffrey Green for the catalogue for the 1976 exhibition at the Manchester City Art Gallery.
69. Shelley Rohde, *L.S Lowry, A Biography*, The Lowry Press, 3rd edition, 1999, p.146.
70. *A Short History of the Bolton College of Art and Design, 1876-1976.*
71. Minutes of Senate of the University of Manchester, 4 July 1922, 20 January 1927, 1 December 1927.
72. *The Journal of Decorative Art*, April 1921.
73. Elisabeth Lee, 'Pierre Adolphe Valette (1876-1942)', Final Year thesis for BA (Hons) course, Department of History of Art, University of Manchester, 1976, p.34.
74. *Op. cit.*, p.33.
75. *Op. cit.*, p.36.

76. *Op., cit.*, p.37.
77. Sandra Martin, *Adolphe Valette, A French Influence in Manchester*, Manchester City Art Galleries, 1994, p.35.

3. *The Return to France*, pp.63-78

1. Minutes of Senate, University of Manchester.
2. Postcard of Adolphe Valette to Maria Lafond written in Moustiers-Sainte-Marie, 15 May 1933.
3. *La Région Illustrée*, No.57, 1931.
4. *La Région Illustrée*, No.79, 1932.
5. Postcard sent from Vernoux, by Maria Lafond to her mother.
6. Postcard of Adolphe Valette to Maria Lafond, written in Moustiers-Ste Marie, 15 May 1933.
7. Elisabeth Lee, 'Pierre Adolphe Valette (1876-1942)', Final Year thesis for BA (Hons) course, Department of History of Art, University of Manchester, 1976, p.39.
8. *Manchester Guardian*, 19 August 1942.
9. *Les Amis du Musée de St-Etienne, Exposition rétrospective des peintres foréziens*, 29 avril-21 mai 1945, Musée de Saint-Etienne.
10. *Jersey Evening Post*, Friday 2 June 1972, 'Exhibition of paintings by Adolphe Valette at A. de Gruchy and Co.'

4. *The Different Facets of Adolphe Valette's Artistic Talent*, pp.79-112

1. Quote after a letter from A.H. Knighton of Somerset to the editor of the *Manchester Guardian*, 24 August 1942 in Elisabeth Lee, 'Pierre Adolphe Valette (1876-1942)', Final Year thesis for BA (Hons) course, Department of History of Art, University of Manchester, 1976.
2. Bernard Denvir, *Chronique de l'Impressionnisme*, Editions de La Martinière, 1993, p.107.
3. Letter of Monet to Alice, 1 February 1901, in Wildenstein 1974-91, III, letter 1591, from Catalogue of exhibition *Turner, Whistler, Monet*, English version, Sylvie Patin, p.189, Tate publishing in association with the Art Gallery of Ontario, 2004.
4. Term coined in *The Studio International*, November 1923.
5. D. Jeremiah, *A Hundred Years and More*, Manchester Polytechnic, 1980, p.32.
6. Whistler, Public lecture, Prince's Hall, Piccadilly, 20 February 1885, from the original manuscript in Glasgow University (Whistler, W 780).
7. Gustave Geffroy (Geffroy, 1924, pp.308-11) quoted by Sylvie Patin, in Catalogue of the exhibition *Turner, Whistler, Monet*, English version, page 192, Tate publishing in association with the Art Gallery of Ontario, 2004.
8. Elisabeth Lee, quoting a letter from Mme Andrée Valette to Geoffrey Green, in Elisabeth Lee, 'Pierre Adolphe Valette (1876-1942)', Final Year thesis for BA (Hons) course, Department of History of Art, University of Manchester, 1976, p.38.
9. *Manchester City News*, 24 April 1926, article entitled 'Modern Painters'.
10. Elisabeth Lee, 'Pierre Adolphe Valette (1876-1942)', Final Year thesis for BA (Hons) course, Department of History of Art, University of Manchester, 1976, quoting the *Daily Mail*, 21 April 1926, 'Basement Exhibition'.
11. Mme Canque to Martine Morion.
12. *Manchester City News*, 25 October 1913, report by William Weatherby.

5. *The Heirs and Facets of Adolphe Valette's Artistic Talent*, pp.113-25

1. *Manchester City News*, 24 April 1926.
2. *Manchester Guardian*, 6 May 1937.
3. *Evening News*, Saturday 11 March 1933, artist by a 'Special Correspondent' entitled 'Returned Artist Talks of Better Days'. In Elisabeth Lee, 'Pierre Adolphe Valette (1876-1942)', Final Year thesis for BA (Hons) course, Department of History of Art, University of Manchester, 1976.
4. Michael Leber and Judith Sandling, *L.S. Lowry*, Phaidon Press, 1987, p.13.
5. Shelley Rohde, *L.S. Lowry, A Biography*, The Lowry Press, 3rd edition, 1999, pp.69 and 70.
6. Michael Leber and Judith Sandling, *L.S. Lowry*, Phaidon Press, 1987, p.13.
7. Shelley Rohde, *L.S. Lowry, A Biography*, The Lowry Press, 3rd edition, 1999, p.72.
8. *Op. cit.*, pp.75, 76.
9. Cotton/Mulineux tapes in: Shelley Rohde, *L.S. Lowry, A Biography*, The Lowry Press, 3rd edition, 1999, p.76.
10. Shelley Rohde, *L.S. Lowry, A Biography*, The Lowry Press, 3rd edition, 1999, p.72.
11. *Op. cit.*, p.75.
12. Interview of L.S. Lowry, North West Sound Archive, 1967.
13. Shelley Rohde, *L.S. Lowry, A Biography*, The Lowry Press, 3rd edition, 1999, p.96, quoting the 'Maitland tapes'.
14. *Op. cit.*, p.88.
15. Sandra Martin, *Adolphe Valette, A French Influence in Manchester*, Manchester City Art Galleries, 1994, p.76.
16. *The Studio International*, November 1923.
17. Mabel Lyon to the author.
18. Alan Fowler and Terry Wyke, *Many Arts, Many Skills, The origins of The Manchester Metropolitan University*, MMU, 1993, p.25.

19. Shelley Rohde, *L.S. Lowry, A Biography*, The Lowry Press, 3rd edition, 1999, p.444.
20. *The Huddersfield Examiner*, 'An Exhibition of Promise', 1994.
21. Sandra Martin, *Adolphe Valette, catalogue of the 1976 exhibition at the Manchester City Art Gallery*, p.17.
22. Jan Green to the author.
23. Document entitled 'Four perspectives', Manchester Art Gallery, in Lowry and Valette Room.

***Summary of Documented Exhibitions by Valette during his Lifetime*, pp.133-6**

1. Sandra Martin, *Adolphe Valette, A French Influence in Manchester*, Manchester City Art Galleries, 1994.
2. Elisabeth Lee, 'Pierre Adolphe Valette (1876-1942)', Final Year thesis for BA (Hons) course, Department of History of Art, University of Manchester, 1976, plate XI.

Index